MW01625297

THE soul
OF PARENTING

MOSAICA PRESS

THE SOUL OF PARENTING

Timeless Wisdom for Raising Today's Children

SLOVIE JUNGREIS-WOLFF

Mosaica Press, with its team of acclaimed editors and designers, is attracting some of the most compelling thinkers and teachers in the Jewish community today. Our books are impacting and engaging readers from around the world.

ISBN: 978-1-957579-71-9

Published by Mosaica Press, Inc.
www.mosaicapress.com
info@mosaicapress.com

To the luminaries in my life

My parents and grandparents

who have illuminated my path

My husband, Mendy

who lights up my life

My children and grandchildren

who brighten my every moment
and give me hope for the future

Dedicated to the *hatzlachah*, *berachah*, and *arichut yamim* of

Our dear parents
and the Kashi and Raofim children

לע״נ

בן ציון חיים בן יהודה

משה בן חנוכה

ע״ה

who were both *niftar* on the fourth night of Chanukah
They were, like a candle, *mashpia* everyone around them with light and *simchah*, keeping their own fires forever shining in our hearts.
With the help of this *sefer*, we can spark the light of *chinuch* in our children always!

And in special dedication to

Rebbetzin Esther Jungreis, ע״ה

a matriarch in her own right who literally illuminated the world

---

We are humbled to have the *zechut* of being part of this special *sefer*, to learn and to grow from the timeless wisdom of Slovie Jungreis-Wolff. It is evident that her teachings come from a long, royal lineage and above all, from her heart. She carries this genuine love for Klal Yisrael on her shoulders as if every one of us were her own children. She has led us with the power of *Nishmat*—to praise Hashem's name and glory, and to be *mefarsem* constant *nissim* in our lives. We are in awe of the way she has stepped into her mother's role as a spiritual mother to us all and touched by her *tefillot* and *berachot* time and time again!
May we all be *zocheh* to raising our children with *kedushah* and endless *ahavah* on the heels of this *sefer*.

SHEENA AND YAAKOV KASHI

Table of Contents

Acknowledgments

I begin with a blessing of gratitude. "*She'hecheyanu v'kiymanu v'higiyanu la'zman ha'zeh.*" Thank You, first, to Hashem, for allowing me the privilege of writing this book, and conveying the teachings and wisdom that I have absorbed throughout my life. I do not take this moment for granted.

I thank my parents, Rabbi Meshulem and Rebbetzin Esther Jungreis, *a"h*, and my grandparents, Harav Avrohom and Rebbetzin Miriam Jungreis, *a"h*, for giving me both life and legacy. Words can never express enough gratitude for their gift of love, their blessings, their *ko'ach*, and their ability to connect me to those who walked before me. I am who I am today solely because of their relentless *emunah*, faith, and passion for our people. Not a day goes by that I do not yearn to hear their voices, savor their presence, and feel their hands upon my head as they give me their blessings. I miss them every single day.

Thank you to my dear husband, Mendy, who has never stopped encouraging me and believing in me. I am eternally grateful to Hashem for sending you to me from across the equator. Your incredible *lev tov*, heart of gold, ability to always see the positive, and steadfast *bitachon* in Hashem, have been my fortress and strength of our family. May Hashem grant us *chayim aruchim*, long lives together, filled with *nachas* from our children, good health, *simchah,* and *berachah.*

My precious children, Moshe Nosson and B.T., Shaindy and Rabbi Shlomo, Akiva and Chavie, Eli and Yael, and Aliza and Yisroel Meir—you are my treasures from Above. Each one of you has brought music to my soul. You've expanded my heart to a place of joy I could never have imagined. Know, forever, that our *neshamos* are eternally connected.

And now, my delicious grandchildren, *chasdei Hashem*, fill my days with laughter and love. May Hashem watch over you, protect you, shine His light upon you, and fill your homes with *shalom*.

Thank you, Rabbi Doron Kornbluth, for your vision and confidence, your infinite enthusiasm, and for making this book a reality. I'd like to express my gratitude, too, to Rabbi Yaacov Haber, as well as the very talented staff of Mosaica Press who have added their professional design, skills, and style.

When Rabbi Nechemiah Coopersmith invited me to write for the incredibly successful site Aish.com, I had no idea that my words would reach thousands and thousands all across the globe. Throughout the years, Rabbi Coopersmith has been a source of incredible knowledge, wise editing, and universal awareness. Thank you, Rabbi Coopersmith, for your constant insights, and to Aish.com, for sharing my articles, many of which the chapters in this book draw upon.

Batsheva Ben-Itzhak has given me her time and technology expertise, and always with a smile. I appreciate your meticulous efforts and diligent organizational skills.

Yaakov and Sheena Kashi, you are the couple who inspire countless others. Your home is always open in the spirit of Avraham Avinu and Sarah Imeinu. You have committed your lives to your family, your community, and your people. When I mentioned the opportunity to dedicate this book, you seized the moment, as you always seize every mitzvah, and how you do it all with joy! Your children have watched you, and now follow in your ways. I have seen your sons' and daughters' gracious hospitality, constant *derech eretz*, and love for Torah and mitzvos. They have learned all this from you. You not only "talk" Torah, but you live Torah. Thank you for your generous heart and for having the belief that this book will touch families and truly make a difference. May Hashem bless your home with *simchah* and true *nachas*.

Introduction

My earliest memories were filled with the knowledge that I came into this world as a child rising above the ashes. I was born after the fire of holocaust had devoured my family. Grandparents, cousins, aunts, and uncles were all a mysterious void. I knew that I would never hold my *zeidy*'s hand, I would never hear the voice of my *bubby* as she sings me a lullaby. The warmth of their hugs and the feel of their kisses upon my head would remain a dream in my mind. My father's parents, siblings, and their sweet babies had vanished.

Miraculously, my mother survived the horrors of Bergen-Belsen along with her two brothers and her parents, my Mama and Zaydah. Hashem, in His great compassion, allowed them to begin life anew. But they, too, lost their most precious loved ones.

These sacred souls who were slaughtered and gave their lives *al kiddush Hashem* became our family legacy. My Zaydah's mother for whom I was named perished in Auschwitz. As she walked into the gas chambers, she was seen holding her youngest grandchild in her arms, and was heard to cry out the *Shema* prayer with her very last breath. I knew this from the time that I could speak my name.

Taken, too, was the world my parents and grandparents had left behind. The majestic rabbinical dynasty of our family and the generations of "*deyukno shel aviv*," the image of a father and mother, which had been an integral part of everyday living, were cruelly snatched away.

They were so incredibly young. Shoved into cattle cars, gasping for air, trying to survive each miserable day, facing a darkness unknown to humanity. Grief. Terror. Shock. Sorrow. All became haunting shadows lurking in their daily existence.

I wonder to myself, how did they go through indescribable suffering and pain, yet raise us with love? I never heard a moment of bitterness, anger, or rage, at all that had been lost. How was it possible to bequeath dignity, unwavering faith, and an endurable spirit? How did they hold onto our glorious past and allow me to taste that which I had never known?

This wonder and contemplation is the driving force behind my life work of reaching out to parents, grandparents, and children, as I impart timeless parenting and relationship insights that emit from my heart and soul.

I have learned the meaning of family. I have been witness to the power of a parent and grandparent to teach me, guide me, and encourage me. **To be an inspired parent means that we are purposeful and passionate, and we persevere.** To love means that we give our children—and ourselves—an opportunity to rise above obstacles and choose to live a life of strength, resilience, and meaning.

I have discovered that we, too, can create and transmit a lasting legacy for our own children, no matter where we have come from or the world that we live in. We can override the challenges and tests that family life brings, that a world filled with chaos thrusts upon us, and construct a home that endures with love, values, and a solid foundation for life.

My mission with this book is to share with you the light of wisdom that my parents and grandparents bequeathed to me, all based on the immutable teachings of the Torah. Life lessons that embolden and fortify me, my children, and grandchildren, until today.

I grew up with stories of courage and faith. Roots, identity, and ideals infused me. I watched my parents and grandparents confront incredible hardship—but they did not simply survive. They triumphed. They nourished me and raised me with the understanding that within us all is a spiritual DNA, a burning flame, a vibrant soul that refuses to die, if we just will it.

In my travels and talks around the world, I have met countless children and young adults gripped with anxiety and a crumbling spirit. I've encountered many parents, too, who have suffered immensely. Relationships in homes have been strained with the stress of a pandemic, economic uncertainty, insecurity that sets in with news of terrorism and war, effects of technology and social media, and simply feeling that the universe has been turned upside down. Family life can be fraught with unexpected obstacles. Emotional, mental, physical, and spiritual health have been compromised. There is a sense that unease and weakness have become internalized, a part of our very being.

It is easy to sigh, raise our hands up, and say, "This seems impossible!"

How can we remain inspired? How do we parent from strength?

When I was a little girl, I would watch my mother kindle her Shabbos *licht*, her candlesticks, every Friday night. There was one proud candlestick that stood apart from the silver candelabra that graced our Shabbos table. I remember asking my mother, "Ema, why does that *licht* stand alone?"

> *Slova Channalah, listen carefully. Before the Rebbetzin Slova Channah was taken away, she and her husband, your Zaydah, HaRav Yisroel HaLevi Jungreis, the rabbi of Nadudvar, went into the courtyard of their shul. It was in middle of the night. Your Bubba and Zaydah dug a deep hole in the earth and there, in the darkness, they buried all their silver. Their kiddush cups, their menorah, their leichters...everything. Soon, after, they were deported to Auschwitz, where they died al kiddush Hashem. The Germans came and dug up the ground. They found the silver and took it all. Somehow, they did not find this candlestick.*
>
> *There was one man from the shul who survived that terrible nightmare. He returned to Nadudvar looking for family, friends, his rebbe, but there was nothing and nobody left. Everyone was gone. He found only this leichter. That was it.*
>
> *When we finally came to the United States of America, we were living in a tiny basement apartment. One day there was a knock at the door. It was the lone survivor. He was holding the Bubba Slova Channah's leichter in his hand.*
>
> *"I made a promise," he said to Zaydah. "I will not sleep, I will not rest, until I bring the candlestick back to its rightful owner.*

> *This is the leichter that your mother lit every leil Shabbos, every Friday night. I came to keep my promise."*
>
> *Zaydah began to cry. He called us together and said, "Kinderlach, we have a message from the ashes. Our bubbas and zaydahs are speaking to us. Know why we survived. We must bring the light of Shabbos into the world."*
>
> *I knew then that Shabbos had kept us alive in Bergen-Belsen. I understood that just as the licht survived, we, too, survived. We were not alone. Hashem is with us. And just as Shabbos lights up the darkest night, our mission is to do the same. Always bring light...never fall into darkness.*
>
> *When you were born and I named you for the Bubba Slova Channah, Zaydah gave me the leichter. Know that you are never alone. Never be afraid. Never forget where you've come from. Always bring light into this world.*

When my mother returned her soul to *Shamayim*, to the heavens above, in 2016, I was given my Bubba's *leichter*. Every Friday night I kindle my lights, circle the flames, and whisper my innermost prayers. Then I take a moment to look at my Bubba's candlestick and remember the impossible journey it has traveled. We are a nation of miracles. We have a mission to seek out the spark within ourselves, within our children, and ignite souls. We are here to continue the path of those who walked before us. To teach the definition of greatness, how to live with compassion, connection, courage, faith, identity, responsibility, grit, love, and the power to make a difference in this world.

I hope that as you read the pages of this book, you will feel the spark within you, reignited. You will draw upon the beauty and strength of our roots, our values, our Divine wisdom, and you will discover the secret to inspired parenting.

CHAPTER 1

Effective Parenting

Parenting Goals for Every Family

How to ensure that your children have a productive year

We begin the school year with blank notebooks, pages fresh and clean. Backpacks are free of crumbs and leaking box drinks. Children wake up early in anticipation. We try to get to school a bit before the morning bell and start the year off on the right track.

But, slowly, the familiar patterns start to appear. Children are going to sleep way past their bedtime, waking in the morning with just moments to spare. Notebooks are left in school, leaving children scrambling to get the work done. Nights are spent struggling over homework, assignments forgotten or left for the last minute, cliques are formed, and disappointments mount—it feels as if we are going backward instead of forward.

How can we make this year different from all the others? How can we take our hopes and wishes for positive change and turn them into a reality?

Transitioning between summer and school can be difficult for children—and for parents. Any change in life, even a change in routine, can bring anxiety, worry, and irritability. Children often have a hard time adjusting to new situations, unfamiliar teachers, and the more rigid schedule that is needed during the school year. When feeling overwhelmed, children may express their emotions through becoming argumentative, fighting more often with siblings, or withdrawing into themselves. And parents can find it difficult to keep calm and not lose themselves in anger when things don't go right.

Instead of just accepting that this is the way our homes are meant to be, we can think about reachable goals toward which we can work. When we create a plan, we can do away with unnecessary failures and strive to help our children feel and be more successful. Here are some suggestions for parenting goals.

MY FIVE PARENTING GOALS

1. Keep My Eyes Open

Sometimes, we notice that something does not feel right with a child, but we get distracted. We have abundant pressures and responsibilities pulling us in too many directions. The child who seems a little "off"—not himself, snappy, or more quiet than usual—is trying to tell us something. It is easy to tuck this information away in a back pocket and, only too late, we realize that something is wrong when a crisis occurs. We then think back and recognize that the signs were there. We were just too preoccupied to pay attention.

Don't allow problems with your child to fester and grow. Open your eyes and observe if a child seems sad, withdrawn, distant, more moody than usual, or angry. Recognize if there seem to be more confrontations between this child and siblings, if friends stop calling or coming over, or if the child can't seem to find his place in school. Because before you know it, half the year can go by, and what could have been a small problem can become a "situation" that requires major time and investment and causes terrible aggravation.

2. Develop a Working Relationship with Teachers

Reach out to your child's teachers before things get out of hand. Many parents feel as if teachers are their opponents and don't realize that we are all here to try and help our children grow in the best way possible. If you think that there may be an issue, it is a good idea to set up a meeting with the teacher and ask how you can work together in harmony.

Too many parents call teachers to demand and accuse instead of saying that they would like to solve this problem together. Before going to the principal with a complaint, see if you can first diffuse the situation.

If there are any special concerns going on in your home, do not wait for the teacher to find out through your child's acting up in class or failure to keep up with schoolwork and poor grades. It would be wise to enlist your child's teacher as your confidential ally and gain their understanding when, for example, a grandparent falls ill, if there is a health concern, or other such issues, such as the loss of a job, marital upheaval, problems with siblings, or any distressing factor that may affect your child's academic or social success. You can believe that most teachers would go the extra mile and extend an open heart to your child.

3. Work on Social Skills

Help your child be successful this year by preparing him not just academically, but also socially. School is not simply about getting straight A's; it is also about learning how to get on with others and knowing how to develop friendships. A child who is happy in school is a child who can focus on studying and doing well. They want to be there and be a part of things. One who believes that school is only about academics and not about social life is, unfortunately, making a big mistake.

How can we better teach our children social skills?

- Set rules and follow through with consequences when needed.
- Set routines for meals and bedtimes that establish stability.
- Develop your child's ability to put himself in the shoes of others and grow more sensitive to the feelings of others.
- Help your child learn how to express frustration, disappointment, and anger without hurting others or retreating into sullenness.
- Establish basic rules of conduct: no hitting, kicking, biting, spitting (no physical hurting allowed), and no wounding others through words.

4. Help Children Become Independent

When children feel that they are gaining skills and becoming self-sufficient, they grow more confident in their abilities. You will watch their self-esteem take off. Each year, every child should be able to point with pride to a newfound skill or added responsibility that comes with age.

We can help our children grow independent and flourish by doing the following:

- Teaching our children to pick out their clothing and dress themselves as they grow older, tie their own shoes, pack school snacks, make lunches the night before, set their own alarm clocks (instead of relying on someone else waking them up), put away their books, and organize themselves
- Allowing young children to complete puzzles and feed themselves and, as they grow, to do their homework and projects by themselves. It is much healthier to tell a child that you will check his work when he is done than it is to sit beside him and correct the answers as he goes along. Making it clear that reports and science projects are not a parent's homework.
- Having children help around the house and gain responsibilities instead of waiting to be served. Assigning tasks to children, such as helping out with putting away the laundry, setting and clearing the table, serving guests, baking, cooking, and keeping their room in order.

5. Communicate with Each Child

Our children should never be afraid to speak with us. No matter how tough the topic, even if they messed up badly, they should not fear that we will reject them or close the door on them. Our love must be unconditional. True, there may be consequences or emotions of disappointment, but they need to know that we are always here for them. After all, we are their parents and if they cannot believe in our love for them, whose love can they believe in?

Work on communicating with your child this year. I am not just speaking about when you must have a conversation about a problem like discipline, poor grades, or after you have received a call from their teacher. I am talking about daily interactions where you share a smile, a good word, a laugh, a story, or a meal together. The main thing is that you put the time and energy in so they know that they matter in your life.

The following are important communication tools:

- Make time to talk to your child every day—even if it's just for a few minutes.
- Put down your phone and turn off your laptop when your child (or you) returns home, at mealtimes and story times, and when you pick your child up from school. Look at them and make eye contact while having a conversation.
- Speak to your child in the tone and with the words that you wish they would use with others.
- Express your love every day, no matter how tough the day. Make it a habit to say "I love you" when your child goes off to school each morning or when you say good night. This communication of love is especially important as children grow older and we may no longer hold, cuddle, or be as affectionate with them as we once were.

I know that some days will bring unforeseen difficulties and that some children seem more challenging than others, but by creating a plan and sticking to it, at least we will know in our hearts that we have tried our best to help our children successfully navigate the road of life.

Family Vacation Tips

Crucial tips for going away with your children

Over the years, I have gathered many lessons to be learned about traveling with children.

KEEPING STANDARDS ALIVE WHILE ON THE ROAD: "U'VELECHTECHA VA'DERECH"

We spend half our lives teaching our children to be polite. "Say please, sweetie." "Be sure to say thank you, honey." But more powerful than any instructions on manners are the words and tone that we use when dealing with others. Our children observe through watchful eyes and listening ears.

There will be times when the rooms that we reserved will not be ready upon arrival, when the "connecting rooms" are really across the hall from each other, the hotel doesn't meet our expectations, and cribs or rollaway beds are not readily available.

What do we do in such situations? Do we put up a big fuss and scream? Do we have a temper tantrum and lose it with the hotel staff? How do we deal with disappointments?

Once, while we were waiting to check in, the family in front of us was informed that the oceanfront rooms that they had requested would not be available. Instead, they would have a view of the parking lot. Not a pretty sight, I admit. But you would not believe the anger and foul language that spewed forth.

As the discussion heated up, so did the sense of entitlement that these parents displayed.

The feeling that came across to all who heard the conversation was clear: *How dare you not provide us with what we want! How could it be that we ordered something and didn't get it? We want it, and we want it now!*

Think of the arrogance these children will inherit after absorbing their parents' attitudes and words. All the discussions these parents may have had with their children about *middos*, character, manners, "please," and "thank you" mean nothing in the face of such behavior.

Imagine the scene when these children return home from school and dinner's not ready or not to their liking:

"What do you mean, supper's not ready? I'm starving!"

"Uch, that's for supper? You know that I hate chicken with sauce!"

Why are we so puzzled with our children's attitudes when it is us they have learned it from? Let's maintain our sense of self-respect and dignity when dealing with life's inevitable disappointments. Let's remain calm, in both manner and tone, so that our children learn from our example, especially while we're on the road handling our frustrations.

MAINTAIN YOUR STANDARDS OF DISCIPLINE

Vacation time is supposed to be fun. We want to take it easy, laugh a lot, and have a relaxing, good time together. We wake up late and may stay out way past bedtime. It becomes easy to lose control as we try hard to make our children (and ourselves) happy. Along with dropping our daily routine, we may find our standards of discipline misplaced.

Many parents mistakenly believe that vacation time means a vacation from discipline. Anything goes till we get home. That's what fun is all about, isn't it?

Though I love fun and good times just as much as anyone else, certain standards should not be compromised, even while on vacation. Children who are given confusing signals do not understand if parents are serious about their boundaries. We also end up disciplining out of anger and frustration when our buttons are pushed to the limit. Often, we can get so exasperated that we speak without being in control of our emotions and thoughts.

On a family vacation, I was sitting with my toddler granddaughter at a kiddie pool. She was making her way down the steps when a little boy decided to splash her.

"Stop it!" his mother said.

The child laughed. He slapped the water even harder and then glanced over at his mother. After giving him a stern look, she went back to scrolling through her phone.

Splash. Now some children began to cry.

"I mean it! Cut it out! Do that again and we're going back to the room."

The boy stopped splashing. As soon as his mother became engrossed in her screen, he threw water on all the children once again. Finally, after twenty minutes of "we're going back to the room," splashing, and more threats, the child left the pool. But it was lunch being served, not discipline, that did the job. This child learned that it's OK to cross the line, especially when mommy is too busy or not serious about her consequences anyway.

If we say something, we must mean it. Empty threats and never-happening consequences lead children to disrespect us. Behaviors that are unacceptable at home must be unacceptable on vacation also.

Hurting others, trashing furniture, leaving wrappers, and spilling soda cans all over the property cannot be tolerated in the name of fun. Good times can be had while maintaining fine character and acting like a mensch.

KEEP ENTHUSIASM ALIVE

The first day away, everything seems new and exciting. You explore the grounds, unpack your things, find out about nearby attractions, and, hopefully, enjoy a delicious meal. You appreciate the scenery and newness of it all. But what happens when you stop noticing the glorious sunset or when your family sits down to a meal and feels like "here we go again"?

We were once on a family trip and while sitting at dinner the first evening, we saw dazzling colors fill the night sky. There were incredible booms as magnificent fireworks burst forth. Sparkles of gold and silver exploded in the sky and then shimmered to the ground. People jumped up from their tables to watch the sight. The next night, the same display brought people to their feet. You heard oohs and aahs with each boom. By the third night, no one looked up from their dinner plates. We all took it for granted. Another fireworks display? Big deal. The extraordinary had become "same old, same old."

Family is one of the greatest blessings that we have. If we are fortunate enough to get away and have time together, let's be sure to appreciate the joy of those precious moments together and never take them for granted.

Things Every Child Needs

How to ensure your children thrive

Our children need to do more than just get by and survive—we need to make sure our children thrive. What can we do to help them?

SELF-WORTH

All children have the need to feel accepted. When we nurture our child's feelings of self-worth, we create a sense of pride. We need to foster an atmosphere of belonging so that our children do not feel the need to find acceptance elsewhere. We want our sons and daughters to know that we love them for who they are and that each of them possesses a unique gift given by God. For each child, the gift is different. It can be brains, personality, sports, art, baking, music, a sense of humor, even the ability to care for a baby. Our role as parents is to help each child discover the magic within them, instead of focusing on the perceived gifts that others possess and making unnecessary, pointless, and hurtful comparisons.

Once we are able to do this, we can help each child feel better about who they are. Self-confident children can deal successfully with the ups and downs that life brings. Kids who possess self-worth will be able to better navigate future relationships, feel resilient enough to try different things and risk failure, and become a source of strength for future generations.

By self-confident, I do not mean a child who is full of himself. Some children perceive themselves to be superior and knock others down. This type of bloated self-esteem creates an arrogant monster in the home. Instead, I am speaking about unearthing and then recognizing that special gift that lies within each child. If we can then show our children that they can use their gifts to make this world better, we transmit to each child a confident awareness that "I make a difference" and "I have value." When a child feels inadequate, we hear lines like, "I can't," "No one likes me," and, "I'm not good enough, smart enough, or popular or pretty enough."

Parents who appreciate their children's differences, interests, and talents, encourage their children to grow confident and be happy with who they are.

SECURITY

We live in a frightening world. Our children are aware of current events, painful tragedies, and images that boggle the mind. A generation is growing up surrounded by loss, anxiety, social unrest, the threat of a pandemic, and scenes of war. And it is not just grim world news that kids must confront. I have spoken to parents whose children are fearful of returning home from summer camp because each year when children return home, there are couples who announce their pending divorce. Do you feel confident that you have given your child a sense of security?

We can help assure our children by creating an atmosphere of trust: "Despite the difficult world out there, know, my child, that you can always count on me."

Here are practical ways to make this happen: rid yourself of chaos and commit to set routines and schedules that work; try to de-clutter so that your home environment does not feel messy and overwhelming. Keep your word—when you say that you will be there, honor your promise, and don't disappoint. Let your child know that you listen to his words and hear what he is expressing.

A lack of consistency in rules makes a child unsure of what to expect. Wishy-washy discipline does not allow a child to anticipate proper consequences and strips away the security of knowing right from wrong.

Most of all, let us recognize the destructive power that we possess when we scream at our children. All it takes is a few moments of outrage to cause a child to feel that he is living with a parent who is out of control. Anger, yelling, sarcastic put-downs, and belittling removes the inborn trust that a child had originally but is now lost. *Why would I want to connect with you if I do not feel safe at your side?* Once the bond between parent and child is damaged, it becomes very difficult to repair. Even if you try to offer soothing words afterward, if you lose it often enough, the harsh image and tone will simmer within your child's heart. Your son or daughter will always be second-guessing: Will this be a safe conversation, or will I feel vulnerable? Creating a stable home will enable your child to grow up knowing what it means to be dependable, reliable, and trustworthy.

RELATIONSHIP SKILLS

Our children need to learn how to deal with others. Too often, parents make excuses for their child's misbehavior or hurtful words. Instead, let us concentrate on helping our children handle their encounters. We can accomplish this by opening our eyes to teaching moments where kids can learn about the importance of making apologies, offering forgiveness, expressing gratitude, sharing, not interrupting, allowing others to be in the limelight, having listening skills, overcoming the desire to hit or scream, dealing successfully with tantrums, and learning how to quell angry reactions.

At the same time, it is important to impart the sense of deference that is required when encountering authority. Discuss the proper *derech eretz*, standards of respect, while speaking to rabbis, principals, teachers, parents, relatives, and elders. Just as crucial is the knowledge of how to act in a shul, at a bar and bas mitzvah, on an airplane, in a restaurant or hotel, and at other people's homes. Lacking social skills produces children who either bully or withdraw into painful silence. Providing the proper relationship know-how gives children character traits like loyalty, respect, unselfishness, and honesty.

SENSITIVITY

Teach your children to be considerate of other people's feelings. When a sibling or classmate has been pained, it is OK and appropriate for a child to be aware and feel empathy. If possible, give your children opportunities to cultivate compassion. The unpopular kid in class who never gets invited—how do you think he is feeling? How can we try to make this situation better? There are many *chessed* projects with which we can get our children involved instead of just focusing on themselves.

A group of bas mitzvah–aged students whose mothers I teach collected hundreds of coats that we shipped off to Israel. We discussed with the girls how there are kids their age who are freezing during the cold winter months because they cannot afford a coat. Some families have only one coat, and they must take turns, sharing that one jacket despite their various ages and sizes. The coats are either embarrassingly oversized or painfully snug. The girls were flabbergasted. It was an incredible day that opened up their eyes and hearts to the suffering of other children. Compassion must be nurtured. It will not happen by itself.

Children notice if their words bring a smile or a tear, recognizing from early on if they've brought pleasure or pain. We cannot afford to shy away from allowing them to confront their behavior and deal with poor decisions that they've made.

As parents, we must replace angry reactions with firm but loving discipline. We cannot expect to raise sensitive children if we ourselves are insensitive to our children's needs or to the needs of others.

LOVE, LOVE, LOVE

Of course, all this is not possible if we lack the ability to make our children feel loved. How can we make our love feel alive?

Be generous with your affection. Hug more, laugh more, and say "I love you" more. Stop making your child feel as if he is never good enough. Allow your children to see that you appreciate and are affectionate with your spouse. Give words of gratitude and admiration.

When you have family time, don't seem bored and uninterested. Watch that the pressures of school, homework, carpools, bedtime, and daily life do not ruin the precious moments that you have together. When you walk in at the end of a long day, be careful to have your device out of sight. Many parents don't realize the off-putting message they are sending when their words of greeting are "I just need to answer this email" or "I need to take this call now."

Our children want to spend time with us. How we respond to their desire can either nourish or diminish our connection.

FORGETTING TO SHOW LOVE AS KIDS GROW

It's easy to show love to an infant. We cuddle, kiss, hug, and sing lullabies. They climb on our laps, and we wipe away their tears. These are all moments of vital physical connection that become a powerful language of love. But what happens as children grow?

We give more orders and show less love. We forget to say "I love you." We don't connect as easily. They are in their world, and we in ours. We get lost in our phones and daily pressures. We stop sharing conversation. Talks are usually reserved for misbehavior, admonishment, and asking if they took a shower or did their homework.

We realize too late that we've left words unsaid and wonder how many more hugs and kisses could have been given to nourish their hungry souls.

All children, no matter their age, need to feel a parent's love.

A mother told me that her children approached her husband after Pesach.

"Daddy, we decided what we want for *afikoman*. We want you to come home early once a week and have supper with us."

The following week the children were anxiously waiting for their dinner time with daddy. Her husband came home, and the children surrounded him. "Guys, I have something much better for you than supper with me. I decided to get laptops for everyone!"

He did not see the shadow on their faces and disappointment in their eyes.

"He just doesn't get it," she said to me, sadly.

Our families are our greatest assets. Let us create homes filled with peace so that we can transmit our legacy to the next generation.

Keys to a Happy Home

How to infuse your home with genuine joy

A woman approached me after a recent parenting lecture. "I own three houses, but I don't have any place that I can really call home. Everyone in my family is unhappy, and it's miserable for us to spend time together." Without joy, even the most beautiful surroundings can feel dark and uninviting. How can we help build an atmosphere of happiness in our homes?

HAPPY FAMILIES TAKE WORK

Looking at everyone else's photos and social media posts can make some people feel as if all other families, except their own, are experiencing bliss. It's as if you are going through your daily grind while others are dancing through life. Scenes of smiling kids, loving couples, and exotic vacations...Don't fall into this "happiness trap." No photo ever gives you the full picture, as everyone puts on a smile for the camera. Every family struggles with moods, dynamics, and challenges. True happiness takes work. There is never a home where it is "all fun, all the time."

Working on creating an atmosphere of joy means that you value your family's privacy. You do not gripe about your spouse or kids to others, nor do you disparage them. You strive to protect your relationships so that a feeling of trust grows between family members. When there is trust in a home, confidence, hope, and stability flourish. There is a reason that we wish a newlywed couple the beautiful berachah of building a *bayis ne'eman b'Yisrael*, a home based on *ne'emanus*, trust and faithfulness, is a home that stands.

As a sense of security is cultivated, parents and children feel happy that they can depend on one another. Instead of comparing your life with others or spending time discussing grievances with friends, make a decision to put energy into nourishing your family unit. Resolve to build rapport between parents and kids as well as siblings.

Strive to see your spouse and children through an *ayin tovah*, in a positive light, with a good eye, by focusing on their good character traits. If you have spent your time seeing the negative, this will take a lot of effort, but understand that everyone has good that lies within and learning to see it takes constant practice.

HAPPY FAMILIES KNOW HOW TO LISTEN

Good communication is not only about talking, it's also about listening. Knowing that we are being heard and understood makes us feel happy.

Are you a good listener?

Here are some tips to reflect upon:

- At times, simply listening is an adequate response to show that you care.
- Be careful not to interrupt.
- Don't always try to offer solutions to fix the situation.
- Give undivided attention and don't check texts and emails while listening.
- Listen without being judgmental or saying things like, "You did what?!" "How could you?" or "What were you thinking?"

HAPPY FAMILIES COMMUNICATE RESPECT

Parents set the tone in the home. Children who observe their mother and father treating each other respectfully know that their home is a safe haven. Of course, there are times that parents disagree, are stressed, or are under pressure. But realizing that even while strained, dignity is being maintained, helps create a sense of peace. Children in such a home know that once they walk through that door, they leave the chaos and craziness of the world behind.

When children grow up in a hostile environment, the foundation of the home is shaken. Some children feel responsible and try to pitifully fix their parents' conflict. Others grow fearful of what may come, and, with time, their pain turns into anger. The joy of family life becomes threatened.

When you disagree or are shouldering a burden, be mindful of your tone and words. Our children learn from us. If it becomes acceptable for parents to put one another down, yell, or be sarcastic, the kids will certainly follow our lead. What a powerful lesson it is for our children to observe that even when parents are stressed, they do not resort to hurting others. We do not stoop to meanness. Instead, we contemplate our words and make a choice to control our temper.

The success of our children's future relationships may depend on the attitude and behavior that they observe at home. We need to model and live the behavior that we hope to instill in our children.

Decide to work on eliminating patterns of disrespect in your home. This includes yelling, put-downs, rolling eyes, sarcastic remarks, laughing at mistakes, and personal attacks. Clearly, physical aggression is never acceptable. Respect translates into an atmosphere where we value the people in our lives and treat each other with honor.

HAPPY FAMILIES SHARE TIME TOGETHER

In today's fast-paced, busy, digital, online world, families have stopped spending time together. Happy families don't communicate while looking down.

Look around. Whether in a restaurant, on a sidewalk pushing a baby stroller, or in your home, most parents are looking at their devices. Our children are growing up thinking that this is the normal way to communicate. You can speak to someone while looking at your phone. You can have a conversation while texting. Dinner time is food with phones on the table.

Watch teens get together. They sit on the couch, phones in hand. Besides the occasional comment about what they are seeing, no one's talking. Kids are missing the opportunity to converse, make eye contact, and connect face-to-face.

This type of social interaction leads to a new type of loneliness. We are "alone but together." We can be texting, in touch with a circle of friends, even sitting beside one another, but we are lonely. Human contact and feeling the physical and emotional presence of others in your life is a sacred gift that can never be replaced by screen time or emojis.

How unimportant do you feel when the person right across from you would rather look at his screen than at you?

It is time for us to say, "Enough." Let's put down our phones, stop interrupting family time as we take photos and share, and really be in the moment. Whether it is having dinner or breakfast, eat together. Studies show that families that share meals together are stronger and more connected. Our Shabbos and Yom Tov tables, too, become a crucial time for family bonding.

Smart parents know that to keep the connection alive we must be present in our children's lives. They create sacred times and spaces so that their children know that family comes first. It is the time together, laughter, family trips, adventures, singing in the rain, and experiences in which we participate that strengthen our family. There is no substitute for our presence.

HAPPY FAMILIES SEE LOVE

Love provides children with a sense of belonging. Homes filled with words of affection, smiles, hugs, and kisses show children that we are happy to be a part of this family.

I met a woman who told me that as a child, her husband was never shown any physical affection. His mother never once said, "I love you," though she is a lovely woman when you meet her. She simply did not know how to express her love. This husband carries the hurt and unhappiness of his childhood, but he won't admit it. As a result, she and their children suffer.

Children who grow up in a home where spouses put each other first, give kindly without resentment, and speak lovingly, enjoy being home. Sons and daughters who feel cherished know that they are valued. Love translates into living a committed life and knowing which priorities are most important. Family and marriage must come first. While words are crucial, it is not enough; *show* that you love and always be generous with your heart.

There are no perfect families that are happy all the time, but we can try to infuse our homes with joy so that we create light, maintain a sense of security, and build a foundation of love.

Family Bonding

Some of the most important qualities every family needs

It is important for us to take the time to think about what matters most. Are there daily choices that we can make that would make a difference in our homes? Can we implement behaviors and attitudes that will help our family grow stronger?

When a family feels bonded, parents and children share life experiences on a different level. Difficult times are filled with moments of strength, connection, and encouragement. Happy occasions become sweeter, brighter, and more joyous.

Here's how to strengthen your family bond:

LOYALTY

In order for families to thrive, there needs to be a sense of security. We create a home that is a haven by allowing each child (and the parents) to feel safe with one another. "Together time" should never evoke sentiments of fear or insecurity. No family member should feel the need to withdraw into a shell to feel protected.

How can we build family loyalty?

- Support each other's dreams and stand up for one another.
- Don't use verbal zingers, sarcasm, or derogatory comments to strike each other down.
- Convey that family sacrifices for one another. Sometimes it is physical, like sharing a crowded space or cutting a favorite piece

of cake in half. Other times, it is emotional, like giving time or a listening ear.

- Parents should model respect when disagreeing with each other; they don't shame each other.
- Create a tone in the home that does not cultivate fear. This means that verbal abuse, yelling, screaming at one another, or looking for someone to constantly blame are all off limits. (Of course, physical abuse and physical fighting are never allowed.)
- Siblings show concern when one is hurting or experiencing pain or disappointment. While we can't fix the situation, the least we can do is care. Indifference shows a callousness of the heart.

ACCEPTANCE

We all need to feel that we belong. Acceptance means that I can lean on you when I fall, and you will encourage me when I fail. If I make a mistake, I am not afraid to confide in you because you are approachable. You believe in me, flaws and all.

This does not just apply to children. Husbands and wives, too, need to feel accepted by their spouse.

Acceptance means that we feel positively about our place in the family, even if we have caused disappointment.

How can we create an environment of acceptance?

1. Get to Know Your Family

As kids grow, parents realize that they are clueless and wonder where "my little guy" or "little girl" has gone. Keep updated. Stay engaged. Be interested. Do activities that your child enjoys. It's not about you; rather, it's about creating connection as years go by. It is also crucial for husbands and wives to continue to make time for one another so that they do not wake up one day and realize that they have become like two ships passing each other in the night.

2. Find Your Child's Inner Star

Some children naturally shine and others need to have the light brought out. But, make no mistake: all of us have been given a Divine gift. Help reveal each child's inner gifts by showing interest in their likes, challenging their curiosity about the world, and joining them in this quest of discovery.

3. Encourage Uniqueness

We are all different, even if we were born to the same parents. Don't try to raise cookie-cutter kids. Allow for individual likes and tastes.

4. Don't Over-Schedule Your Child

Seeking exceptionality brings parents to overexpect. Children are made to feel as if they are inadequate if they do not invent a start-up, star on a team, score high on their exams, or excel at playing a musical instrument. What about just being a wonderful human being who is kind, sensitive, and a pleasure to be with?

5. Don't Cause Feelings of Rejection

Never do something that creates the feeling that a child is rejected from the home. Be careful when upset not to say something that can be interpreted as being hateful. While we can dislike the behavior, we must not allow a child or spouse to feel discarded from the family.

UNCONDITIONAL LOVE

Unconditional love means "I love you no matter what." You are not being judged by your grades, looks, abilities, or difficulties. You are loved for who you are, not for your accomplishments. This understanding is especially needed when we find ourselves navigating through difficult times. There will be moments where the parenting road seems muddled and dismal. Unconditional love is the light that shines through the fog, guiding us as we find our way. The connection between parent and child is unbreakable.

This does not mean that we always approve of our child's behavior or actions. It does not mean that we never discipline or give consequences. It does mean that despite the disappointment, our children know without a doubt that they are loved. Children who enjoy this type of relationship with their parents will not fear being abandoned emotionally. Lacking unconditional love, children can feel confused and insecure. Do Mommy and Daddy love me even if...? We want our children to never feel isolated within our family. Unconditional love means that I do not ever have to explore elsewhere to feel accepted.

Children raised with conditional love grow up to be teens who reflect this type of love back to their parents. If I am happy with you, I will listen to you. If you frustrate me, I will ignore you. The home becomes filled with resentment. Anger and pain sets in.

We assume that our children know we love them, but our actions do not always translate into their perception. We drive them, shop for them, prepare their meals, take them on trips, and care for them. To us, this means "I love you," but children may still not interpret our actions as love. Unconditional love is the universal language that speaks to our children.

Like plants, our children need nurturing to grow. Did you ever notice how a plant will twist and turn as it seeks the sunlight? Our children, too, will search and go toward the warmth and unconditional love that they are shown. We must be sure that we are the source of that love. Negative social influences and the pull of peer pressure can be countered by positive family experiences and affection.

Each Friday night, my siblings and I received a blessing from my parents. No matter how difficult the week, despite anything that happened, I knew that both my father and mother would place their hands upon my head and give me their blessing. I can still recall their glistening eyes, their private words, and their tender kiss upon my head as they whispered "I love you."

Until today those moments sustain me and nourish my soul. And now it is I and my husband who have been privileged to place our hands upon our children's and grandchildren's heads, whisper our private prayers, and kiss them as we, too, say "I love you."

After I shared this thought at a parenting talk, a young mother asked to speak with me as I was leaving. Tears were streaming down her cheeks.

"Why are you crying, *bubelah*?" I asked.

"All my life my parents never once blessed me. I have no idea what that feels like, but I want so much to bless my own family. Please, show me how to give a berachah to my children."

No matter how pressured or chaotic life becomes, let us resolve to convey to our children our unconditional love, loyalty, and acceptance, as we create an environment of connection that anchors our homes.

Parenting-Style Mistakes

Open your eyes to common parenting mistakes

Like everyone, parents aren't perfect. As much as we try to do our best, sometimes, we, too, make mistakes. But not all mistakes are equal. Let's take a few moments to focus on some of the common parenting mistakes that can lead to producing over-indulged, ungrateful children—the exact opposite of what we are all hoping to raise our children to be.

THE "AS LONG AS THEY ARE HAPPY" ATTITUDE

When I pose the question, "What would you like for your kids?" the most common reply I receive is, "We just want them to be happy."

Big mistake.

We keep buying and looking away at bad behavior, overindulging, and going against our better judgment—all in the name of happiness. We confuse the idea of loving children with constantly doing for them and trying to make them happy.

My goal is not happiness. My mission is to give my child **tools** for happiness.

Character, kindness, grit, resilience, *middos*, and morality is the end game. When all we desire is happy children, we'll do anything not to deal with their whining, tears, and tantrums. We bend the rules, ignore better judgment, and look away at bad behavior—all in the name of happy kids.

There will be times that our children will be unhappy despite our best intentions. They will get upset with our decisions. But sometimes the answer is no. As hard as we try, we will encounter their tears.

This does not mean that we are bad parents. It means we are doing our job and teaching our children that they can't always have everything that they want in life. Life holds disappointments and failures.

The as-long-as-they're-happy parents are the parents who stop all conversation as their five-year-old enters the room. While on the phone, they allow themselves to be constantly interrupted. When the children are little, these kids are stuffed with treats and prizes. Their parents give in too easily to nagging and kvetching.

As their children grow, parents become reluctant to ask them to help out. Not wanting to deal with the anger or back talk, they stop guiding them to sweat more, give more, and do more for others.

Solution: stop equating good parenting with happy kids. Your child in tears does not mean that you are a bad parent. A happy life does not come from prizes, toys, or never experiencing discomfort. Pleasure and joy come when there is a feeling of contentment. Happiness is created when we learn to be satisfied with what we have and grateful for what we have been given. Making children feel as if they are the center of our universe from the time that they are little creates arrogance.

Don't be afraid of your children's tears. Resolve not to give in to tantrums because they make you feel unsure of yourself as a parent. Allow your child to see that others can come first. It's not the end of the world when they are asked to be uncomfortable or to go out of their comfort zone. These are the moments where character is born.

THE "BEST CHILDHOOD EVER" PARENT

Parents who want to give their children all the luxuries and experiences that they never had growing up often go overboard. They indulge and pamper. It becomes difficult to set limits. Sons and daughters binge on excessive material junk food. Thinking that they are being great parents, mothers and fathers keep overextending themselves, creating an environment of entitlement and lack of appreciation. Luxuries become necessities.

You find two-year-olds with their own devices, kids needing the latest and trendiest clothing, and teenagers living on endless credit cards. Extravagant vacations, constant ordering on Amazon and Uber eats, and bar/bas mitzvahs that defy imagination, are all part of the "best childhood ever" package.

When given too much, children grow bored easily. They stop appreciating. Parents must constantly feed their expectations with more and better.

Solution: Be consistent. Discipline wisely. Create limits and stick to them. Don't allow children's bullying to make you cross lines with which you are uncomfortable. Resolve to look at needs versus wants. Stop overindulging. Concentrate more on time together and less on things.

Children who are given everything lose their sense of wonder. The magic of this universe and awe at this incredible world in which we live are emotions that keep us growing. When dullness sets in because we've "been there, done that," we forfeit our passion. There is nothing to look forward to. Everything is boring.

THE "FIX IT ALL" PARENT

There are kids who can't pick up after themselves. They are missing homework assignments, forgetting books, and sleeping through the morning alarm clock despite talks and threats. They come down in the morning and ask where their lunch is when they are highly capable of preparing their own.

Parents are rushing to school with books left at home, writing excuse notes, bringing forgotten mitts to the baseball field, and calling the coach to demand better positions on the team. While their child is sleeping, parents are typing the book report that is due in the morning. Clothing is scattered until mommy hangs it all up. What's wrong with this picture?

These children don't know the meaning of consequences. They assume that parents will always be around to remedy the situation. Responsibilities are not taken seriously. After all, if mommy and daddy will take care of it, why should I?

But this is not real life. At some point, the child will have to be away from home, answer to higher authority figures, and be a spouse and parent who must take care of others. These children can't possibly stand on their own two feet. They will cave in to the pressure of deadlines, late night feedings, and stress that life and relationships inevitably bring. We are not helping our children when we constantly step in—in fact, we are harming them. They will wind up clueless when it comes to handling real life. Disappointments become overwhelming.

Solution: Stop fixing. Instead, work on helping your child find solutions. Allow your children to make mistakes, experience failures, and see how natural consequences happen. Recognize their efforts at doing better. Try not to express impatience if they are working at a slower pace or don't keep up with your quicker ways.

It is important, too, to allow a child the space to experience being bored or hungry. Instead of you, the parent, resolving the frustration, let your child come up with a solution. Some children grumble and whine, "I'm so bored; there's nothing to do," when there is a house filled with games, gadgets, and siblings, and the outdoors is calling. Or they complain, "There's nothing to eat in this house. I'm starving." Instead of suggesting activities or rushing to prepare a snack, guide your child to figure out what he can do to help himself in a positive way.

Take a step back from undertaking your child's responsibilities. Speak about how to set up a study schedule, house rules, and maintain agreed-upon accountabilities. Being part of a family means that everyone is required to pitch in and help. Do not allow children to get away with laziness because it's easier for you to just do it yourself than chase after them to do it. Responsibility leads to respect.

Parents, find the courage to say no. Realize that happiness comes from within. Allow children to taste success through hard work and sweat. You will find children who contribute more, appreciate life's blessings, and bring goodness to this world.

Ways to Help Your Child Be More Successful This Year

Focusing on these daily habits will help your child flourish

Regardless of your child's age, there are steps that you can take to help your child thrive and flourish more this year. The key is focusing daily on these habits. Our children recognize our priorities when we don't drop the ball despite the pressures and stress of family life.

DAILY RESPONSIBILITY

Putting homework and books into knapsacks nightly, clearing away plates and cutlery from the dinner table, and placing laundry in the hamper are all examples of daily tasks that teach children to be responsible.

When you realize that the mess you make is yours to clean and that no one but you is accountable for your tasks, maturity is gained.

Waking up in time to make it for the bus or minyan is a part of being accountable for our time. While it's OK to sometimes give a child a pass when they've stayed up late studying or at a family celebration, we need to be sure that sleeping in and lateness (and after a while, laziness) does not become a pattern of behavior.

Parents often give lectures about being responsible, but the real way of transmitting this essential character trait is through making sure that we live what we preach. Many parents have told me that as their children have grown, they've been forced to take a hard look at their own daily schedules and habits. The truth is, when we parent our children, we parent ourselves as well.

Our next step is to confront the situation in a constructive manner. If you see that your child is sleeping in too many mornings, it is time to address this issue, together. Speak about natural consequences, such as going to sleep earlier, owning the situation by setting one's own alarm clock, and dealing with the ramifications of being late to school. Try to understand from your child what he or she is thinking and how they would like to overcome this hurdle in a positive way.

Successful children understand that they can be self-reliant and independent.

GOOD PEOPLE SKILLS

Children who are socially happy in school and know how to settle conflicts with peers will be more successful students. If you see that your child is getting bogged down in arguments with siblings or friends, make a mental note of what is happening. Is your child overly sensitive? Is she easily explosive? Does he always have to get his way? Does your child know how to give space to others—both physical and emotional? Is shyness or lack of self-confidence preventing socialization?

Social skills are not automatic. As children grow, we may notice that they are being excluded. Some children are socially awkward. Others don't know how to read social cues properly. And there are those whose parents hovered when they were little so that they are now inept in grade school, high school, and even college.

A twenty-year study at Penn State and Duke found that kids with good social skills became more successful as years passed; it behooves us to help guide our children.

How can we help our children with their social skills?

Pay attention to the way that your child deals with peers and family members. Instead of jumping in, allow your child to navigate situations. If you must, speak privately to your child about the right way to apologize and forgive. (Some adults may need to brush up on these skills themselves before trying to teach them to their children.) Open your child's eyes to feeling empathy, giving a helping hand to someone in need, and being sensitive to another's challenges. Help your child read and learn how to respond to social cues.

Many of our children sit in front of their screens completely oblivious to the people around them. Facial expressions, eye contact, and body language may be completely ignored or misread. They do better with emojis than living, breathing human beings and real faces. Texting all types of emotions is easy, but saying, "I'm sorry," "I'm so happy to see you," or, "I'm excited" feels clumsy. The power of a kind word, reassuring gesture, and sympathetic eye cannot be minimized. Our children are losing this vital human connection through which relationships are built and endure.

Linger and spend extra time chatting with your child. Talk about the little things so that the lines of communication remain open. Remember that talking together requires your time and patience. You will be teaching your child the art of conversation while building bonds of love as you speak.

GOOD STUDY HABITS

Children require calm and adequate time to study. Pushing off studying and procrastinating until the last possible minute is a bad habit to get into. Checking texts or devices while doing homework ensures a distracted mind. A noisy environment does not encourage concentration. If you know that your child is a procrastinator or that assignments are consistently missed as the year passes, set a goal to tackle the issue this year. Ask your child before the problems begin: What can we do to make this year better? Involve your child in the solution. Good study habits bring children to feel more secure and self-assured as they face their school day.

Parents should be careful not to put down their children's teachers and authority figures. We must model the behavior that we expect. When we speak respectfully of teachers and school rules, children understand that their behavior toward school and authority matters.

VALUE OPPORTUNITY FOR GROWTH

We have come to fear failure. Many parents would rather stay up the entire night and complete the science fair project than see their child grapple with a poor grade. Take a step back and recognize that even when not doing well, there is an opening for growth. Embrace the opportunity to grow through challenge. There is no life that will not be touched by disappointment. Each person will find himself in a situation where he has fallen and must pick himself up and try again. If never allowed the experience, how will our children know the power of their efforts?

Resilience cannot be taught; it must be lived. Give your child space to grow.

ENCOURAGE LEADERSHIP AND VISION

Our children are capable of greatness and of accomplishments beyond imagination. We must allow them to think big, to soar, and not to limit their dreams because we think their visions are impossible.

After a Chanukah party where my daughter spoke to young girls and their mothers about the courage of the heroine, Yehudis, one preteen asked if she could speak with me.

"I want to be like Yehudis," Lily said. "I want to do something for the Jewish people."

I loved seeing the fire in her eyes.

I told her about a coming event that we would be having for our Hineni women and girls. "Maybe you could do something for that event? We will be celebrating and speaking about the joy of Shabbos...let's think together with your mom."

This young girl came up with a plan. She decided to make slime and sell it. She would take the profits and use it to create something special for our upcoming event.

Instead of saying "impossible," Lily's mother encouraged her. Her grandmother cheered her on and had her friends buy slime for their grandchildren. She sold her slime to friends and neighbors. Somehow, this ten-year-old girl managed to raise one thousand dollars from all her hard work.

Now the real effort began. Lily transformed her dream into reality.

The night of our event, each family received the most magnificent silver and gold embroidered challah cover, sponsored by Lily.

On the inside, Lily composed these words:

Created with love by Lily Mark

In memory of our dear Rebbetzin Esther Jungreis

With wishes that we all feel the light of Shabbos in our hearts

Children who think beyond themselves, and try to make a difference in this world, grow to embrace success. We must fortify their hopes and allow their dreams.

The Stress of Modern Parenting

The power of a parent's love is more valuable than any after-school activity, technology, or pair of sneakers that money can buy

I received a call to give a lecture to a group of parents who were dealing with anxiety.

"What are they anxious about?" I asked. "Everything" was the response.

The next day, the front page of the *New York Times* read: "Stress, Exhaustion, and Guilt: Modern Parenting."

What's going on in our homes?

The article describes parents who, regardless of their economic situation, are constantly monitoring their children. There is tremendous anxiety over trying to get children to climb higher and ensure that their children succeed or, at least, do as well as their parents financially. Trying to get their children into after-school activities, the right high schools and post-high school programs, paying for numerous tutors or being sure that high grades are achieved through constant oversight is taking a hard toll. Parenting is grinding. Parents are getting worn out.

It begins with infanthood, as parents (and grandparents) are pressured to buy the top name-brand strollers and baby gear. Baby monitors record a child's every movement and whimper. There is stress to join the latest classes for tots, and the strain to continuously keep up with their classmates' after-school activities only increases with time.

Adult conversation and time together between husband and wife have suffered.

Of course, family time is valued, but a balance must be found.

What is the effect of this "constant contact" on children?

Psychologists and others have warned that our children's over-dependence on parents and hyper-intensive mothers and fathers have produced kids who are living with more anxiety. They are less satisfied with their lives. They are filled with stress. When children are given the opportunity to play freely and have leisure time, they build social skills, develop emotional security, and learn how to function in various settings.

THE REAL ISSUE

There is more going on here than the pressure of increased time and monitoring of children by their parents.

FOMO, fear of missing out, due to comparative living on social media, has caused tremendous damage to our family life. Parents feel inadequate when others post their children's accomplishments, trophies, acceptance letters, and star roles in productions or on the hockey team. Photos of vacations, Chol Hamoed trips, shopping expeditions, and over-the-top experiences pressure parents to prove to themselves that they, too, are great parents who can give it all to their kids.

Mothers and fathers worry that they are not doing enough, providing enough, or investing enough. Regardless of education, income, or race, parents feel that the most hands-on and expensive choices are best. Social media only fuels the fire.

Parents exhibit their own insecurities, which trickle down to their children. Why must we post our inner lives for the world to see? Why are vacations more enjoyable if we take the world with us? Why must we publicize high marks, gifts of jewelry, lavish *upsherins*, villas in Orlando, expensive new sneakers, or evenings out? I ask in my talks: "Why does sushi taste better if we post it?" We cannot base our lives on the lives that others live. Counting other people's blessings prevents us from seeing our own.

THE TOLL ON MOTHERS

All this stress has taken the greatest toll on mothers. Though fathers have increased their participation in children's lives, the real expectation falls on mothers. The time that women spend trying to help their children keep up is coming at the expense of sleep, time with their husbands and friends, leisure activities, and other household needs. The pull between career and time spent with children can also produce great angst.

The power of a mother's love is more valuable than any after-school activity, technology, or pair of sneakers that money can buy. Living with a stressed-out parent, no matter how hard she is working to maximize a child's experiences, frays the bond between parent and child. Better to stop comparing and sending the message to children that our self-worth is intertwined with other parents' posts and activities that we keep checking.

Be authentic to the type of parent that you believe you should be. Be true to the experiences that you want your child to have, and don't do things merely because someone else decided it's *the* thing to do. Reflect on a woman's true mission in the home: to imbue each child with strong roots, spirituality, and a life legacy, as she transmits her mother's milk of faith. A mother guards her child from harm even as she carries the newest soul in her womb. As the child grows, the mother continues on this path and tries to teach her child the difference between right and wrong, nourishing his or her soul and spirit with holiness and values. "*Chochmas nashim bansah beisah*—The wisdom of women builds their home."[1] Women have a vital role in their children's lives.

---

1 *Mishlei*-Proverbs 14:1.

Not every day will be perfect. We will make mistakes. We must be able to forgive ourselves and know that we are trying our best to build strong, loving homes. Don't fall into the trap of pressure, exhaustion, or guilt. Parenting can be the most magical and joyful experience—if we allow it to be.

Take a moment of introspection to ponder your parenting journey. Don't look back at these years with regret because you were caught up with everyone else's desires. Live your life, know your children's needs, see your blessings, and build a home filled with love. Leave the stress and guilt behind.

Over-Zealous Parenting Is Harming Our Children

How to raise independent kids in today's world

One of my favorite childhood memories is riding my bike Sunday afternoons and pedaling through the leafy sidewalks of North Woodmere. I lived in a quiet suburban community with open spaces, shady trees, and lots of winding roads.

These were the days before Amber Alerts, 9/11, raging terrorism, the pandemic, ugly anti-Semitism, constant after-school programs, and hours spent texting or checking out your phone. We kids loved to be free and explore our world. Today's children are growing up in a totally different environment. It can be stifling.

Andrea Petersen's article "The Overprotected American Child" in the *Wall Street Journal* laments the lack of independence in our children today. Fewer kids walk to school on their own. Parents have been charged with neglect when they allowed their sons and daughters to play or walk unsupervised. As a result, psychologists are seeing more children and young adults with anxiety disorders. "Over-zealous parenting can do real harm," Petersen writes.

The connection between anxiety and lack of independence is strong. The more autonomy a child is given, the less anxiety they exhibit. When we enclose our children in bubble wrap, we mistakenly believe that we are safeguarding them for life. In reality, we are making them even more anxious.

Overprotecting children doesn't shield them from harm. Instead, it conveys the message that the world is frightening and dangerous. Children feel ill-equipped to handle stress. They remain over-dependent on mommy and daddy, seeking their parents' solutions instead of finding their own as they grow. When decisions need to be made, they doubt themselves because their parents have always stepped in.

We don't want our children to be scared of life, thus lacking the necessary skills needed to navigate daily living. We want them to become self-sufficient, self-reliant, and self-assured.

Torah gives us this message of the importance of children's independence and self-reliance in a most beautiful way. When Sarah Imeinu weaned her son, Yitzchak, the words used are "*Va'yigdal ha'yeled, va'yi**gamel***—The child grew and was weaned."[2] The root of the word for weaned, ***gamal***, can also mean "to give," such as when we say *gemilus chessed*, to give kindness. We must understand that we are truly giving our children the greatest gift by weaning, stepping back, and allowing them to rely on their own resources and efforts.

Yes, we need to deal with the reality of the world today. There are some really awful stories out there. Parents need to have a sense of safety and awareness and guide their children accordingly. Different cultures and different neighborhoods bring different rules. I recall being astounded when I visited my daughter in Israel and saw young children crossing streets and running errands for their mothers at the local supermarket. But that does not mean that just because you live in a more guarded society, your children cannot find their own spirit of independence.

The question is: How?

First, examine if you are doing for your children that which they can do for themselves. Parents struggle with time crunch, pressure, and tight schedules. We often let our children off easy.

---

2 *Bereishis*-Genesis 21:8.

If you'd like to teach your child independence, begin with age-appropriate skills that they can learn in the home. As children grow, they can be involved in their food prep and even cooking with a parent's watchful eye. Teaching safety and techniques allows for self-reliance instead of greater expectations for parents to do it all. The result is self-confidence and self-esteem, not based on empty praise, but because they themselves see how they are naturally growing into capable and competent young adults.

Independence outside our home is more difficult to achieve, but it is possible. Again, it is up to a parent's wisdom and discretion. Besides thinking about how to navigate street crossings, mall outings, and venturing outdoors, here are some guidelines for parents to keep in mind:

- Provide clear rules and understandings about curfews, distances, what to do when feeling lost or unsafe, and expected responsibilities.
- Speak about consequences if rules and responsibilities are not followed.
- Teach children to own their behavior. Explain: You are responsible for your mistakes, causing harm, damage, and bad behavior. If you hurt others, you need to make amends. Don't make excuses or seek to blame others. It's not about who else did it, who pushed you to do it, or it somehow being everyone else's fault, but what you did. Be accountable.
- Allow children to overcome fears, take risks, and gain courage. For example, talk together about how shyness can be conquered in small steps, or seek solutions instead of remaining frightened of dogs or heights. Empower your child.
- Realize that we cannot manipulate our children's friendships, sleepover invitations, and social lives. Yes, when they are small, we can help with playdates. That ends early on, though, and then our children need to navigate on their own. We can try to guide them, help them recognize the meaning of true friendship, and open our homes and hearts. Ultimately, we hope they will make good choices because we have taught them well.

- Guide children to help and do for themselves. They can fulfill their needs and requirements without expecting parents to come to the rescue. One gym teacher told me that I would not believe the number of students who blame their mothers for not packing their sneakers.

MAKING CHANGES

If you desire to bring more independence to your child's life, begin with these five ideas:

- Communicate that you would like to see more self-reliance. Say something positive like, "Now that you are in junior high school, you can..." And be clear about responsibilities.
- Give your children a sense of time with clocks, watches, and phone alarms that they can use to stick to a schedule and learn how to appropriately balance their time.
- Acceptance: Don't get stuck on perfection. Recognize efforts and then work on bettering skills.
- Begin with the positive. If your son dressed himself, recognize that before mentioning that his shirt is on backward. Energize instead of criticizing.
- Teach solution skills. No matter the age, you will find your child struggling with something. Don't rush in to fix the problem. Instead, encourage them to find solutions.

When we cannot step back and allow children to make mistakes or discover life's magic on their own, they lose the power to spread their wings. As children grow, they want to rely less on us, but still be aware of our love and inspiration. We have the ability to help our sons and daughters flourish, gain independence, and nourish their souls so that they can make a difference in this world.

Remember, we cannot possibly protect our children by outsmarting tomorrow. But we can provide them with a toolbox today.

Harmful Habits That Impede Children from Creating Healthy Relationships

How parents unknowingly hinder children's abilities to form strong relationships later in life

Young men and women often tell me about their frustration with the quality of the relationships that they've been in. Issues with commitment, lack of responsibility, and an inability to give of one's time wholeheartedly were all part of their dating experience.

It made me wonder if parents may be unknowingly doing things that hinder their children's abilities to form strong relationships later in life. What can parents do while raising their kids that will help them create stronger commitments when they grow up?

DRONE PARENTING

This is "helicopter parenting on steroids." These are parents who shield children from pressure, overprotect them, and micromanage their lives. Through technology, parents are now able to be involved by monitoring children and tracking them from afar. Children get used to parents being a constant silent presence, managing their lives and removing obstacles that create stress. Such parents may do their child's homework or dominate their school projects so that they get the best grade possible. There have been incidents of parents accompanying their adult children to job interviews, calling high school teachers and college professors about poor grades and difficult assignments, and joining children at college orientations intended solely for students.

Children require the ability to act on their own, make real decisions, and deal with life independently. How can young adults move on with life when their parents are hovering above them? Learning to navigate relationships requires a sense of fortitude that comes with overcoming obstacles. Sometimes sweat and hard work are called for. If a child has not faced difficult circumstances, he or she will not be able to handle the ups and downs that every relationship entails.

THE TEACHER IS NEVER RIGHT

While it is crucial to listen to your child, the way that you speak about your child's teachers will impact the way that he learns to treat others. We live in a culture where, most times, it's assumed that the teacher/school/coach/principal/camp director is wrong. Arguing, disrespecting, and even yelling by parents have become normal behaviors that children observe. Children are made to feel as if they are always right. I've spoken to teachers who told me that they encounter students who flippantly say, "Just wait till my father speaks to the board about you."

Marriage requires respect. Husband and wife must honor one another. No one is always right. There are times that apologies are required in a relationship. If a child grows up believing that he or she is never wrong, they may end up destroying their relationships with their arrogant behavior, and this is the kind of behavior that can kill a marriage.

LACK OF RESPONSIBILITY

How many children are given real responsibilities today? We've created an overindulged generation. It's just easier to do it all ourselves than deal with griping and complaining children. There are also parents who harangue and scream the same lines over and over again without seeing results or imposing any consequences. Seeds of selfishness sprout entitled young adults.

Relationships work when we feel responsible for our words and actions. Giving time and energy and being sensitive to the needs of others are crucial ingredients for forging lasting bonds. Relationships cannot flourish without selflessness, a dedication and devotion beyond oneself. The word for "love," ***ahavah***, has the root word "***hav***," which means to give. Because the more we give, the more we love. Instead of asking, "What does he do for me?" we must teach our children to ask, "What can I do for him?" or, "How do I make her feel?"

We need to give our children responsibilities that expand their abilities to contribute and look beyond themselves.

RAISING TAKERS

The world is made up of givers and takers. What is your child?

Givers are happier people. They feel more joy in life. They are not entitled. They live with a sense of purpose and mission.

Takers are never content. Whatever you give them, it is never enough. They always want more, and they want it now.

When children sit as their parents constantly do everything for them, they're never given the opportunity to taste the joy that comes with being a giver. They also believe that relationships are more about taking than giving.

Marriage comes with sacrifice. We sometimes must look away at our own needs and desires and think about the wishes of another. There are moments when we don't feel like doing what our spouse wants to do, but we do it anyway, and with a smile. Why? Because we know that we are giving to the person that we love and that makes us happy.

But this will only happen if we practice a life of giving with our children while they are under our roofs. Once they are on their own, it is too late to transmit this life lesson.

If we take the time to think about our parenting now, we can help our children build a foundation that will ensure that they succeed when they are ready to build their own homes with joy.

CHAPTER 2

Building Character

A Lesson in Self-Esteem

Teaching our kids who they really are and what makes them special

Dear Slovie,

My twelve-year-old son, David, is in seventh grade. At his middle school, there is a clique of "popular kids" who have begun having bar mitzvah parties. My son, though he is kind, funny, intelligent, and warm, has always had a hard time making many friends because of his shyness in social situations. It's hard for him to be social, and he's not invited to most of these bar mitzvah parties. Most of the kids hand out sweatshirts as swag favors at their parties. The Monday after their party, all of the kids who were at the event come to school wearing the sweatshirt. My son comes home many Mondays feeling sad.

Last week, my son attended a party of a boy whose father does business with my husband (which is why he was invited, since this boy doesn't really talk to my son). When Monday morning came, my husband and I told David he was not allowed to wear the sweatshirt to school because I remembered the lessons you taught us about teaching our children compassion. We told him that just as his feelings were hurt on so many Mondays, other children will be hurting now. And it's also like bragging that you went to a popular boy's bar mitzvah. He listened but wasn't happy. When he came home, he said that all the kids who were wearing their sweatshirts made the others feel bad anyway so why couldn't he wear his? I told him that regardless of what others did, he knew he hadn't caused others pain.

I feel like it was a character–building experience that he will one day understand. Please let me know if I did the right thing.

Sarah

I read the email and had to pause for a moment. I was incredibly moved by this mother's courageous determination to teach her child a lesson in compassion. After all, wouldn't most parents want their children to finally "fit in" and wear the "right shirt"? But the truth is, this mother not only taught her child to open his heart, but she also gave him the gift of self-esteem.

Later that night, we spoke.

"The first thing I want you to do," I began, "is to sit down with your son and have a conversation. Tell him how proud you are of the way he respected your decision, even though it was difficult for him to carry through. Too often we criticize our children, but neglect to tell them how proud we are of them.

"Next, I would like you to explain that when he feels hurt by others in life, he should always try to remember that feeling so that he never inflicts pain on anyone else. It would be so much easier, of course, to just forget about the other kids who are feeling sad and leave them behind. But then what? You are acting the same way as those who hurt you. The point of going through something is not to grow insensitive, but, rather, to grow from the experience and become a kinder, more compassionate human being. That way, you know in your heart of hearts that you have taken the higher road, and that is the greatest road to take in life."

"That is exactly the lesson I wanted David to walk away with," Sarah replied.

"But here is the greatest lesson of all," I added. "Ask David this question: If these kids are being nice to him and including him only when he wears the 'in' sweatshirt, what kind of friends are these? What happens next week, when he's back Monday morning without the right sweatshirt on? Are they back to not including him because he wasn't at the big weekend party? If someone is your friend only for the label on your shirt, is that called a true friend? And then, if you lose the label, do you lose your friends? Do you lose your sense of self? Are you only as good as the sweatshirt on your back? Ask yourself, without this shirt, who am I?"

"I never thought of it like that," Sarah said.

ANGELS ON EARTH

"Listen, Sarah, I want to tell you a story, and I want you to relay this story to David. When my children were little, we would often stay at my parents' home for Shabbos. My siblings would join us with all their little ones and, though space was tight, incredible love and laughter filled the house. Friday night, after finishing the meal, all the cousins would gather together and ask my mother to tell them a story. 'Bubba, can you tell us about when you were a little girl?' they would say.

"No matter how exhausted she was, my mother would settle down with her grandchildren around her, waiting to hear their Bubba's tales. One of my children's most requested stories was my mother's description of Shabbos in Bergen-Belsen. Each week, my Zaydah, my grandfather, would set aside his meager portion of stale bread. When Friday night would arrive, Zaydah would gather his children close, together with Mama, my grandmother. My mother described the scene to all the grandchildren who surrounded her."

> *"Close your eyes, kinderlach," Zaydah would whisper. "Imagine that you are home, and the Shabbos candles are lit. The licht are dancing and Mama's challah is warm. The house is filled with light." Zaydah would take out his hidden crumbs and share them with us.*

> *Zaydah then began to hum Shalom Aleichem, the prayer that we sing to welcome the angels of Shabbos into our home. For those few minutes, we were back home, away from all the darkness. One week, my little brother called out, "Tatty, you are singing to the malachim, but I don't see any malachim here!" Zaydah began to cry. He looked at us and said, "You, my most precious children, you are the malachim."*

These thoughts were the lightning rod that electrified my mother's life, my life, and the life of my children, until today. We are the *malachim* of Shabbos! And then my mother would add:

> *You know what, my children? Each morning I had to stand at roll call in the freezing cold. I was dressed in rags. My head was shaved, there were sores all over my body, and I was covered with lice. I was starving. I looked at those Nazi guards standing across from me in their shiny boots, warm woolen coats, and vicious German shepherd dogs. But to me they had nothing, and I had everything. I would never in a million years want to be one of them. I would rather be starving and freezing, but still be me, the daughter of Zaydah and Mama, the daughter of kings and prophets, a bas melech, and an angel here on earth.*

"Sarah," I said, "here is your opportunity to teach David an incredible lesson for life. It's not your sweatshirt, your phone, your sneakers, or your car that defines you. It is your heart, your soul, your deeds, and how you impact others in this world that tells you who you are. Especially now, when the world is in chaos, we need to give our kids a true sense of what really counts in life. Who you really are, and what makes you so special."

"I can't wait to speak to David," Sarah said. "There is so much I want to share with him. You're right, we have been feeling stressed from all the pressures right now...and I know that if I give David an understanding of who he is, I'll be giving him one of the greatest gifts a parent can give a child."

Recently, I received an email from Sarah:

> *Dear Slovie,*
>
> *I just dropped David off at school. It's Monday! As he was getting out of the car, David turned to me and said, "Look Mom, there are all those kids in those silly sweatshirts," and then he laughed. And I laughed too. Thank you for helping me teach my son one of the greatest lessons of his life.*
>
> *Sarah*

It is up to us parents to ask ourselves: Who am I? What defines me? And how do my children define themselves? If we are able to discover our sense of self beyond the cars that we drive and the labels on our backs, we will then be able to impart to our children a greater understanding of self. They will then be fortified to climb the many mountains that life's challenges bring. And that is true self-esteem.

Not Gifted? Get Over It

How we can stop raising a generation of narcissists

Researchers at the University of Amsterdam studied 565 kids and 705 parents over two years to understand what makes kids narcissists. They went beyond the presumption that smartphones and trophies given for participation make it easier today to create a self-absorbed generation. Instead, they focused on the parenting style that produces narcissist kids, those who "feel superior to others, fantasize about personal success, and believe that they deserve special treatment."

They found that parents who worship their children and teach their sons and daughters that they are "extraordinary," "amazing," and "the best" encourage overblown views of themselves. At the same time, these kids have been found to look down with disdain on others. As they grow, so does their arrogance and self-love.

The problem is that the world does not think of them the way that their parents do. Take twenty-two "amazing" kids and put them into a classroom, and you will find twenty-two children who can't understand why their teacher does not find them "amazing." Their inflated perception leads to a road of disappointment, anxiety, and feelings of inadequacy.

YOU'RE SO GIFTED!

Parents mistakenly praise the smallest accomplishments, believe their children are entitled to extra special treatment, and overstate their kid's achievements.

How often do we look at our children's drawings and say, "Wow! Unbelievable!" At Little League games we call out, "You were amazing!" I have heard parents tell their Lego-building kids, "No one can do what you do!" And after a dance recital, "You were the best! A superstar!"

Self-esteem is not developed through grandiose compliments.

Children lavished with overblown praise who possess an inflated sense of self can easily grow into arrogant kids. They have learned to expect compliments, require constant affirmation, and find it difficult to accept constructive criticism. The late Jeffrey Zaslow wrote an article titled, "The Most Praised Generation Goes to Work" for *The Wall Street Journal*, in which he recounts the difficulties that bosses and spouses face as they live with those who have been "uber-stroked" since childhood. We hear of companies that give praise through "Celebration Voice Mailboxes" (giving employees consistent praise throughout the day), accolades for simply showing up to work, and hire consultants to teach managers how to compliment employees. Zaslow adds that as this generation, which has been thought of as "gifted" by their parents grows up, "bosses, professors, and mates are feeling the need to lavish praise on young adults or else see them wither under an unfamiliar compliment deficit."

This constant need for compliments and applause has deep social ramifications. Inappropriate or constant accolades cause young adults to feel insecure if they are not receiving the constant compliments that made them feel "special" throughout their childhood. A psychotherapist and divorce attorney quoted in the article adds that "young married people who've been very praised in their childhoods, particularly, need praise for both their child side and their adult side." When we live with people who require more ego stroking, relationships can be taxing.

And that leaves us to ponder: What is the right way to help our children achieve self-esteem?

THE BEST PARENTING STRATEGY

What is true self-esteem? We can derive an answer from the Talmud that asks why God created Adam, the first man, alone. Why didn't He create the world fully populated? Our sages teach us that we are to learn from this that every one of us should look at the world and say, "The world was created for me." Every individual is vital and has a unique mission that only he or she can fulfill.

Knowing that I count, that I make a difference, and that I have a significant spiritual fingerprint that can impact this world makes me feel pride and secure in who I am. I do not require others to constantly tell me that I am "special" or "amazing." My self-respect should never be dependent on other people's words or their lavish praise.

Each child should be raised with the understanding that there is a singular, unique spirit that lies within him. If we are able to help our children discover that uniqueness, we will give them the gift of self-esteem. Here is the vital message to impart to each of our children: There is only one of you in the entire world. God created you for a reason. Realize your purpose. You have a unique mission that only you can accomplish. Discover your unique God-given gifts and use them to make this world better.

To help our children harness this singular spirit, parents can work toward generating a positive identity. This becomes the spiritual dimension of self-esteem—guiding our children to reveal their true self-worth.

HOW TO CREATE A POSITIVE SELF-IMAGE

1. Teach Children the Value of Their Actions

We can teach our children that they are unique because they have the ability to impact others through their kindness and good deeds, giving them a legacy by which to live. It's easy for children to impact others and feel good about themselves: Their smile can brighten up a room. Their music lifts a dark mood. Their phone call to grandparents elicits joy. Their shared snack invites friendship. Their invitation to join a game dispels loneliness. The possibilities to create blessing in this world are endless. Our children will feel pride that the world is a better place because they exist; this is true self-esteem. The talents that they have been given are not an end in themselves, but a means through which they can touch people. Such an idea can be empowering.

2. Focus on Efforts and Real Accomplishments

Instead of lavish praise, we should focus on their efforts and real accomplishments. Too many parents reward their kids for tasks they are expected to do. Children are left with the impression that they deserve praise for putting their plate in the dishwasher, picking up their laundry, or doing their homework. Ultimately, these children grow to believe that the world revolves around them, which demands no effort on their part; they just have to show up, and they receive accolades.

Helping children discover their self-worth is the path that comes not through over-praising our kids but through harnessing the unique spirit that lies within their souls.

The Angry Child

Tips to empower parents

Dear Slovie,

My ten-year-old son is getting increasingly out of hand. He yells out his demands and gets infuriated when they are not met. If I reprimand him or put him into time-out, he takes out his anger on his siblings and me. He speaks very disrespectfully and tends to be quite negative. His behavior is detrimentally affecting everyone in the house. I am out of ideas. I would appreciate any advice you can give me; I am at my wits' end.

Thank you,

Mom at the end of her rope

Dear Mom,

There are times that we must deal with an angry child. We confront heavy silences, sudden outbursts, feeling estranged and deep pain as harsh words are flung at us. Often, we want to explode.

Here are practical tips on how to deal with an angry child.

1. Don't React to Anger with Anger

We accomplish nothing by losing our temper, yelling, or giving emotional ultimatums. When we are out of control, we say things we don't mean. Often, we are left with regret. We certainly don't solve the problem and may, in fact, cause greater damage. Parents who yell encourage children to yell back louder or retreat into a shell.

2. Don't Slap or Get Physical

Many times, I receive questions from parents about hitting. Usually it goes something like this:

"My parents/in-laws/husband/wife says that what this kid needs is a good slap. That was the only thing that worked when we were growing up, and it is the only thing that will set this child straight."

Sorry, today this will just not work. You will only be teaching your child to hit when he is frustrated or angered. You will also begin to notice that your children are using their hands against each other. Nothing was accomplished. Ask yourself how this child will handle his frustrations as a husband or father one day.

The Gemara gives us the reason why hitting an older child is not allowed. The parent is placing a stumbling block in front of the child that could bring the child to rebel and mimic his parent's actions by raising his hand and hitting back.[1] But it has

1 *Kiddushin* 30a.

become understood that in our world today, this logic applies not only to teens and preteens, but even our younger children. The bond between parent and child can be damaged beyond repair with harsh physical discipline. A child's self-confidence will be destroyed as well. Anger will build and transform into rage.

3. Don't Give In to Nagging

When a child sees that constant nagging forces you to retreat from your position, he learns exactly which button to push. He comes to understand that whining or refusing to take your no as a final answer will yield results. Whenever he does not get his way, he will go into tantrum mode until you surrender. It makes no difference if you are dealing with a toddler or a teen, as a parent you cannot be afraid to say no. Be consistent and stick to your decision.

4. Wait for Calm to Talk It Out

Our sages teach us that we should not approach a person in their moment of anger. Trying to reason with your child in the midst of his outburst will not cede the results you are seeking. Use minimal words and say, "When you are ready to speak calmly and respectfully, I am happy to listen." Younger children can be told that they can sit in a "calm down space" until the tantrum is over. There is no problem in saying to an older child, "You obviously need a breather. I am here when you are ready to speak."

Our goal is to teach children to find a way to calm themselves in angry moments.

5. Discover the Trigger

It is a good idea to ask yourself, "What triggered this outburst in my child?" Children often explode because they are feeling embarrassed, left out, anxious, frustrated or hurt. They respond in anger because they feel helpless. Anger is an emotion; figuring out the source of the emotion can go a long way.

6. Create Alternative Solutions

Instead of simply criticizing or disciplining the angry outburst, explore better responses together. In a calm moment—certainly not in the eye of the storm—ask your child for other options besides rage. Explain that he or she can be part of the solution and not the problem. But we need to provide the tools. You can role-play or discuss together how this can be handled more appropriately next time.

7. Focus on Your Own Physical Reaction

When we start to pay attention, we recognize that our bodies give us warning signals before we reach the explosive territory of no return. If we take a step back, we realize that our hearts are racing or that we are clenching our jaws or fists. We breathe differently, narrow our eyes, and become enraged. As we grow more attuned to our body's "red flags," we can learn to step back at that crucial moment. This can be life transforming as we rid ourselves of angry, out-of-control reactions.

8. Allow Children to Experience Failure and Frustration

Too many kids today do not know how to handle failure and disappointment. They crumble as they taste defeat. Thinking that they are helping, parents intervene from the earliest days so that their children can grow up happy and stress free.

"Won't that be too difficult for him to deal with?"

"Won't she be sad if that happens?"

But this is not real life. Instead of helping our children, we are hindering them. When children don't know how to deal with a poor grade, the loss of a game, school deadlines, or difficulties with friends, they grow frustrated and angry. You will hear them say, "It's not fair!" They will give up easily, blame others for their mistakes and not take responsibility for their actions.

We can only appreciate the thrill of success if we sweat, climb, and sometimes fall. Everyone must deal with loss sometime. We cannot shield our children forever.

9. Communicate Love

Children who feel cared for feel secure and safe. Even if they are upset, they know deep inside that they are loved. No matter what happens in life, this is one belief that will never be altered. Show your children that you love them by expressing interest in their ideas and interests. Try to join them at dinner time whenever possible. Put down your phone and really listen. Share your thoughts with them and talk about your day. Be involved in their activities instead of just dropping them off and carpooling them back and forth. Laugh, smile, and don't take everything so seriously. Your child will enjoy your time together, and your connection will grow and be strengthened. Don't wait for a gap to form and then wonder how you can bridge the divide.

10. Role Model

The first nine tips are meaningless if our children watch us lose control when we are confronted with frustration or disappointment. How we deal with our challenges is the greatest teaching moment of all.

A calm home is a happy home. Let's help our children learn how to navigate life successfully and lose the anger.

Kids with No Patience

Teaching our kids patience, anticipation, and humility in today's hassle-free world

Back to school means lots of waiting in line. Stores are filled with parents and kids checking off their long lists of supplies. Even buying shoes for school can become an ordeal. I sat with my daughter-in-law and granddaughters in a crowded children's shoe store and could not believe I watched night fall before it was our turn to be helped.

But what some see as a terribly frustrating experience can become a tremendous opportunity to teach our children an incredible life lesson. As we are confronted with these long waits, it is important to recognize that we are teachers for our children in this awesome classroom called life. Parents who insist that their kids are unable to sit and wait, and try to cut the line, are shortchanging their children. There will be future situations when, no matter who you are or how effectively your parents were able to circumvent the rules, you'll need to draw upon this character trait of *savlanus*, patience.

THE GIFT OF PATIENCE

There will be times when your child will confront frustrating situations: sitting in heavy traffic, waiting for a teacher to call on him when there are twenty-five kids in the classroom requiring attention, not understanding the math homework despite working on the problem for thirty minutes, or wanting the latest scooter now even though he already has a perfectly good model from last year. These are all real scenarios where our children can gain an added dimension to their character growth. Patience is key to helping our children handle moments of exasperation through good *middos* and self-control instead of losing themselves to anger and frustration.

We want our children to react calmly to life's twists and turns. Many parents become upset when they realize that their children cannot deal with even small disappointments. They speak about kids who erupt in anger when carpool is late, homework seems impossible, or supper is not ready on time since they are "starving."

Think about it. You are teaching your child to ride a two-wheeler, and he keeps falling. Would you simply say forget it? Or would you encourage him to keep on trying? That moment that he "gets it" and rides on his own because you did not allow him to give up is exhilarating. You taught him not only to ride his bike. You taught him how to grow patient with himself, to carry on despite frustration, and to endure.

These are the little moments through which we can teach our children to remain composed while they confront their frustrations. Reacting calmly, working through the situation, and not losing it despite being irritated empowers a child to lead with his mind and not just his emotions.

Lashon hakodesh, the Divine language, gives us an added dimension to the importance of *savlanus*, patience. The word for tolerance is *sovlanus*, related to the word *savlanus*. The word *sovel* means "suffer" and also means "carries a load." *Seboles* is endurance, and a *sovel* is a hotel porter. The connection between all these words gives us deep practical wisdom. We are all spiritual porters, carrying our challenges as we journey through life. When we haul a heavy life load, even suffering at times, and go through the hardship successfully, we have learned tolerance. We have discovered the gift of endurance. The *middah* of *savlanus* is born.

We want to raise children who are not complainers. Tolerance and patience help children counter their natural instinct to grumble and kvetch. We all know adults who could work more on their patience/tolerance muscle as well. Helping children grow their *savlanus* muscle when they are young impacts their future abilities to be successful in life, at jobs, and in relationships.

THE GIFT OF ANTICIPATION

Many of us have fond memories of taking our film to be developed. We would anxiously wait for the allotted day and eagerly sort through the package of photos. Some have childhood memories of collections—coins, dolls, stamps, stickers, or stationery. Each time a new piece was acquired, there was a thrilling feeling. Shopping trips meant waiting our turn and knowing that when the next salesperson would be free, we would be helped. I recall checking the mail each day waiting for friends who were overseas to respond to my letters. When I finally spotted the familiar writing, I would rip the envelopes open and hungrily read their words.

Our culture has trained us and our children to live in a world of instant gratification. In a split-second, pictures appear on our cameras and phones. Food is zapped in the microwave. Uber Eats quickly delivers complete meals to our doorway without having to step out of our homes. Emails, WhatsApp, and texts appear instantly. We click, buy online, and our children scroll through Amazon and shopping sites with ease. There is no learning to wait our turn.

Our easy, hassle-free lifestyle has robbed our children of the gift of anticipation. Waiting for a moment to happen or anticipating a desired object makes us appreciate things so much more. We value what we have because we have invested our time and energy in obtaining it. When we are given things too easily, we don't appreciate them, and we stop cherishing our blessings.

COUNTERING ARROGANCE

As we try to make life easier for the next generation, there is another character trait that has remained out of reach: humility. When children are not given the opportunity to see that others come first, they grow arrogant. Waiting means that we open our eyes and see that this world does not only revolve around us. There are other people with whom we share this universe. I am not always number one.

The root of chutzpah and disrespect is *gaavah*, sheer arrogance. Thinking that they must always come first enables a child to speak and act with disdain for others. A person who lives with arrogance pushes away the presence of Hashem from their life. They become so "full of themselves" that there is no room for others—even God.

Let's help our children learn to confront the inevitable ups and downs of life with a more positive spirit, teaching them that patience, anticipation, and humility make this world a better place for us all.

Raising Millennials

How to instill empathy and sensitivity in an age of narcissism and entitlement

Once, waiting in line for a salad, I observed two teens in front of me. They took their iced coffees but, before they drank, there was a ritual. They stuck their straws into their mouths, stood cheek to cheek, and made identical "kissy" faces. They held their phone a few inches away and clicked. As they checked out their image, they giggled together.

Welcome to the iGeneration. We have iPhones, iPads, and iPods that accompany kids throughout their waking hours. They fight sleep as their text messages ping through the night. You need to be sure that you can keep up. You have grown up watching peers post their every move, the dance steps, their sushi rolls, and even their teary-eyed sad faces.

AGE OF NARCISSISM

Here is some shocking hard data that *Time* magazine presented in their article, "The Me Me Me Generation" about millennials—those born between 1980–2000:

- The incidence of narcissistic personality disorder is nearly three times as high for people in their twenties than for the generation that's now sixty-five and older.
- Millennials got so many participation trophies growing up that 40 percent believe that they should be promoted every two years despite performance.
- They are fame obsessed, and convinced of their own greatness.
- They are their own moral guides, with 60 percent believing that they will always just feel what's right in a situation.

When I read all of this, I am reminded of the mother who raised her hand during class with a great parenting tip that she had hoped to share: "A famous politician changed the way that we bring up our son. He said that he believes that he became so successful because, as a child, his parents would always applaud him. So now every morning when our son comes down to the kitchen, my husband and I applaud. "Hooray for Noah!" we say, and then we clap. We feel that we are really giving Noah the gift of self-esteem."

I was floored. How can we applaud a child for simply waking up in the morning and walking into the kitchen? This is not the gift of self-esteem; it's creating a monster.

If this is considered "the norm," how will this generation then raise their own children?

And what happens when these kids grow up and realize that relationships and careers are all about sweating and giving? When your baby wakes up crying at 3 a.m., there is no one applauding you. When your child needs you to hold her hand and you are scared and frightened yourself, no one is telling you how amazing you are.

ARROGANCE AND ENTITLEMENT

Think about it. When you need to figure something out on your new phone or when you need help with your laptop, to whom do you turn? Usually, it is your kids. After a while, our children start rolling their eyes at us, whom they see as ignorant and "left behind." It is difficult to respect somebody if you feel superior to them, especially if that somebody is your parent. This leads to incredible chutzpah and arrogance.

Our children are mostly interacting with their friends and peers. Parents are often shut out and have no idea what their children are up to. I have spoken to parents who were shocked when they discovered secret online accounts, horrifying pictures, and parental blocks that somehow had been bypassed. For some teens, it is a world devoid of adult wisdom. Imagine arriving at your twenties having missed out on years of guidance and inspiration. There is simply a lack of communication. Screen time with peers has overtaken family time. If a teen is skilled, he can text and maintain eye contact at the same time. We are alone, together.

WHAT CAN WE DO?

1. No-Screen Zone

The first thing that we must do is recognize the problem. When parents themselves sit at a breakfast or dinner table and keep half an eye on the screen, they are setting an awful example. We cannot expect more from our children than we do from ourselves. We need to establish a "no-screen zone." This means that mealtimes, both at home and when out, must be set aside as family time.

The same goes for picking up kids from school or while doing an activity with them. Even our toddlers sit in their strollers scrolling on an iPad. Older siblings are shocked when they realize how easily their younger brothers and sisters maneuver their devices. We are quickly becoming disconnected from the ones with whom we are supposed to be sharing our lives. When children see that we are more interested in the person on the other side of the screen, it will not take long for them to get the message that they are number two. They will also infer that tuning out from family is totally acceptable behavior. It is not.

2. Nurture Empathy

Next, we should work on encouraging our children's ability to feel empathy. We can counter narcissism if we ignite the spark of sensitivity and compassion that lies within each child's heart. Allow children to see that this world is not just about them.

We can encourage our children to use their connections to better this world. Imagine if instead of snapping photos of their drinking iced coffees, they would share messages of joining coat drives, marathons, or bake sales for charity. This generation has the world at its fingertips. They can connect to hundreds of peers in an instant. Empowered by their optimism and knowledge, they can be driven when they choose to be. Why not use these gifts to accomplish greatness?

3. Set Limits

There is no doubt that we are growing more addicted to our devices each day. (How many times did you check your phone while reading this chapter?) It is difficult to do any activity without our phones nearby. When kids do homework and try to study while constantly checking their messages, their schoolwork becomes affected. When they stay up late through the night answering "just one more" text, their ability to concentrate in class the next day is impaired. We need to set firm limits. Phones cannot be used throughout the night. Nor can they become part of homework and studying time. This is about self-discipline and self-control. (And for those who wonder how they can enforce these rules—we cannot fear setting limits in our homes. This is where effective discipline and natural consequences come in.)

4. Taste of Shabbos

While trying to conquer this growing addiction, we have been blessed with a built-in formula for success. Once a week, we have been given an incredible gift to reconnect with our families. No phones, no iPads, no iPods. Only Shabbos candles dancing and precious family time. Each week I look around my Shabbos table and am so grateful that I have been given this opportunity to shut off all the stress and pressure of the past few days. We laugh, we speak, we bond, and we rediscover the magic of our family.

One Thursday night, I invited the women I teach to join me, together with their daughters, for a Shabbos Experience. In a beautiful white tent under the stars, we danced, we sang, we shared a Shabbos-type meal, and told stories about the magic of Shabbos. At the end of the night, a woman approached me.

"There is a young girl inside and she is sobbing. Maybe you can find her and see what's wrong?"

I followed the sound of this child's cries. There she was, in the living room, together with her mother.

"Why are you crying, *bubelah*?" I asked.

She took a few moments to catch her breath.

"Because," she sobbed, "I want Shabbos."

"You want Shabbos? And that's why you're crying?"

She nodded solemnly.

"You are crying for Shabbos? I can't believe it! Wow!" I turned toward her mother. "Mommy, your sweet daughter wants Shabbos!"

Her mother nodded. "I know...and I told her I would light my Shabbos candles, and we will have Shabbos."

"So why are you crying, *bubelah*? Your mommy said she will give you Shabbos."

"No," she said sadly. "We can't. We can't have Shabbos." Now fresh tears began to fall.

I bent down to look into this young girl's eyes. "But why can't you have Shabbos?" I asked gently.

"Because...we used to have Shabbos, but then my father died...And then we just stopped." Her sobbing grew louder. "And once you stop having Shabbos you can never ever have it again."

I took this precious *neshamah* into my arms. Now all three of us were crying.

"Listen to me," I said. "Of course, you can have Shabbos again! There's no such thing that you can't bring Shabbos back! Do you know what? Tomorrow night is Friday night. Your mommy is going to light her Shabbos candles again, and the Shabbos lights will fill your home. And in the heavens above, there are *malachim*, angels of Shabbos. When they will see your Shabbos candles lit, they are going to dance and clap, and sing and cry out, 'Look who's back! Look who is bringing Shabbos into the world again!' And do you know who they will be talking about?"

This most precious *neshamah* smiled through her tears. "Me. They will be talking about me."

At that moment, the words of our sages spoke to me: "More than the Jewish people have kept Shabbos alive, Shabbos has kept the Jewish people alive." Let us all give our families the joy, the connection, and the magic of Shabbos.

Teaching Children to Step Up

Torn between a child and her mother

Dear Slovie,

Last month, my dear father passed away after a long illness. My mother is seventy-five years old, but she is not in the best of health. She is diabetic and also has a heart condition, and my father's passing has put her in a very depressed state. I imagine our dilemma is not unique, but for us it has been causing a lot of anguish and a rift in my family. It was decided among my siblings, and I agree with the decision, that we cannot let my mother sleep alone, and each of us will do our share and take responsibility for one night of the week. Some of my sisters don't have young children at home, so they are sleeping with my mother, while other siblings are sending their teenage daughters. My daughter, who is fourteen, is refusing to go. She says that she will not sleep in the same room where my father passed away (my mother lives in a one-bedroom apartment). She also is the child who very rarely went to see my father, because she found it difficult to see him in a compromised way. She is the kind of child who hates changes; she hates sleeping anywhere other than her own bed. I cannot sleep with my mother because I am nursing an infant. My siblings are furious that my husband and I are "letting our daughter get away with it; that we are letting her be selfish, and a child must learn to do chessed" and so on and so forth, and "it's all on their backs now." But my husband and I feel that regardless of whether we think she is right or wrong, we cannot force a fourteen-year-old to do something she doesn't want to do. We don't want this to become a "war" between her and us. My questions are as follows: Do you believe we should force our daughter? What should we tell my siblings? And most importantly, what should we tell our daughter? Should we try to continue to persuade her? And if yes, would you have tips on how to persuade her? And how should we react to her not going? Should we show her that we disapprove of her behavior?

Mom in the Middle

Dear Mom in the Middle,

I would like to first express words of nechamah for your loss. No matter our age, losing a dear parent is most difficult. Coupled with the illness of your mother, dealing with siblings who are "furious," and trying to figure out how to balance your child's needs along with your family—you obviously are handling many emotions right now. There is pain, too, from the anguish and rift in the family. The greatest nechamah would be shalom. There is of course no easy answer to your predicament. Perhaps your resolution will not satisfy all involved. But the main thing is that when looking back at this time of your life, you feel sure that you did the right thing. Regret eats away at the peace of too many people.

You ask a few questions: Should you force your daughter? What do you tell your siblings? And, as you write, "Most importantly, what should we tell our daughter?" I believe that you are correct that communicating well with your daughter is the most important issue here. The rest will follow and fall into place once you have gained clarity. Let us begin by understanding our goal here. The goal is chinuch, and Rashi explains that this refers to the breaking in of a person into the role or task each is destined to perform.[2] *You would like your daughter to step up, to do a chessed, to be mechabed, honor, her grandmother and not allow Bubby to sleep alone. The question, is how could you teach these middos to your daughter? How can you help her step into a role that she is reluctant, even afraid, to carry? What are your choices? You ask if you should force her or show disapproval. Force, threats, and harshness will never yield long-term growth. You may think that you have achieved results, but the child is left with resentment and anger that simmer inside. The short-term results cannot contain the damage done. The key is effective communication. You describe your child's nature. "She hates change. She hates sleeping anywhere but her own bed." She found it difficult to visit with your father in his compromised position and is also fearful of sleeping in the room where her zeidy died. Your mother is unfortunately not well, battling diabetes and a heart condition, and now she is severely depressed. "Chanoch la'naar al pi darko—Educate a child according to his own way,"*[3] *his inborn nature. If we force a child on a path that is inappropriate for his nature, there will be difficult consequences. This does not mean that we cannot expect greatness from our children. But we must figure out how to work with this child's particular nature. Your daughter is sensitive, loves routine, and is expressing a fear of sleeping in a bed that she associates with loss. She is expressing a need for security and safety. She may be afraid of the responsibility of caring for an elderly grandmother who is ill. What happens if there's an emergency while she is there? She may also be afraid of her bubby's depressed state. For some children, none of this*

---

2 *Bereishis*-Genesis 14:14.

3 *Mishlei*-Proverbs 22:6.

would matter. But for your daughter's nature, it is difficult. The question is how do we help your child grow, move out of her comfort zone, extend herself, and experience incredible spiritual and emotional strength?

I suggest three steps: First, make space for your child to be heard. She needs to see that you want to listen to her concerns and understand her needs. Allow your daughter to voice her worries and unease. Tell her that you will address her discomfort in a practical way. It's important that you deal with your daughter's fears. When we are scared, we have an "avoidance reaction," where we walk away from our fears instead of confronting them. This will not be the only time in life that your daughter will be afraid. Children express fears like sleeping alone in their rooms, sleepaway camp, taking exams, trying new experiences; we don't just say "forget it." We help them overcome. It's OK to sometimes be uncomfortable, to stretch in life. This is how we build emotional muscle and resilience. You are helping your child gain "grit," which is a key for success. The goal is chinuch (education), which refers to the breaking in of a person into the role or task each is destined to perform. Next, I would ask that you help your daughter open her heart to her bubby. It is most difficult to require help as one grows older. As a sensitive child, I believe that it is important for your daughter to put herself in her bubby's shoes. What does it feel like for Bubby to sleep alone, to be lonely, to miss Zeidy, and to not feel well? A better understanding elicits empathy and a desire to do chessed. This is not the same as making a child feel guilty by saying things like, "I can't believe you! Why can't you just do this? Why are you being so difficult?" The problem is not selfishness; it is fear. At this point I'd like to add an additional thought. You write that your daughter very rarely went to see your father, because she found it difficult to see him in a compromised way. I do not want to, chas v'shalom, cause you any pain. But for the sake of those reading this response,

I would encourage parents to both role model and help children gain the ability to see grandparents through the many seasons of life. When I was a child, my mother would always take us to visit my Zaydah and receive his berachah even when my Zaydah was very ill. He could not speak and was unable to move. I overcame any fear because I saw the way my mother related to her beloved Tatte. I will forever remember my Zaydah's hands being placed upon my head for a berachah. I was taught and came to learn that this was my greatest zechus. How I wish I would have the opportunity today for just one more such moment in my life. Finally, you work on options together. Perhaps your daughter can sleep over with a cousin (perhaps in the living room) and not go alone at first. Maybe she can bring a friend so that she has company. Perhaps an option is that you join her for the first few times along with your infant—not comfortable, but maybe the bridge needed for her to go it alone. Another idea is that your mother comes to spend Shabbos with you, and that becomes your family's night. Your daughter should be given opportunities to honor her bubby, serving food and drinks, helping Bubby be comfortable and getting to know Bubby better, so that you can segue to the desired long-term solution. We want to give your daughter the confidence needed to overcome her fears. This will help her beyond this situation; it will be life changing. Be truthful with your siblings. You are here for them even if it's not exactly the way they may believe you should be. This may take some time. You are trying your best to come up with a solution that works for everyone's needs. As you kindle your Shabbos licht, add a tefillah to allow your words to enter the hearts of those you love. May you see nachas from your children and give nachas to your dear mother.[4]

4 As published in *Ami Magazine*.

The Entitled Child

We are raising one of the most selfish generations ever—and what to do about it

"Whatever" (sigh).

"Fine" (roll of the eyes).

"Daddy, you have to take me to gymnastics."

"Ma, there's nothing good to eat in this house!"

"I have that already!"

Sound familiar?

Did you ever drive a carpool and notice that the kids just slammed the door shut without even saying a thank you?

Did you ever sit in a restaurant or airplane and watch children being served? Did you hear a thank you or appreciative words given?

One mother said to me, "Forget about gratitude, I'm just happy if my kids don't complain."

Is a thank you so crucial to our children's character, or is it just another polite display of good manners?

Waiting on a line in a shop, I watched a scene in front of me unfold. A teenage girl had piled the counter with clothing. Her mother was standing there waiting for the items to be tallied.

"That will be $464.00," said the saleswoman.

I see the mom wince. The young girl barely looks up. She is busy on her phone.

"Are you sure this is what you want?" the mother asks.

Her daughter snaps her bubble gum, still looking down. "Yeah," she replies without meeting her mother's eyes. She is texting.

Her mom slowly counts out every dollar. Her wallet is now empty. The saleswoman hands her the bag. The young girl has still not acknowledged her mother's presence—forget about the gift of clothing. They leave the store without any exchange, not even a smile. The words "thank you" are never uttered. And guess who's shlepping the bags to the car?

I feel sad for both mother and daughter—the mother, for trying so hard to make her child happy and not feeling appreciated despite the obvious sacrifice, and the daughter, for growing up with such incredible disregard and arrogance. They are on a journey of disrespect and unhappiness.

It is our job as parents to teach our children how to appreciate, voice thankfulness, and grow with character, despite the many hurdles that we face in trying to mold our children's characters. A great part of parenting is setting limits while being loving. Buying more stuff doesn't help us gain entry into our children's hearts.

Too many parents are afraid to tell their kids how to live and act better. They are scared of their children's reactions, frightened that their kids won't like them. Knowing that their disrespect is tolerated, sons and daughters simply mouth off or blatantly ignore their parents.

Parents are also faced with a personal dilemma that stems from their own childhoods. As one mom told me, "When you grow up without, you want your kids to have it all. So, you keep buying whatever they want." We mistakenly equate acquiring things with acquiring love, but the two are not the same.

As parents, *hakaras hatov*, an attitude of gratitude, is one of the most crucial character traits that we can teach our children. Gratitude is the foundation of a home that embodies an atmosphere of respect. When we appreciate our possessions and people in our lives, when children realize that things don't just suddenly appear in our closets and on our plates, then we arrive at an awareness of thankfulness that permeates our life. We come to value and respect both our families and our things, and learn to stop taking it all for granted.

Hakaras hatov goes beyond simply seeing the good. It means we *recognize* the blessings in our life, because there are times when we see something but do not recognize what we are looking at.

WHY GRATITUDE

In a 2008 study published in the *Journal of School Psychology*, children raised with a sense of thankfulness were found to be more optimistic, to have better grades, to be less likely to be depressed, to have a better attitude toward school and family, and to show more satisfaction with life. They also spoke more respectfully and took better care of their things because of their appreciation.

Grateful teens are found to be less envious, depressed, and materialistic than their less appreciative peers. They also use their talents and strengths to improve their surroundings while being engaged in schoolwork and hobbies.[5]

Grateful adults are happier, possess greater self-esteem, and live with more feelings of hope, empathy, and optimism.

GRATITUDE SHAPES CHARACTER

We are given spiritual solutions for living in the Torah. At the onset of the first plague in Egypt, it was Aharon, not Moshe, who was commanded to strike the Nile. As an infant, Moshe's mother had secured him in a basket and placed him in the river. God now wanted Moshe to acknowledge and appreciate the water that had kept him alive.

Would the Nile even know the difference? Did the river go out of its way to carry baby Moshe?

Of course not.

It was not the Nile River that God was concerned about. God was shaping the character of Moshe, future leader of the Jewish people.

This lesson in *hakaras hatov* was to be inculcated within Moshe, and within us, forever.

How do we foster an attitude of appreciation in our homes?

MOMENTS OF DAILY THANKS

Thankfulness should become common in our vocabulary. Look for moments, big and small, about which to express gratitude. You found a parking spot easily? The family is going out and eating dinner together? Make sure your children hear you voice your gratitude. You will find that you yourself will begin to see your world with a more appreciative lens.

THANK YOU, HASHEM

A beautiful way to end each day as we say the *Shema* is to teach our children to thank Hashem for their blessings before they go to sleep. Help younger children think of people, experiences, and things for

---

5 From a 2011 study published in *Psychological Assessment*.

which they are grateful. This will foster a positive awareness that will grow as they do. Open children's eyes to the many blessings we have been given and teach them to habitually say "*Baruch Hashem*" and "Thank You, Hashem."

Parents who make a point of saying their berachos clearly and out loud, and not mumbled in a rush, teach children each day to be mindful of living with expressions of gratitude to God—even for the many delicious foods that we eat.

GRATITUDE BEGINS AT HOME

We often take the people in our lives for granted. We stop seeing all that they do for us and assume that if it's their responsibility, there's no need to express our thanks. We make an awful mistake teaching children that spouses do not deserve to hear that we cherish their efforts and hard work. Even if we are expected to bring home a paycheck, make dinner, or drive carpool, that does not excuse an attitude lacking appreciation for such things. Make a point to verbalize your words of gratefulness. Show your family that you cherish and admire your spouse. When you show your children that you value your spouse, they will follow your lead.

As my Shabbos meal comes to an end, my husband gives me a most precious gift. In front of my children and guests, he says, "Thank you so much for our beautiful Shabbos." Week after week, year after year, my husband's appreciation is cherished. Yes, Mommy will make Shabbos for us each week, but that does not mean that we may take her efforts for granted. And whether we are joined with our children and grandchildren or having a quiet Shabbos together, I am blessed with the gift of my husband's words of gratitude.

I, too, have tried to follow this path of appreciation. As our children grew, when we were fortunate enough to take a family vacation or even buy Shabbos/school/camp clothing, I would make a point of taking a moment and thanking my husband for all that he does for us, as did each of our children. We are not entitled. Our children must learn to never take life's blessings for granted.

What better way to teach our children appreciation than by being examples and role models ourselves? A seed has been planted. We are instilling within our children the education of appreciation. When husbands and wives live together with words of gratitude, the foundation of our home is based on mutual thankfulness and respect.

Children who grow up lacking gratitude and appreciation become selfish and arrogant. They walk around with attitude that nothing is ever good enough. They become accustomed to their parent's filling their every need. "Selfies" allow them to focus only on themselves. They see no reason to express their thankfulness—it's what a parent is *supposed* to do for them. A high school teacher told me that her students were befuddled with the question of why they must express appreciation to parents for all that they do. "But Morah C.," they insisted, "Our parents are *supposed* to pay for all our things, buy us clothing, send us to camp, and take care of us. We didn't ask to be born! Why do we need to express *hakaras hatov*? It's our parents' job!"

Entitlement cannot become a way of life. It is time for the "Me Generation" to become the "We Generation."

Open your children's eyes to the people who do for them. Give them a greater awareness of the people who put energy into making their days flow. This also goes for anyone whom we tend to overlook. The doorman, the food server, the bus driver, the babysitter, the math tutor—there are too many people we disrespect by ignoring their presence in our lives.

TEACH HUMILITY

Gratitude and humility are linked together. One leads to the other. Jewish wisdom guides us.

We wake up each morning and the first words out of our lips is a prayer: *Modeh Ani*. We thank God for the gift of a new day. These two words provide us with a path for life, a road for living each day with character.

Modeh ani does not only mean thank you—it also means "I admit." You see, if I thank you for something, then I must admit that I owe you. I couldn't do this without you. And no one likes to think that he owes anyone anything. It's uncomfortable and humbling to be beholden to someone else. It's much easier to just assume that I'm self-made and that I have it all coming to me. Without expressing gratitude, we grow arrogant.

The words "*modeh ani*" literally mean "grateful am I." Why don't we say "*ani modeh*—I am grateful," which would be less awkward sounding? The answer is a huge life lesson: never should the first words out of our mouths each day be "I." Instead we must begin our day with the word "grateful," to imprint within us an attitude of gratitude and humility.

Judaism teaches us that we must begin each day with an appreciation for our time here, for the incredible gift of every moment. Saying thank you is much more than polite manners; it is character building. I actually owe God for my very breath.

BEGIN WITH "THANK YOU"

So, the next time you ask, "Would you like to go buy sneakers after school?" or "Would you like some macaroni, sweetie?" don't accept "fine" or "whatever" as an answer. Instead of, "You need to take me to soccer, Daddy," or "Mommy, you need to drive me to school," take a moment and implant within your children an attitude of gratitude. A simple thank you can bring our children to recognize the daily gifts and blessings that they have so often taken for granted.

GRATITUDE FOR TIME

Time spent together with family is a gift we often overlook.

My children returned from Israel to spend Pesach with us right as COVID hit. Much about dealing with the pandemic was unknown then, and vaccines were still a dream of the future. My son, his wife, and baby came to visit. We had not seen each other for many months. Our time together was spent masked and outdoors, since we would not be having Yom Tov together, and they'd only "move in" after Pesach. When it was time to say goodbye, I stood beside their car and watched them through the window.

"Mommy, a berachah?" my son mouthed.

I placed my hands on the glass and gave each child my blessing. As my son waved goodbye, I saw his eyes moisten. I, too, began to cry. How painful to be so close and yet be unable to put my hands on my children's heads for a berachah, to give a hug, a kiss, to pick up my granddaughter and hold her in my arms.

Had I ever appreciated these small acts of love?

Time together has become even more precious. Life is fragile. In an instant, the world can find itself steeped in chaos and confusion. We must take these days we have lived through and realize that nothing is the same. Even placing your hands on your child's head to give a blessing is a moment to savor and say, "Thank You, Hashem."

The Disappointed Parent

What does your child see in your eyes when she comes down the stairs in the morning?

Sometimes we need to look in the mirror to see what's in front of us. We are faced with a challenging situation, and we look everywhere but at ourselves.

Bella is eight years old. She has soft blond curls and a beautiful smile. She easily makes friends in school. She can also be messy and disheveled, and has trouble following directions.

Bella's mother, Dina, is exasperated. "Mornings are impossible!" she says to me. "By the time Bella leaves for school, I am at the end of my rope. We've had too many power struggles, over everything from her outfit to what she's going to eat for breakfast. Her homework is all over the place. I just end up yelling at her and losing it with the rest of my children. As Bella gets on the bus, we are both in tears. When she comes home, it starts all over again. I have to tell you the truth—there are days that I just don't like my own daughter...and I feel terrible about it. We are like oil and water. What can I do to change this situation? How can I make this better?"

I know Dina. She is well-groomed and immaculate. She loves everything "perfect" and in order. But life is not always perfect. Sometimes, the neat mother is given the messy daughter. The athletic father may find himself with a son who can't hit a ball.

And we are disappointed. We struggle with our children and find ourselves in a battlefield. We never realize that we are fighting ourselves—our lost dreams that we've held onto for so long.

"What do you think Bella sees when she sees your face?" I asked Dina. "When she comes down the stairs in the morning, what's the look in your eyes?"

"Here's the truth," Dina replied. "When I was growing up, I was the girl who always got the main part in the play. I was the one who always looked great and brought home straight A's. I met my husband, and he was the most awesome guy. I always thought that I'd get married, have amazing children, and we'd have this perfect family—white picket fence and all, you know the scene."

"But Bella, she just doesn't fit into the picture. My PTA meetings are upsetting. She always looks like a mess. She is not coordinated. It's just not what I imagined."

"And maybe she sees that in your eyes," I said. "Maybe she feels your disappointment in who she is."

"Perhaps, the place to start is within. I am not saying that you shouldn't work with her and try to teach her to be orderly and neat. But first, look in the mirror and see your reflection. See what she sees each time you glance at her. You have this expectation of life, even of your mornings, that it will be easy and carefree, just as you've grown used to. Along comes this child who breaks the mold. You are exasperated. Can she not be sensing this?"

Dina was silent for a moment. She took a breath, looked down, and whispered, "You are right. She sees it. She hears it. She knows it. It's my tone, the way I sigh when I look at her, and the way I lose it with her over the smallest things. I need to start the work here with me."

Each of us must ask ourselves these questions: When my child sees me, what does she see? Do my body language, my facial expressions, and my tone convey my love?

COMMUNICATING JOY

I recall having one of those tough mornings when my children were toddlers. After tantrums and tears, I decided that it would be best to take the children out of the house. We'd all cool off a little. A change of atmosphere and some fresh air can work wonders for both parent and child.

As I watched my children running and playing outdoors, my then four-year-old son climbed onto my lap. "Mommy, are you angry?" he asked.

"Of course not, sweetie," I answered. "I'm so happy to be outside with you. And don't you see the smile on my face?"

"So, why are your eyebrows angry?"

We are constantly communicating with our children. Look at how children read our faces. Even our eyebrows transmit a message. Beyond words, our attitude and expressions reveal our innermost thoughts.

We need to ask ourselves how we convey our feelings toward our children. Do we impart joy as we parent or do our children hear a deep sigh as they enter the room?

You can serve the tastiest dinner, but if it's slammed down on the table or given resentfully, the food is tasteless.

The look on our faces as we sit down to read a book to our toddlers, the lackluster "yes" we give as we respond to helping with math homework, the way that we drive our children to school in the morning—everything we do, and the way that we do it—tells our children how we feel as we interact with them.

And as our children grow, we need to honestly examine our attitudes. Do we scrutinize their achievements through our own hopes and dreams, or do we accept each child for who he is?

When we make every effort to communicate joy, love, and acceptance in our homes, our children respond to our open hearts. We can then try to help each child reach his or her great potential and find the blessing that lies within their souls.

I would like to add a message to parents and educators who will, at some point, deal with a child who brings real displeasure and distress. What thoughts can you harness to see you through the challenge so that you are not left with disappointment in yourself and the way you handled the situation? After all is said and done, your reaction will have a lasting impact not only on this child, but on his children and the children who come after him. I have met with today's adults who are still harboring the hurts of yesterday. Some express feeling as if they were discarded like a piece of trash. They speak of the way they were treated in school, or post high school in yeshiva and seminary. You do not want to be the cause of anguish and pain because of a lack of vision or understanding.

Before Yaakov Avinu, our father Jacob, left this world, he called for Yosef to come see him, along with his sons, Ephraim and Menashe.

The two boys are standing before their grandfather, and Yaakov asks, "*Mi eileh*—Who are these?"

Can it be that Yaakov Avinu did not recognize his own grandsons?

The Midrash teaches that Yaakov wished to bless the young men in front of him, but suddenly the Divine Presence left him. Yaakov realized that future descendants, unworthy of blessings, would be the offspring of the two boys, and he grew frightened. In shock, he questioned Yosef. "Who are these? How can this be? Where did these sons come from?"

Yosef responded: "*Banai hem asher nasan li Elokim*—These are my sons whom God has given me."

Yosef assured his father that despite the disappointment he was feeling, these boys were worthy of his blessings. Indeed, they were his gifts from Above.

And what was Zeidy Yaakov's response?

"*Kachem na eilai, v'avarchem*—Bring them to me, and I will bless them."[6] He asked that Yosef bring the two children close; he kissed them and hugged them, and then he placed his hands upon their heads and blessed them.

This must be our response. Bring the child close. Open you heart. Give hugs and kisses. Bless this child and show your love.

Parents and educators, your understanding that every child has been given to you as a gift from Above will sustain you throughout the difficult moments. Watch your words and guard your reactions. Don't push the child away. You have been chosen to be the person in this child's life at this particular time. Through your empathy and vision, you can bestow your blessings and anchor this child through your love. Children who receive your berachah aspire to be a berachah.

---

6 *Bereishis*-Genesis 48:8–11.

Mean Kids

Teaching our children that cruelty and unkindness will not be tolerated

The voice on the line was insistent. Though we had never met, she asked that I tell her story.

"I was sitting in shul on Yom Kippur, and behind me sat two little girls, around eight years old. I caught some snippets of their conversation and finally couldn't hold myself back.

"Do you know Ariella?"

"Her? Ugh, I hate her!"

"I hate her too!"

On and on they went, tearing this little girl apart.

I turned around and said to them, "Girls, you are talking *lashon hara* and gossiping about somebody—hurting her—in shul! And it's Yom Kippur! Don't you feel bad?"

The girls didn't even pause to think.

"No," they laughed. "It's fun."

And then one girl's mother turned toward me and glared, as if to say, *how dare you start up with my daughter!*

On Yom Kippur, the holiest day of the year, we stand trembling before God, asking for forgiveness and a chance to start again. How can our children sit there and miss the message? Where did we go wrong?

Yes, you can say that "kids will be kids, and this is what kids do." You can tell the parents of this little girl that the other children will grow out of it and that she should just ignore them and try to help her daughter find other friends.

But here's the thing: these kids were mean. They spoke unkindly. And there is no place for meanness in the hearts of our children. It doesn't matter if they are four or fourteen. We can expect more. We can do better.

And keep in mind: mean children grow up to become mean adults. They especially hurt the ones that they love and then argue that everyone is being too sensitive. They destroy marriages and wound children, never taking responsibility for their actions.

I cannot begin to convey to you the calls and emails I have received through the years from parents in pain, as they describe the meanness that their children have faced.

A couple emailed me and told me that for a Chanukah gift, their daughter asked if they could find her a friend. It seems that her classmates decided that she was a "loser." When she sat down at the lunch table, the girls who were sitting there got up and left, even those who had once been her closest friends.

A father asked how he could help his son who was hurting after he was unable to find even one roommate for his eighth-grade graduation trip.

A mother described dropping off her five-year-old daughter in school and having her heart broken.

"She's crazy."

"She's a cuckoo head."

"No one wants to play with her! Go home!"

These three sentences, uttered by five-year-olds, brought a mother to tears.

CAUSES OF DESTRUCTION

The Gemara writes:

> *Why was the First Temple destroyed? Because during its period there were three cardinal sins: idolatry, immorality, and blood shed...But the Second Temple—we know that they studied Torah, performed the commandments, and did kind deeds—so why was it destroyed? Because there was purposeless hatred among them.*[7]

During the time of the First Beis Hamikdash, the First Temple that stood in Jerusalem, holiness and prophecy were found everywhere. You could actually see miracles manifested before your eyes. During the Second Temple, there was no prophecy and no holy Ark in the Temple, but the strength of our people was seen in our unity. We cared for each

7 *Yoma* 9b.

other. We cried for one another. It was when we reached the new low of petty bickering, humiliating, and, eventually, even hating one another that we forfeited our Divine grace. Our oneness was lost, and our magnificent Temple was destroyed.

Our sages teach us that by loving one another again, we have the power to bring redemption and see the Temple, the Beis Hamikdash, rebuilt in our times. Until now, we have faced persecution, Inquisition, Holocaust, and deep anti-Semitism as we've been exiled throughout the four corners of the earth. Perhaps, being subject to the hatred of others will inspire us, once again, to be kind and compassionate toward each other. Maybe, we will finally learn to unite and cherish our brothers and sisters.

Why hate each other when we are confronted with such vile hatred against us in the world? What a great tragedy!

CREATE COMPASSIONATE KIDS

It is time for us to bring *achdus*, unity, to our nation. It is up to us teach our children, the next generation, that cruelty and unkindness will not be tolerated. Even if a child is not your friend or "not your type" and "no one else is inviting him, anyway," you must be kind. We are one people. There is no room for meanness in our lives.

It is vital for parents to pay attention to our children's character traits and ask ourselves these questions:

- How does my child play and interact with other kids?
- Does my child use hurtful words and sarcastic put-downs easily?
- Does my child know how to apologize if he or she hurts others?
- Does my child react compassionately if someone is hurt?
- Is my child often involved in bickering and conflicts?

Recognizing our children's character flaws is the first step toward creating compassionate children. If we are able to pinpoint the areas of weakness, we can then work on strengthening and building.

When your child has a birthday party or bar/bas mitzvah, do not allow the "kids who no one likes" to be left out. That's mean. When your children are invited to a party of an unpopular classmate, be sure that they attend.

I know children who were crushed, waiting hours anxiously by the door, as their parties were ignored, and no one showed up. Their pillows were soaked with their tears. How painful!

We have come to measure our children through their success on and off the field, their popularity, and their grades. If they do well, we believe that we are raising successful children.

We are wrong.

Children who are mean and unkind are not being raised successfully no matter how popular they are or how incredible their straight A report card seems. We can demand more from our children. We need to stop making excuses and stop blaming those who tell us that they have been hurt by our child.

REMEMBER FAMILY KINDNESS

You have just returned from the supermarket. You walk into the room with six bags weighing heavily on each hand. Your son looks at you without moving.

"I'm starving," he says. "Supper's not even ready yet!"

Now is your moment. Don't lose it. Don't mutter under your breath. Teach him to actually look at you and see how he can lend a hand.

"Sweetie, do you see me carrying all these bags? Wouldn't it be the right thing for you to come and help me now instead of complaining about supper?"

Rather than being resentful, teach your son how to become more sensitive to those around him.

Children need to be taught about "family kindness." Charity really does begin at home. Let us try to teach our children to be sensitive and generous in both word and deed. There are no acceptable circumstances that permit children to act unkindly.

MODEL SENSITIVITY AND OPEN YOUR CIRCLE

If we are real role models and treat the world around us with sensitivity, our children will understand the true meaning of growing kinder each day. This means that we, as parents, live with graciousness and inclusivity toward others, as we teach our children how to live with character and *middos*.

I have spoken with many couples who feel slighted and irrelevant in their communities. They hear of crowded Shabbos meals, Chanukah and Purim parties where the "in crowd" and their children are having the time of their lives, and they are never thought of. If we truly want to raise children with open hearts, we must stop and think: What do my children see? Do we make room and widen our circle, or do we exclude others from our table? Are we warm and welcoming to new faces in our community?

Our children are capable of great kindness. Let's take a stand together and teach our children that through caring about one another we can rebuild our Temple, our holy Beis Hamikdash, brick by brick, one kindness at a time, and eventually we can change the world.

Children and Lying

Are we teaching our children to lie?

Who doesn't want to raise an honest child?

We want to bring children who cherish truth into this world, but listen to this: Researchers have concluded that really smart kids begin to lie at the age of two or three.[8] They found that the savvier the child, the greater the chance that he will grow up to become a habitual liar.

Here are some shocking facts:

- 98 percent of teens admitted that they lied to their parents.
- The average teen lies about friends that they were with, which clothing that they wore when they were out of the house, how much money they spent, whether chaperones were present at parties, and what they did when their parents were not home. They lie about what they've watched, technology, dating, substance abuse, and friends who were drinking and driving.

---

8 See research done by Dr. Nancy Darling, Penn State University, and Dr. Victoria Talwar, McGill University.

- Most of these kids said that they lied a lot. But, when asked, they also said that lying is wrong. Why the disconnect?

DO WE TEACH OUR CHILDREN TO LIE?

I do not doubt that most of us parents believe that we are honest human beings.

We don't steal, rob, or live fraudulently. We try to teach our children well, expect them to answer truthfully, deal with others honestly, and not cheat on their exams. Deceitfulness and untruthfulness are not tolerated.

But there are the little moments, the encounters that go unchecked, that our children see and hear throughout the day that impact their understanding of living life truthfully.

They see us do it!

Imagine this scene. You've just come home, and you're exhausted. You had a really hard day. The phone rings. Your son comes to tell you that Rabbi Schwartz from Organization X is calling. You know what he wants. And you're just not in the mood to get involved. Or it could even be your mother-in-law on the phone.

"Tell him that I'm not home."

Oops. You just taught your son that it's OK to lie.

What about that trip to the amusement park that you took over summer vacation? All children under ten can buy discounted tickets. As you're about to pay, you say that you have three children under the age of ten.

Your eleven-year-old looks at you quizzically. You give her a wink and count your change.

You have just transmitted a life lesson more powerful than any speech on honesty.

Our children are sponges. They absorb every action, every encounter, and every conversation that they hear. Nothing goes over their heads. We speak in vain about truthfulness if we ourselves are not truthful. When we seek the easy way out or shortcuts in life through dishonesty, we are telling our children that these little white lies are insignificant. They grow comfortable with dishonesty. Eventually, it is we, the parents, who become victims of our own untruths. Our children end up lying to us and we wonder why.

HELPING KIDS TELL THE TRUTH

All children lie one time or another. It's upsetting, but we can use the experience to help our children learn to tell the truth in the future. Our reaction to the situation can make all the difference.

Here are some tips to help keep our children from being dishonest.

1. Never Shame a Child for Lying

Instead of embarrassing a child or yelling at him, let him know that you are disappointed in his actions. It is not that he is a bad person, but that what he did is simply unacceptable. Give him your decided consequence or speak to him about your feelings. Then let him know that you are confident that he will make the right choice in the future so that he can once again earn your trust.

2. Never Set a Child Up to Lie

You know he ate the cookies. There are crumbs on his shirt and chocolate smeared all over his fingers. So why ask him if he did it? Instead, tell him that you know he ate the cookies even though you had told him not to eat them, and now you can deal with the situation.

3. Look for Patterns

Try to figure out if this is becoming a habit. Ask yourself if your child is dealing with self-esteem issues, trying to impress others, or having problems with siblings or in school. If lying is becoming second nature, you are facing a problem that needs help.

OF COURSE, we are the greatest role models for truth in our children's lives.

A mother who attends my classes told me about the following incident, and I was moved to share it with you.

Jill was at a class that I had given where we spoke about modeling character traits for our children. The next week, she was driving with her kids and talking on her cell phone. Sure enough, she heard a loud siren blaring behind her. She checked her rearview mirror, and a police car was right behind her. Jill quickly threw her phone under the seat and pulled over.

"What seems to be the problem, officer?"

"Were you on your cell phone?" the policeman asked.

"No, officer, I wasn't," she replied.

"Are you sure? I thought I saw you on your cell."

"No, officer," Jill said. "I definitely was not on my phone."

"Well, all right then. Go ahead."

Jill was thrilled to get out of an expensive ticket and be on her way. It took just a second till she heard a little voice from the back of the car.

"But mommy, you *were* on the cell phone! You didn't tell the truth! And to a policeman!"

Uh oh, Jill thought to herself. *All those parenting classes I've taken, all those times I've tried to teach my kids to do the right thing, and now it comes down to this.*

With a sinking feeling, Jill knew what she had to do. She drove ahead and chased the police car down three blocks until she found him. She honked and honked. Finally, he pulled down his window.

"It's you? What is it?" the policeman asked.

"Officer," Jill said. "I lied."

"You lied?" he said in astonishment.

"I lied. I really was on my cell phone. I am so sorry for lying."

"So, why did you come back?"

Jill pointed to the back seat. The policeman nodded.

She turned around and saw her son's eyes open wide. She knew that she had just delivered the greatest life lesson on honesty that she could possibly give.

What would you have done?

Bully!

"They don't let our son play. They never include him when they make their birthday parties or have sleepovers. My son wants to be their friend, but they make fun of him. He's not the best ball player and he does have a learning disability, but does that give them a right to call him names and be mean?"

The couple stood before me, broken-hearted. I had just finished a parenting lecture and they were visibly anguished.

"How old is your son?" I asked.

"Eight. He is just eight years old, and he's already had a lifetime of pain," they replied sadly.

What is there to say to these parents?

Allow me to share a personal memory. Growing up, I attended an all-girl's yeshiva elementary school. There were not many private school children to service at the time, so the district combined two other community schools onto one route. This meant that I shared the long bus ride home with middle school kids who attended the neighborhood coed schools.

For some reason, two boys on the bus spent their days taunting me. I remember sitting silently, often holding back my tears, as they would mock my more religious school, my mode of dress, and especially the fact that I was a daughter of a rabbi and *rebbetzin*. They would use shocking curse words, throw their sticky lollipops in my hair, and laugh at me all the way home. As we would pass my father's shul, they would make nasty comments. The bus driver remained silent. I remember staring out the window, trying hard to be stoic as I pretended not to hear them.

No one called it bullying then. But we all knew that it was mean and wrong. Why didn't I say something? The family of one of these boys belonged to my father's synagogue. Though I was just a child of ten, I realized the awful predicament I would be putting my parents in. I didn't want to ask them to confront a member of their shul, forcing them to acknowledge their son's gross misbehavior. I knew the daily difficulties my parents faced as they grappled with building the shul and maintaining relationships with the members. I'm not advising children to be silent while facing bullying, I'm simply telling you what happened to me.

I should've discussed the bullying, but I did not. I swallowed the mean insults, the mockery, and the disgusting lollipops tangled in my hair.

And I made it through those years confident in my parents' love for me, incredibly proud of the mission they lived and the legacy that they bequeathed. Those boys' ugly behavior reeked of weakness to me. I made a promise never to be like them. Ever.

But still. It hurt. I know how it feels to be bullied as a child.

The papers are filled with stories of bullying. Somehow the meanness seems to begin at a younger age. I receive countless calls and emails from parents who ache from their children's distress. And it is not just teens and preteens anymore. Even preschoolers and first graders have come home with stories of heartless callousness and cruelty. Being made fun of, teased in hurtful ways, and purposely excluded and ignored are behaviors that worry parents and their children.

A mother of a Pre-1A child told me that she was new to her community. After one year in the local school, she asked to speak to the principal.

"Each week our children learn parashah. They hear stories about *middos*, not speaking *lashon hara*, and doing *chessed*. But with all that they've heard, my little girl is still coming home in tears. Every time she sits down on a chair, another child says, 'This seat's saved.' Not one child invited her for a play date, not one! How can that be? How can she feel so excluded? Is there not one child who is nice enough and kind enough to say, 'Would you like to come over too?' Is there not one mother whose heart is open to my child's pain?"

The principal had no response. There was nothing to say.

Can it be that our children are picking up on the unkindness that they see in the world around them? Can they be reflecting these insensitive attitudes in their behavior?

Perhaps, if we take a moment to observe the world of our children, we can gain enough understanding to make a difference and come to raise a kinder generation.

G.O.Y. KIDS

No, I did not coin this phrase, and I was as surprised as you are when I read the latest acronym branded by parents and educators. G.O.Y. kids are *not* what you tend to think when you hear the word "*goy*."

G.O.Y. stands for Growing Older Younger—today our children are seven going on thirteen. Even the youngest children have tech tools that kids their age have never possessed in the history of the world. Handing over these gadgets to kids without a backward glance is a huge mistake. To me, it's like handing over the car keys and saying nonchalantly, have a good time!

Think about this: An eleven-year-old girl took a humiliating picture of her classmate that caught her in an awkward moment. She then sent the photo with a "cute" remark to her group of friends. You can imagine what happened next.

Each child forwarded the photo to their friends, who had a good laugh as they passed it on. In no time at all, the child was the buzz of her entire school…and beyond. She found herself in cyber grief and, quite understandably, refused to return to class. Her parents called me in tears. Do you think this harm could possibly be erased?

Today's technology allows bullying and shaming at the push of a button. Instead of speaking to just one friend, you can reach dozens in an instant. As the pain spreads, so does the torment and there is no stopping its wild course.

What can we do about it?

The first thing we need to do is teach our children responsibility. There is no such thing as hurting another and not facing the consequences of our actions. You are responsible for where that mean text or photo ends up. It doesn't matter that you just sent it to one or two friends. Know the immense impact that your actions caused.

Our children must understand that real harm is done with each "send."

Perhaps, it is not seeing the victim's face that prevents our children from understanding the anguish that they've caused. Cell phones can seem so innocent. But the child whose image is sent or who has the mean text written about them meets with derision and laughter over and over again.

Our children must be made aware of the terrible damage that they can cause with the click of a button, akin to the firing of a weapon—total and utter devastation. If you use this phone or device, you must use it wisely.

IS OUR WORLD MEANER?

Our children definitely watch videos and clips that do not channel kindness. These videos and clips make rude behavior seem normal, even funny.

So, our children grow desensitized as they are entertained by watching people hurt people or by mocking someone who is caught in an embarrassing situation. That person who is being laughed at is someone's father, brother, mother, sister, or child. That person is a human being who has been shamed and the clip keeps getting forwarded as it goes viral.

How can our kids not be affected?

Some feel that parents today are, somehow, more hardened. I would not want to think that this is true. I do know that we are stressed and pulled in many directions. Many homes are emotionally squeezed, and marriages are strained. Single-parent homes have the added burden of juggling roles.

The result can be that we are not tuned in to what's really going on until trouble hits. We are happy if all seems quiet on the home front, and the kids are not bothering us.

If your child was invited to an "in" party along with her group of friends, you'd be thrilled to know that she was included. What would you do if you heard that there was a girl who was left out and hurting? What would you do if you knew that another child in the class was being taunted, excluded, or bullied? Would you teach your child to take a stand?

These are difficult questions. Some would say it depends on your child's age, her social standing, and the relationship that you have with your child or the other mother.

Whatever our response, we need to realize that our actions speak louder than any speeches that we try to give our children on compassion and kindness. Training our children to include those who are hurting can be a life-altering lesson. Going on without even a thought while feeling smug that at least our child was included can easily create a child who grows cold-hearted and insensitive to the tears of another. And one day that "other" may very well be family.

WHAT CAN WE DO IF OUR CHILD IS BULLIED?

Every day, countless children are afraid to go to school, get on the bus, sit down for lunch, or join their classmates at recess.

The children who are bullied can be taunted for the way they look, dress, speak, act, or their home life. No matter the reason behind the cruelty, the child who is being bullied grows fearful and loses self-confidence.

While young children are encouraged to confide in a trusted adult like a teacher or parent, preteens and teens would be reluctant to bring someone else, especially an adult, into the picture. They are afraid of even more taunting, "So, you had to go to your mommy? What a baby you are!" Instead of sharing their pain, many of these children grow silent. They keep their anguish inside. Childhood becomes an emotional album of painful memories.

HELPING KIDS COPE

Experts advise parents to build a child's self-esteem so that the bullying will not destroy feelings of self-worth. The better your child feels about himself, the less likely that the taunting will leave a child battling inner devastation. It is a good idea to encourage hobbies, extracurricular activities, healthy connections with others, and friendships made outside of school. Relaying to your child what you love about him, as well as reinforcing his strengths and positive qualities, also build a child's self-regard. Some children also need parents to role play and help them learn how to ignore the bully or use humor to get around the situation. It is important to practice confidence, positive body language, and not give the bully the response he is looking for. Forming emotional intelligence skills allows children to learn needed life abilities for future experiences.

KINDNESS OF CHILDREN

I still believe in the kindness of children. I still have faith in the spark that lies within every child. It is up to us adults to seek out that light and ignite a flame of compassion within the heart and soul of every child.

If we can teach our children to think before they speak, to ponder the effects of their actions before they act, to at least feel when they hear of another's hurt, imagine the generation that we could raise.

The Blessing of Enough

How to raise content kids

Did you ever notice how so many children today seem to grapple with feelings of discontent?

No matter how much they have, no matter how hard we try to give them more, they never seem satisfied. They should be the happiest kids who ever lived. They have traveled to islands, swum with dolphins, gone jeeping through the deserts of Israel, enjoyed Yom Tov in beautiful vacation villas, but there is still a sense of discontent.

There are children who have devices, gadgets, electric scooters, Nintendos, American Girl dolls, and basements filled with toys. Summertime brings talk of going to sleepaway camp, travel camps, shopping with long lists in hand, or planning trips to faraway places. Even with a difficult economic situation, the reality is that we would rather do without ourselves than have our children feel as if they are lacking.

A father called me. He said that each summer, he rents a home for his family in beautiful surroundings. It is a neighborhood where some people buy lavish homes and others rent. Even though he has always enjoyed their summer place, his thirteen-year-old daughter made it clear that she was unhappy.

At 2 a.m. she decided to have a meltdown.

"I am ashamed of the house that we stay in every summer," she cried. "All my friends have much better houses, why can't we? If we take this same house as always, I don't want any of my friends coming over. Don't even think about inviting them!"

She stomped to her room and slammed the door, leaving her father hurt and perplexed.

"I try so hard," he said to me. "What is she thinking? Doesn't she see how much I sweat to make a buck?"

How do we combat the malcontent?

Of course, there are many reasons our children act miserably. Some will say that it is awful chutzpah, too much stuff, absence of parental involvement, or deficient discipline. Others will say that there is not enough one-on-one time, that our children do not feel really accepted, that they lack self-esteem, or that it's just plain arrogance.

But at the root of the misery lies a basic glaring lack of satisfaction and appreciation for all that we have been given. After eating a meal, we say in *Birkas Hamazon* these words from the Torah: "*V'achalata, v'savata, u'veirachta*—And you shall eat, and you shall be satisfied, and you shall bless."[9] Our children have mastered the "*v'achalta*"—they eat and consume effortlessly. But do they know the feeling of "*v'savata*"—and you shall be satisfied? Because if all they do is consume but never stop to feel satisfied and content, they can never arrive at the next step: "*u'veirachta*"—and you shall bless. When children are not gratified and cognizant of their blessings, they do not begin to realize how much they have been given and how much they have to be grateful for.

TEACH CHILDREN THE BLESSING OF ENOUGH

I explained to this father that it is time that he sat down with his daughter and introduced her to the concept of *dayeinu*. On *Pesach* we recount all of God's many kindnesses. After each kindness we pause and say, "*Dayeinu*—It would have been enough for us!" We are encouraged to recognize each gracious act of giving and realize that every deed deserves thoughtful appreciation.

We don't take anything for granted. We stop to feel fulfilled and appreciate what we have. We savor and contemplate the blessing of enough.

I asked the father to compile a list of blessings for his daughter.

I received an incredibly long list that had been drawn up for this thirteen-year-old. Here's part of the list:

- We have a beautiful home.
- We rent a lovely summer house in a gorgeous neighborhood.
- We have traveled to Israel.
- We have traveled to Paris.
- We have traveled to Italy.
- We have gone skiing in Utah.

---

9 *Bamidbar*-Numbers 8:10.

- We eat in delicious restaurants.
- We have gone to Miami every Chanukah vacation since you were a baby.
- We have celebrated your bas mitzvah with an amazing party.
- We have sent you to sleepaway camp since fourth grade.
- We have a loving family.
- We have grandparents who cherish us.
- We have good health.

After each line, the father wrote "*dayeinu*." And then he explained to this child, who had been blessed with more than she had ever understood (and more than most could ever imagine), that it was time to appreciate what she had been blessed with, instead of focusing on what she thought was missing from her life.

We are given the opportunity to internalize this teaching every time we enter or exit a room. The mezuzah on our door has the letters of Hashem's name: *shin*, *daled,* and *yud*. Did you ever wonder why this particular name of God was chosen to grace our doorways?

When we look at the mezuzah, the message is that *daled* and *yud* together spell the word *dai*, enough. Know that everything you have is exactly what you need to live your complete life. Within this home, within every single room, lies *dai*—the blessing of enough. Take a moment before entering and exiting. Reflect upon the timeless truth that the mezuzah is giving to you. Be satisfied, be gratified, and recognize your life's blessings.

Children who grow up ungrateful and dissatisfied feel discontented and empty inside. They are always looking for the next thrill. But nothing seems to fill the hollowness that lies within. Misunderstanding the void that gnaws beneath the surface, they run after more "things" or believe that certain extreme behaviors will bring them the pleasure they seek. The search is endless. There is never the feeling of being satisfied with "the blessing of enough."

There is one more missing link here—the presence of parents who must live with the motto of *dayeinu* in their own lives. When children hear their mother or father constantly commenting on other people's homes, enviously recounting the way that others vacation, or having conversations about the expensive clothing and furniture that their friends seem to have, they are implanting the ugly roots of discontent and unhappiness in their children's hearts.

How can we teach the blessing of enough when our days are spent wanting more and more?

It is not only financially and materialistically that we come up short in our minds. When a husband or wife feels that their spouse does not give or do enough, the relationship is diminished. If I am always concentrating on what my spouse does not do instead of recognizing the good that he does, I end up destroying any potential for joy that I may have. My life becomes filled with negatives, and I grow bitter and unhappy. The children will echo the sentiment.

Let us take the lesson of *dayeinu* to heart. It is time for us all to contemplate the blessing of having enough.

Raising Kids to Stand Up for Kindness

In our self-absorbed society, how do we instill compassion in our children?

My son emailed me a clip titled, "Danny's Day," which touched me deeply. Danny Keefe, age seven, is a high school football-team water coach. Little Danny calls out, "Do you need a water?" But it is very difficult to understand his words. Danny had bleeding in his brain after birth and suffers from apraxia, a motor disorder that makes it hard to speak. His father says that the doctors were extremely pessimistic about Danny's prognosis. They said, "Whatever you do, don't expect much. He may never walk. He may never talk."

Danny defied the odds. He has not only come to love life, but he also loves to dress colorfully as well. Since the age of two, Danny insisted on wearing a button-down shirt, jacket, tie, and often a fedora. In school, kids have made fun of Danny and bullied him. They could not understand his words; they could not understand his attire. "Hey, listen to this kid. He's speaking Chinese!" they mocked. Danny's mother cries as she describes his request to bring a world globe to school to show that he really does come from the same country. Danny is eager to make friends, but kids in school have acted in hurtful ways. They took off Danny's hat and threw it into the mulch, then they threw mulch on his hair. Danny looks into the camera and says that this made him feel very sad.

Danny's older brother Tim and his best friend, Tommy, play on a football team. Tommy is the team quarterback. When he heard about the bullying, Tommy decided to do something to boost Danny's spirits. He got his football teammates and friends to declare "Danny Appreciation Day." They dressed like Danny, wearing suits and hats, and cheered his name, "Danny, Danny!" A fire truck came to pick Danny up and brought him to their school. The boys surrounded him with friendship and played football with him. When asked why they did this, Tim and Tommy responded: "To show that he's a person too. He may dress differently or talk differently, but he has feelings." Danny describes the moment as, "The most best day."

We all want to raise kind kids who take a stand against bullying and show incredible compassion. Are we succeeding?

A PARENT'S MESSAGE TO THEIR CHILDREN

A group at the Harvard Graduate School of Education led by Dr. Richard Weissbourd released the following information based on a study that they conducted: About 80 percent of the youth in the study said that their parents were more concerned with their achievements or happiness than with whether they cared for others. The interviewees were also three times more likely to agree with the statement that "my parents are prouder if I get good grades in my classes than if I'm a caring community member in class and school."

Parents may believe that they're sending the right message, but only 20 percent of kids interviewed felt that their parents genuinely believe that caring for others is a greater priority than acquiring happiness or achievements. We are sending our children a mixed message: yes, we want to raise moral and kind kids, but a successful, happy child is the real goal. Have we stressed achievements and grades over moral character?

Perhaps, we've become too consumed with our children's accomplishments, neglecting our responsibility to mold them into more compassionate beings. In a world where there is great pressure to perform, be in the *aleph* class, maintain a high grade-point average, and join after-school activities, where does kindness fit in? How can we help our children focus on the needs and feelings of others?

Dr. Weissbourd and his team[10] recommend the following five tips to raise moral, caring children:

- Make caring for others a priority. Help children balance their needs with the needs of others.
- Provide opportunities for children to practice caring and gratitude. Daily repetition makes caring second nature.
- Expand your child's circle of concern. Challenge your child to learn to care about someone outside his circle.
- Be a strong moral role model and mentor. This means that parents practice being caring, honest, and fair. We demonstrate how we want our children to live with others.
- Guide children to manage destructive feelings. Dr. Weissbourd points out that our ability to care for others is often overwhelmed by negative feelings like shame, envy, or anger. We need to help our children learn how to cope productively with these feelings.

How can we actualize these points? How do we teach a child to open his heart and become more caring and kind? How do we raise a child to become "*gadol*," a great human being?

When Moshe was in Egypt, growing up in the luxury of Pharaoh's palace, he had a choice to make. Either he could remain the prince of Egypt and say to himself, "There's nothing I can do anyway. At least let me stay safe," or, he could step out of the comfort and security, seek out his people, and contemplate their suffering.

---

10 Making Caring Common initiative, based at the Harvard Graduate School of Education.

"***Va'yigdal*** *ha'yeled*...***Va'yigdal*** *Moshe va'yetzei el achav va'yar b'sivlosam*—The boy **grew**...Moshe **grew** and went out to his brethren and saw their burdens."[11]

At first Moshe grew in years. But the moment he walked out of those palace doors and decided to feel the anguish of his brothers, he attained a different type of growth. He grew spiritually. Here, we are given the secret to nourishing inner greatness and the magic of becoming *gadol*, great, in the eyes of God.

We must teach our children that they each have the potential to become *gadol* like Moshe.

DON'T BE AFRAID TO TEACH YOUR CHILD TO FEEL THE PAIN OF ANOTHER

When we feel for others, we become mindful of their hurts. We help our children break out of the shell that a comfortable life brings. When I was a little girl, many people would pour out their problems to my parents, the rabbi and *rebbetzin* of the congregation. I recall once having my parents tell us to say *Tehillim* for a child who was ill. A visitor watched the scene and said, "Now, really, Rebbetzin, isn't this too much for these children?"

I'll never forget my mother's response and the fire in her voice as she spoke: "Some children cry for licorice. Others for chocolate or toys. My children? My children will cry for the pain of another."

REACH BEYOND YOUR COMFORT ZONE

We are our children's greatest role models. If we wish to raise children who are kind, we must exert ourselves and sometimes reach beyond our own comfort zones. This means being nice to people who may frustrate us and are different from us, and helping others instead of looking away. In a world that stresses "self-care," can we grow greater and not only care for ourselves?

Sometimes, we overlook those who are closest to us. We reach out and feel for everyone—everyone but our spouse, children, or parents. Those

---

11 *Shemos*-Exodus 2:10–11.

whom we are supposed to love most shouldn't think that they matter least. How is it that we have kind words, endless patience, and time in abundance for everyone except for the people with whom we live?

THE GIFT OF GRANDPARENTS

Grandparents are not only a gift for children to cherish but become endearing instruments in grandchildren's lives to help them grow more compassionate. Seeing the need and confronting a grandparent's potential for loneliness allows children to step up and make a difference.

When my mother moved down the block from my home after the loss of my father, we began a tradition where we would share our Shabbos meals together. My daughter Shaindy, though she was only nine years old at the time, would wake up early Shabbos morning, walk with her Bubba to shul, and daven at her side. Those years of meaningful conversations they had each week, and of davening together side by side, shaped the person and educator my daughter has become. As Shabbos came to an end, my eldest son, Moshe Nosson, would make *Havdalah* for Bubba. This became their special time. When he went off to study in Israel, my son Akiva, and then my youngest son, Eli, happily took over this privileged responsibility. Cherished memories were made each week as they bid farewell to Shabbos together. After my mother broke her hip, she was not thrilled to use a walker. My daughter Aliza decided to surprise her Bubba and decorated the walker with shimmering sequins, silk flowers, and ribbons. How my mother laughed and called her walker "Bubba's Bling."

We must ask ourselves who was the true giver here? It was not the children who gave, but indeed, their Bubba who was the source of giving. She gave each child the opportunity to open their eyes to the need of another, to grow more compassionate and sensitive, and to know that they have the power to illuminate this world through their actions.

When the World Is Falling Down, Raise It with Kindness

Compassion is a mighty force of strength that transforms sorrow into joy

How do we keep our world intact when it feels as if everything we've known is falling apart?

Finding ourselves under lockdown, anxious and confused about all the unrest and illness that occurred, can bring us to a place of sadness. There is uncertainty mixed with grief. We worry about our future and our children's futures; we worry about our world.

Amidst all the chaos we have the power to bring light.

King David says it best: "The world is built through kindness."[12] When the universe around you is falling down, you have the ability to raise it up. Compassion becomes a mighty force of strength that transforms sorrow into joy. Every time you connect with another soul, you create a link of unity. Hope for the future is born.

Friday afternoon, as I was about to turn off my computer to get ready for Shabbos, I noticed an email that had popped into my inbox. The subject intrigued me. "Touching base. It's been over forty years."

I began to read the message.

> *Dear Slovie,*
>
> *I don't know if you remember me. We went to camp together and I'm pretty sure we haven't spoken since then.*
>
> *Anyway, while quarantined, my husband started looking through old papers. I found the attached card you sent me some forty-three years ago.*
>
> *I don't remember the incident. However, the fact that you sent me a card, and I kept it, shows how much the hakaras hatov*

---

12 *Tehillim*-Psalms 89:3.

> *meant to me. I thought you would enjoy seeing a card that you and your father jointly wrote.*
>
> *Quick forty-plus update: I'm married for forty-one years, thank God, blessed with kids and grandchildren. I would love to meet you and say "hi" if you ever come to my neighborhood. You are always invited if you need a place to stay.*
>
> *Have a nice Shabbos.*

The letter was signed along with a phone contact.

And there below was a sight that took my breath away.

A photo attachment of a Rosh Hashanah New Year card in my teenaged scrawl along with my father's bold handwriting. I had no recollection of the card or the incident, but seeing my father's distinct script brought me back to being my "Daddy's little girl." I read and reread my father's words and then my own and got a picture of the story. My heavy trunk needed schlepping. It was the last day of camp, and everyone was busy with her own stuff. This one girl stopped whatever she was doing and helped us lug the trunk and duffel bag to my father's car. Before Rosh Hashanah, I had sent her a thank you note. What made me now stop and pause were my father's words at the bottom of the card.

> *You have recently fulfilled the mitzvah of "hakem takem immo" (helping one lift his burden) by helping to carry Slovie's trunk. Thank you. May you be written and inscribed for a good new year.*
>
> *Rabbi Jungreis*

I felt a tear slide down my cheek.

Besides feeling as if I had received a hug from above after all these years, I could not believe that my father had actually taken the interest and the time to add to my teenage letter. It struck me what a force of light he must've been for me growing up, in subtle ways that I could not even appreciate at the time. What I had taken as simply ordinary was, in truth, extraordinary.

I called the phone number in the email, and we reconnected. We reminisced, caught up, and wished each other a good Shabbos. I was touched to my very core.

It was not just about a young girl on a hot summer day who had taken the time to stop what she was doing, see the need, and help me and my father. At this moment, the kindness took on a new life of its own.

Forty-three years later, that young girl, who is now a grandmother, stopped what she was doing and returned my father's words back to me. Greater than carrying my loaded trunk was her carrying the load in my heart; missing my father while trying to make sense of the world in which we live. Once again, she stopped and thought of me, not even realizing the great impact that her message would make.

We all feel vulnerable. Connecting with others unlocks the constraints that we all feel. Knowing that we have/had parents, friends, and family who love us, care for us, and watch over us, empowers us as we grope through the darkness.

We all have the ability to reconnect with someone now and create a moment of kindness.

Think of someone who has impacted your life. It can be someone from long ago like a third-grade teacher you've never forgotten, a mentor, an aunt or uncle who used to take you on family trips, or a friend who had been there for you with whom you've lost touch. Think of the person who helped you get your first job, introduced you to your spouse, or invited you for a Shabbos that ignited a spark within.

Take out a moment from your day and find the time to say thank you. Reconnect and build a bridge between souls.

Now, think of the people in your life whom you take most for granted: your parents, your grandparents, your family, or good friends. You know they will be there for you. You know you've gone through challenges and strains; maybe you had words and encounters that hurt. But you've also discovered the power of friendship, loyalty, and love. When there was no one else to soothe your pain, they had listening hearts—a balm for your soul. You have stories that bond and memories and private jokes that only the two of you share.

Take out a moment from your day and find the time to say thank you. Reconnect and build a bridge between souls.

We combat darkness with light, desperation with hope, and anguish with consolation.

Let us build our world through kindness.

(And thank you, R., for taking the time to reconnect and bringing me solace and joy.)

CHAPTER 3

Parenting in Unity

Mommy, Daddy, and Our Parenting Mission

When Spouse and Child Are Against You

How to ensure that you and your spouse are united and build better bonds in your family

Do you find yourself in cahoots with your child against your spouse? Do you ever feel as if you're standing alone as your spouse and child form an informal pact together?

When one parent is allied with a child, it creates an unhealthy bond. This environment becomes ripe for disrespect as the seeds of chutzpah are sown. A child who learns that parents are not on the same page sees the possibility of putting down a parent and casting his opinion aside. A parent and child versus the other parent is a recipe for dysfunction.

A mother asked me about the relationship that her husband has with their eleven-year-old son. Describing their exchanges, she felt that her husband was unduly harsher with him than with their daughters. He expected more, demanded more, and corrected him about the slightest mistakes. Somehow, it felt as if they were in competition with one another.

They were in competition; they were competing for her alliance.

I wanted to know what her reaction was when these happenings took place.

"I tell my husband that he's being too hard and that he should just let things go. After all, he is the father, and he needs to act like the adult."

"And do you say all this in front of your son?" I questioned.

"Well," she replied, "I do try my best to whisper. But I guess I'm whispering out loud, and he hears it all."

I assured her that not only did her son hear, but he understood quite clearly that he had discovered a powerful wedge between his parents. Anytime in the future that he had an issue with his father, he now perceived his mother as on his side. His relationship with his father will suffer as he grows into his teens. The relationship between husband and wife will also fray.

There is a question of loyalty, trust, and parenting on common ground. Parents who display favoritism for a child over a spouse create resentment and anger in their marriage. It is the father and mother who must stand united, not the child and parent.

Of course, there are times when a parent comes down hard on a child or is unreasonable in his expectations. How can we resolve this type of situation and stand together with strength so that our children perceive a home environment that feels safe and secure?

Understand that resolving this is vital. When kids see parents behaving lovingly and respectfully with one another, they feel as if they are in a stable home that will endure. A firm foundation gives sons and daughters the sense of steadiness needed in a chaotic world. Children also learn to respect parents when parents display respect for one another. Casting a spouse's opinion aside thoughtlessly, disparaging a husband or wife, and treating each other disrespectfully only hurts us, the parents. Children pick up these disrespectful cues and then act the very same way toward us. Nobody wins.

STRATEGIES FOR A HEALTHY HOME

Here are some dos and don'ts to ensure you and your spouse are united and build better bonds in your family.

DON'TS:

- Don't put down your spouse in front of your child.
- Don't sabotage the relationship of the other parent by criticizing the way your spouse is handling a situation. Saying things like, "You always make her cry" or "That's how you discipline him?" is not productive.
- Don't use your child as a pawn to get back at your spouse.
- Don't attempt to fix your loneliness or hurt through becoming your child's partner.
- Don't argue about your child while he is present. Besides teaching him to be disrespectful, many children end up feeling guilty that they have caused bad feelings between parents.
- Don't show favoritism to one child or become that child's defense attorney. You must be honest here. If you find yourself constantly sticking up for a child, take a step back and figure out what is happening in your home.

DOS:

- Do discuss differences of opinion in private, using the respectful tones and words that you would expect your children to use.
- Do agree that you will not put each other down or use disparaging remarks to get your point across—especially in front of the children.
- Do agree that there must be standards of respect in your home so that when a child is upset or angry, he may not put down a parent. Saying things like, "She drives me crazy" or "He doesn't know what he's talking about" is completely unacceptable. A child may express frustration or sadness, or ask for more time or understanding, but everything must be expressed with honorable words and actions. Children should never perceive a parent as a vessel for complaints against another parent.
- Do communicate that you are on the same page as parents.

- Do decide to sit down together and discuss how to handle the times that you disagree. Are there certain situations that keep on cropping up, pitting one parent against another? Is there one child in particular who brings out this unhealthy alliance?
- Do be sure that children hear positive words from both parents. Sometimes, a parent falls into a negative spiral with a child. Every interaction is about what the child did not do or how the child could do better. When the other parent hears this, a defensive posture is taken. This tug of war must stop. Children need to hear positive words, encouragement, and love from both mom and dad.

Emotional crossfire wounds both parents and children. Being a parent means that we set our egos aside, stop indulging ourselves, and start focusing on the health of our homes. Our children need us to lead them into the future, a future that is intact and based on mutual respect and dignity. Children who see parents aligning together understand that theirs is a home filled with love and wisdom.

What's a Father For?

The definition of being a father

What is the definition of being a father?

Is his self-worth simply based upon his financial income and the type of car that he drives? Or is he here to provide more, to endow his children with a spiritual income, as well?

In addition to his financial portfolio, has he thought about the spiritual portfolio that his children will come to inherit one day?

There are many challenges facing today's families. Life is expensive. Tuition, insurance, camp, clothing, food, after-school activities, orthodontists, mortgage payments, medical bills, various therapies, and tutors—the list goes on and on. Though I know that often it is both husbands and wives who are working long hours and worrying about the bills, I also know that men feel greatly responsible for their family's financial situation.

And then my mind wanders to memories of my father.

No, we did not have much "stuff" growing up. We never took exotic vacations or had the latest "must-haves" and toys. But my parents provided us with so much more to carry us through our days: endless love and faith that have anchored us throughout life's ups and downs.

Though many stories pop into my mind, there is one story in particular that imprinted within me the sense of "what's a father for."

It had been a long, hot summer. My husband had undergone delicate surgery for a dislocated shoulder and was warned to watch the movements of his arm. He was wearing a sling while dealing with a lot of pain. I was in my later months of pregnancy, and you know that scorching days and expectant mothers are a difficult combination.

I took my children outside to play, and my five-year-old daughter fell off her swing. Her hand lay limply at her side.

I drove to the pediatrician hoping that he'd tell me this was just a bruise or sprain. He gave me the news that my daughter's hand seemed broken, and I would need to see an orthopedist. My child would need an adult to lift her, accompany her into the x-ray room, and calm her fears. I also had a toddler who needed someone to watch over him in the office while my daughter was being examined and having a cast put on.

Since I was expecting, that "someone" who was needed in the x-ray room could not be me. My husband was completely incapacitated. I drove home, thinking of my various options. My mother was lecturing, and I knew that my father had left that morning to visit my sister and spend a week with her family in their Catskills bungalow.

As I entered the house, my phone rang. I picked up the receiver and heard my father's voice.

"*Sheifele*, how are you?"

I could not speak. I just started to cry.

"What is it, Slovelah? Why are you crying?"

I sobbed a bit more and then relayed my story to my father. I described my husband, immobile in his sling, my daughter, wailing and needing to have x-rays taken of her arm, my seven-year-old, just getting off the day camp bus, and my two-year-old, doing what two-year-olds do. The orthopedist's office was an hour away. I didn't know how to manage. I felt overwhelmed.

"Don't worry, my *sheifele*, I'm coming to help you."

"Abba, what do you mean?" I asked. "You just arrived this morning. You spent three hours on a bus getting there, and you're staying for a week. How will you help me?"

"I am going to take the next bus home—don't worry. I didn't even unpack yet, so it's fine."

"Are you sure, Abba?" I asked incredulously.

I was astonished. I knew how my father had been waiting for this week. My parents never took a vacation. This was to be my father's "big getaway"—a week in my sister's bungalow. His greatest pleasure was spending time with his children and grandchildren, taking walks on the country roads, and breathing in the natural beauty of God's world. He had schlepped up by bus, and I learned later from my sister that my father had arrived sopping wet, drenched in sweat from the heat of the trip.

But he made no mention of any of this to me. It was clear that he would just turn around and come home. I was overwhelmed with his kindness. I decided to ask one more time.

"Are you sure, Abba?"

I heard my father's wonderful laugh over the phone. And then he said something that I will never forget.

"*Slovelah*, of course I'm sure. What's a father for?"

As we grapple with uncertainties and a topsy-turvy world, at least let us hold onto this one unshakable truth. Fathers exist in the lives of their children with a role that goes way beyond paying the credit card bills. Fathers are here to lead, to provide spiritual and emotional nourishment to both sons and daughters.

Fathers can be the moral compass that steer children through their life's journey.

And then, when we grow up and wonder if we are doing the right thing or how we will possibly make it, we can hear our father's voice and see our father's image in our mind. We can look back on the small kindnesses, the little talks when we seemed troubled, and the reassuring arm around our shoulders that let us know that we are loved and never stand alone.

And if right now, you are feeling hurt and lacking such memories, know that today is your opportunity to create this legacy with your own children.

After all, what's a father for?

Manhood and Tough Finances

How we respond to challenges makes a profound impact on our children

When families go through economic turmoil, marriages suffer. Intimacy suffers. Relationships with children suffer. (This is true, too, for any times of unexpected chaos and tumult that a couple confronts).

There is a sense of fatigue. Emotions of sadness, irritability, and loss of energy overwhelm and demoralize. Withdrawal of love and outbursts of fighting can devastate the entire family.

I have met with numerous couples who are trying hard to hold on to a life that they once took for granted.

Husbands and wives whisper about credit card bills, tuition fees, and mortgage payments that sit on their desks waiting to be paid. The threat to their *shalom bayis*, peace in the home, is real.

How can we help our kids resist the urge to grow despondent while sensing a hopeless shadow constantly hovering above?

I cannot say that I have all the answers, but I do know this.

There will come a time that our children will look back at times of challenge and they will reflect on their memories.

Perhaps, they will be going through new challenges of their own; perhaps, they will be reminiscing about their childhood.

When they think of you, what will they remember?

A SON CALLS HOME

Lisa and Josh seem like the perfect couple. They easily complete each other's sentences and have a great rapport between them. Josh had a fabulous job as an investment banker in NYC, until the market collapsed.

The day that he was let go, I received an email from Lisa.

"My husband has given his life to his company. What will he do? I am afraid he'll fall into a depression. What will happen to us? I am so frightened."

Lisa has attended my classes for years. I encouraged her to share the wisdom she has gained with her husband. Couples who study together grow united. Torah's wisdom anchors us; it strengthens our souls.

The year passed slowly. While searching for a job, Josh took on running. One day, while on a jog, he fell and broke his leg badly. He needed surgery, then crutches, and months' worth of therapy.

Lisa and I exchanged daily emails. We spoke about never losing hope. We spoke about the power of a good word, about the smile that gives life to another. Though times may be difficult, we still have the ability to touch each other with goodness. I asked Lisa and Josh to never let a day go by without doing something kind for their family…even the smallest act of kindness helps a family remain connected.

It was a very tough time.

Josh finally found a job. His leg healed. Lisa took on a part-time position to help ease the financial load. Their eldest son left for college.

One night, Lisa and Josh asked to speak with me. Their son had called home and told them that everyone had been asked to give a talk about their hero. When it was their son's turn, he spoke about his father.

"Dad, I told them how you taught me that no matter how tough life gets, we never give up. I told them how you lost your job and busted your leg, but you refused to lie down and surrender. Dad, I told everyone you're my hero."

I ask parents everywhere to ask this question: When your children will look back on difficult days, what image will come to mind?

Will they recall a father sitting hopelessly in his chair with a blank look in his eyes, night after night?

Will they conjure an image of a mother's sharp outburst in response to the slightest request for help?

Or will they know in their heart of hearts that despite all the stress and exhaustive pressure, you, their parents, never gave up—not on faith and not on each other.

You never lost your love of life, your dedication to family, your ability to hold on.

You never gave in to despair.

A FATHER'S AND MOTHER'S IMAGE

When Yosef was just seventeen years old, he found himself living as the only Jew in the land of Egypt. He had been sold into slavery by his brothers, lost connection with his family, and did not know if his father Yaakov was even alive. One day, Yosef was left in solitude with the wife of his boss, Potiphar. She had tried to entice the handsome young man in every way possible for months, but to no avail. On this holiday, Potiphar's wife feigned illness while the entire household was out, celebrating in their temple. Again, she tried to tempt Yosef. His resistance almost cracked...but in the last moment, Yosef resisted and ran out of the room. Where did Yosef find the incredible strength needed to resist such strong temptation?

It was "*deyukno shel aviv*," the image of his father that saved Yosef in the last moment. His father's face reminded him of who he was supposed to be, the great potential that lay within, his roots, and his destiny. How could Yosef betray his father's legacy?

Rabbi Ami adds that Yosef saw the image of his mother, Rachel, and his blood ran cold.[1]

At that moment, he saw his mother's face. He remembered her sacrifice on her wedding day so that her sister, Leah, would not be publicly shamed, and he was struck with awe: How could I possibly fall so low when I come from such greatness?

We are each creating our very own "*diyukno shel aviv*." When our children think of us and ask themselves, "What would Daddy do?" or "What would Mommy say?" they are tapping into the legacy we have paved for them.

---

1 *Bereishis Rabbah* 98:20.

I pray that we give our children an image that inspires them to always choose the right path, and to remember that they come from strong roots. And, though we may not have dreamed that we would travel down this road, the journey has taken us to places that helped us discover the true meaning of faith, courage, and love.

Peter Pan Parents

Some parents never want to grow up

A letter from a teenager to an advice columnist caught my eye:

> *I am a fourteen-year-old girl, and I get along with my mother pretty well. But she tends to wear clothes that are appropriate for girls my age—and totally wrong for a forty-two-year-old mother. I feel humiliated when my friends see her dressed up like that. But when I try to discuss the issue calmly, we end up screaming. What can I do?"*

I have spoken to children who have described how ashamed they felt when their father ruined a bar mitzvah celebration, a night out, or a meal together, by drinking himself into the most humiliating of experiences. I have tried to help children find peace after speaking about mothers who dress in inappropriate outfits, thinking they look fashionable, but in their daughter's eyes, they are only a source of embarrassment.

The issue goes beyond "not in good taste" and a little too much alcohol. As parents, we are responsible for setting certain standards of behavior in our family's lives. The way we dress, the way we celebrate, and the way we speak all impact the way our children see us. And if our children believe that we are belittling ourselves through our behavior or clothing, we become diminished in their eyes.

There is a trend in our world today where parents are just not interested in the responsibility that parenting entails. Too many fathers and mothers are trying to raise children while they have not yet finished growing up themselves. We don't want to look older, act older, or miss out on the fun. We find blogs complaining about having to be home at night, doing carpool, or needing to sit down and concentrate on boring math homework. "Been there, done that—I need to get away from it all."

I call them "Peter Pan parents." Every neighborhood has them. We find fathers and mothers who would rather be out or on vacation than deal with the pressures of family life. Some dress in beat-up sneakers or wear the same outfits as their tweens and teens so that they'll still feel young. As their children grow, they become stuck in time, refusing to move on.

The trouble is that in the process, we lose our dignity. And when our dignity goes out the window, so too does the esteem that our children should have for us. It is important for us to remember that children need parents to respect. Of course, we want to create a warm and loving environment in our homes. But, at the same time, we cannot fall into the trap of thinking that we and our children are simply BFFs. As a parent, I have a most crucial mission: to guide, to lead, and to inspire. I am here to mold character and raise a child with soul. How can I possibly accomplish all this if I did not yet accept the responsibility that honorable parenting brings?

We are our children's greatest role models. If not us, who will our children seek out for direction?

Athletes, celebrities, and famous politicians have immersed themselves in indecent behaviors. Social media and popular videos encourage our kids to mock decency. Popular culture screams out that coarse and crude are "in."

If we want our children to speak and carry themselves with respect, we must be the first in line. Judaism teaches us to revere both body and soul. We dress with dignity. We give thought to our words and language. The way we live reflects the majesty that lies within.

When Noach left the ark after the great flood, the first thing he did was plant a vineyard. After drinking wine, he became drunk and "uncovered himself within his tent."[2] Cham, the son of Noach, saw

---

2 *Bereishis*-Genesis 9:21– 22.

"*ervas aviv*," the uncovering of his father, and mockingly told his two brothers about their father's disgraced condition. Rabbi S.R. Hirsch teaches that "*ervah*" is an expression of weakness and shame, such as when a person sinks into a degrading position as a result of his drunkenness. When a parent dishonors themself, they also dishonor the parental image that their children hold onto. Their behavior causes them to become shamed in their child's eyes. The entire relationship between parent and child becomes diminished as does the reverence that children have.

Honor and respect are basic foundations of our homes. Effective discipline is contingent upon the relationships that we have with our kids. Parents who live with dignity give their children an image to revere, admire, and respect.

Your children need to honor you—not because you crave admiration or obedience; rather, your children should gain inspiration and learn life values from you. You are the primary giver of *mesorah*, the transmission of our heritage, a chain that links us back to Sinai. Respect is a cornerstone of our relationship. When children show respect, they are accepting their parents as their life guides. The greater their reverence, the stronger the bond of transmission that grows between parent and child. This cannot be accomplished by parents who act as if they are still in college (or high school).

We begin by living with dignity and honor. We begin by taking a good look at ourselves.

There is a part of parenting that requires us to dig deep. We must let go of our selfish needs and finally grow up. We may be tired. It might not always be fun. But, when we finally reach the moment where we are prepared to live with dignity, to parent with honor, to seek out moments that define us as parents, then we have come to a place in our life that will be cherished beyond our days.

When You Stay Together for the Kids

How to make a difficult situation better

Dear Slovie,

I recently watched your talk on living with joy. Here's my question: I decided to stay together with my husband because of the kids. What advice do you have for me? When a spouse just doesn't connect, and you decide to be there for the children, is there anything more you could tell me?

Thank you,

Stuck at Home

My Dear Friend,

Thank you for your email, and I am glad that you reached out to me. Let's talk.

This is not a response to whether you should stay or go. You've made your decision. I am sure you have put lots of thought into this and I appreciate your sacrifice and desire to create a home that you feel is best for your children. Now the question is: What more can you do to make a difficult situation better?

I am going to give you three thoughts, and I'd like you to contemplate each one.

1. Own Your Decision

You sign your letter as, "Stuck at Home." The truth is, you have made this determination to remain in the marriage for your children. Now it's time to own your decision. There is no one in this world who can judge you. You cannot be stuck if it is a position that you have arrived at after careful consideration. The more stuck you feel, the less empowered you become.

Living life as a victim is an awful way to live. When we make choices in life, we must accept and even embrace the road that we have chosen. This is called strength. To see yourself as stuck is to say, "I am weak and everything I do now is useless and futile." But that is not true.

Are you victim or victor?

For starters, get rid of the idea that you are a casualty. Don't wake up each morning feeling defeated. If you have resolved to remain for the children, respect yourself. Believe in your path. This is a role that you have taken on, so do it with energy and positivity. I'm not saying that this is an easy journey. There is much here to which I am obviously not privy. But if you are there for your children, then be there in both body and soul.

To help bolster your confidence, think about the conclusion of Judith Wallerstein, who wrote The Unexpected Legacy of Divorce. She is convinced that children are almost always better off if the family remains intact, even if the parents are not in love. This is definitely not speaking about situations where abuse, anger, or addictions are taking place. She is talking about homes where mother and father can work on remaining civil. Of course, we would all prefer a home filled with perfectly happy mothers and fathers. But her research found that if parents could avoid exposing children to fights and nasty arguments, the children do well. These thoughts should bring you comfort and strength.

2. Rid Yourself of Hostility

You ask if there is anything more that I can tell you.

I am not here to cast judgment on your decision or to sway you in either direction. This is an individual choice to make. There is no clear answer here. I am sure that some days you question yourself and look at your disconnected spouse with hurt, even with antagonism. It is easy to fall into hostility. But what is accomplished?

If you are in this situation, it is best to leave contempt behind. Otherwise, you will look in the mirror one day and find yourself unrecognizable. You will wonder at the bitterness, the negativity, the resentful person you have become.

You may be asking, "But how? How is it possible to live with one who is disconnected and not breed anger? How can I live with rejection and not lose myself?"

Remember, you have chosen this path so live actively and not reactively. This means that there should never be one person in your life who holds the on/off switch to your emotions. Do not allow others to be your sole source of joy or self-worth. Do you only react to your husband's disconnect, or can you actively find a way to discover peace within, through other roads? What makes you a happy and fulfilled woman? Develop a relationship with yourself, see the greatness inside of you, and explore the unlimited potential that is waiting to be discovered. Perhaps, you can become part of a shul or chessed community, take classes online, or discover a hobby or career path that has been unexplored. You have more power than you realize.

Every Yom Kippur, my mother, Rebbetzin Esther Jungreis, a"h, would give all who were at our davening services a most beautiful blessing. "I wish you nachas,"[3] she would say. "You should have nachas from your families, nachas from your children, but, most of all, nachas from yourselves." And this is my wish to you, too, that, despite the loneliness and pain in your life, may you find nachas not only from your children to whom you are giving your all, but also from yourself.

3. Seek Good Help and Support

I cannot assume that you have taken this route, staying in it for the kids, without trying to professionally repair your relationship. There are some wonderful people out there who can help you. Did you meet with a wise therapist, Torah teacher, rabbi, or rebbetzin?

---

3 *Nachas* is one of those Hebrew words that is hard to translate, but it means "inner joy," the type that fills your heart.

Sometimes, we assume that a situation is hopeless, when really it is not. I have spoken to couples who were in the same situation in which you now find yourself. I cannot guarantee that you will be able to make your marriage work again, but I also cannot say that it is an impossibility. At times, there is disconnect and friction because of a situation with a child or in-law, or there may be a financial or health crisis. With time, good advice, and deep investments of energy and effort, the darkness lifts. Couples who never thought it possible to live together as an intact family have found themselves reconstructing their relationship.

Sometimes, rebuilding after going through turmoil brings a more steadfast home. I ask that you try to find that go-to professional person who can be your emotional and spiritual guide.

I know that this must not have been easy for you to share.

I wish you strength and blessings on your journey.

Mommy and Daddy: Stop Fighting

Things that a child wished her parents knew about fighting

At the conclusion of a lecture on *shalom bayis*, how to create peace in one's home, I asked the audience if they had any comments or questions. A hand shot up in the back. It was the teenaged girl who had come to help set up the room for the program.

"Everything you said tonight is true," she said. "Especially what you said about the fighting. If only my parents were here to hear your words. I get so upset, sometimes even frightened, when there is all this arguing going on in our house. I wish I could tell this to my parents. So all of you sitting here tonight, please take this message home."

Here, then, is this young teen's wish—perhaps her parents may be reading my words. There are too many kids out there who cannot express themselves but who hope that their parents can come to a better place of understanding.

1. Stop Fighting in Front of Us

Our family is in turmoil. Behind the social mask that we wear, we are disconnected. Whenever you fight, it makes us feel vulnerable. We know that it is not possible to always get along, but why can't you disagree with dignity? Why can't you have your discussions privately and respectfully? Why must you wage your battles in front of us? Why do we have to see you treat each other like this? Whether it is a cold war or heated arguments, it doesn't matter. Both wear us down and make us feel as if our home is not a safe haven. We do not want to live in a battle zone. We will start looking for other places and people to spend our time with. We will seek an escape.

2. Don't Argue about Us

Too often you quarrel about the way the other one parents. You accuse Daddy of not knowing how to do anything right with us. You accuse Mommy of letting us get out of control. You act as if we are a burden. When we see you fighting because of us, we feel responsible for your arguments. We think that we are the ones to blame because you can't seem to get along. We find ourselves feeling guilty and trying to make the hurt disappear. We struggle to help you find resolution. "Don't worry," we say, as we try to wipe away Mommy's tears. "It's OK, Daddy," we say bravely, when things don't turn out perfectly. We just want to live in peace.

3. Don't Use Us as Pawns

Don't give each other the silent treatment and expect us to carry messages between the two of you. "Tell Daddy I'm going out"—when Daddy is standing right in front of you, or "Tell Mommy I'm not hungry now"—when she is sitting at the same table as you. This makes our life dark and complicated. How can we ever expect to learn how to communicate with our own spouses if we see such dysfunctional communication between the two of you? We are your children, not chess pieces that are manipulated until you reach a moment of checkmate.

I will never forget the anguished face of the ten-year-old child who asked to speak with me privately. "Why does my father say tell your mother I'm ready to go to the wedding, and then my mother says, tell your father I need ten more minutes, when they're both right there? This is not good, right? My mother thinks that I don't hear her crying in the night after she puts us to sleep, but I hear everything."

What is there to say to this child?

4. Don't Undermine Each Other

When we ask Mommy if we can go to a sleepover and she says, "No, not on a school night," and then we run to Daddy, and he says, "Yes, what's the big deal?" we smell weakness. We see that you are not in sync, and we know that we can manipulate you. It may sound funny, but we would rather believe that the two of you stand together and firm as one unit, even if we don't like what you say; we feel strength when you agree and say it together. It means that our family is solid. We need you to speak with one voice. It removes the confusion and does not allow us to speak with chutzpah. Because you must know, Mommy and Daddy, that chutzpah and disrespect come when you do not respect each other's opinions. How can we respect you if you do not respect each other? And a home filled with disrespect has toxins in the air.

WHILE IT IS NOT ALWAYS EASY for us to live together as families, we can decide to live by certain rules of dignity, even when we disagree. No matter how stressed or challenged we feel, we must know in our heart of hearts that we have been given precious children to watch over and take care of. Let us resolve to build homes in which our children feel secure and loved. Let us wake up each morning and ask ourselves what we can do to successfully raise the next generation. And one day, we will have the joy of watching our children build their own havens, knowing that we have shown them the way.

Targeting Stay-At-Home Moms

Are stay-at-home moms weak and dependent?

Does being a stay-at-home mom while your husband is the breadwinner define you as a weak and dependent woman?

In a penned op-ed in the *New York Times* titled "Poor Little Rich Women," Wednesday Martin describes her culture shock when she moved to Manhattan's Upper East Side. She coined the term "Glam SAHMs," for the glamorous-stay-at-home-moms whom she met at playgrounds, playgroups, and nursery schools where she took her sons.

Though they had graduated from distinguished colleges and business schools, these women do not currently work. Instead, they spend their days "toiling at extensive mothering."

Martin bemoans these highly educated women who "tend to give away the skills they honed in graduate school and their professions—now organizing galas, editing newsletters, and running the library and bake sales—free of charge."

"Tell anyone you're a stay-at-home mom at a party in New York," she adds, "and the conversation just dies there. And when you're not culturally valued, it makes you anxious."

She concludes that these stay-at-home moms who have chosen to put their energies into their families are "dependent and comparatively disempowered."

I am not here to debate the lifestyle choices of working versus non-working mothers. It is not up to us to peer behind people's doors and throw out opinions on their lives. I believe that mothers are trying hard to build strong, loving homes and do their best to raise successful, well-adjusted children. It is the mother who transforms a house into a home.

What does bother me, though, is the inference that women who choose not to work are somehow lesser, smaller, and disempowered. It is time to stop making women feel as if they must battle one another, embroiling us in a constant mommy war between those who work and those who opt to stay home. Why must it be that if I use my talents in an office or the corporate world, I command more respect than if I take those very same gifts and use them for my family or child's school?

One of the most difficult jobs in the world is called "mother." There are some moms who work all day, return exhausted, and are disrespected or, at best, ignored in their homes. And the same can be said for some mothers who stay at home, give all they've got to their families, and yet, are disregarded and taken for granted by their children. It has nothing to do with salary earned or how much money has been amassed in a bank account. Both these women feel weak and belittled. We cannot always equate cash with clout. These mothers who try hard, yet somehow parent in pain, are the mothers whom I feel badly for.

At the same time, there are mothers who are cherished and appreciated. Their voices are heard, their opinions respected. They walk with a force of grace and dignity. These are mothers who parent from strength.

It's not about whether a mother works or stays at home. It does have to do with parenting style, family dynamics, kids' natures, effective discipline, and praying for success and peace in the home. To love and be loved, to hear and be heard, to own self-respect and be respected—this is the ultimate feeling of empowerment for a mother.

Indeed, it was Adam, the first man, who gave words to the essential life force called woman. Adam called his wife "*Chavah, eim kol chai*—Chavah, mother of all the living," for she was the one who gave life to all the living.[4] Chavah denotes spiritual life, for not only does this woman/mother give physical life, but a spiritual and emotional life as well. She created an incredible legacy that is eternal as she gave life to the next generation. Despite death, the destiny of man continues. It is the mother who has been charged with this noble and mighty task.

Judaism reveres the powerful role of mothers. Through their loyalty, sacrifice, strong faith, heroism, deep love, and Shabbos lights, mothers have paved the path that we follow until today. The root of our nation's faith, *emunah*, lies in the *eim*, the mother, who nourishes the *neshamah* of each generation. Far from being dependent, it is the women upon

---

4 *Bereishis*-Genesis 3:20.

whom Am Yisrael depends. Mothers ignite the sparks that are waiting to be kindled within the hearts of the next generation. Children raised on their mother's milk of faith grow to become the next torchbearers of our nation. Mothers teach their children the meaning of compassion, connection, and endless love. Shlomo HaMelech implores, "*Al titosh Toras imecha*—Do not forsake the Torah teachings of your mother."[5] Mothers carry life, give life, and shed tears as they pray that each child lives with blessing, meaning and purpose. To me, this is the greatest, most empowering mission of all and one that I feel incredibly privileged to have been given.

5 *Mishlei*-Proverbs 1:8.

CHAPTER 4

Journey of a Jewish Home

Powerful Lessons to Impart about Holidays and Roots

Teaching Kids about Yamim Nora'im, the High Holidays

Practical ways to transmit the beauty of our heritage

"I'm Jewish too, you know."

These were the opening words of the passenger sitting next to me on a flight I took. I was returning home from a speaking engagement, and in the first few moments of conversation, I found out that this father of three was Jewish and that his children had almost zero connection to their roots. Though not at all religious, he had always felt strongly about his Judaism.

"I see this spiritual bond lacking in my three girls, though, and I don't really understand why. It's not as if I grew up observant, you know."

"You at least grew up with a real image," I said. "I am sure you had a *bubby* in your life."

He nodded.

"Holidays came with traditions and special foods. Maybe you can even remember Shabbos candles and some Hebrew prayer melodies. You have memories that linger deep inside and still touch your heart. But honestly, what have you given your children? The High Holidays are coming. When your girls think of Rosh Hashanah and Yom Kippur, what is the picture that pops into their minds?"

My seatmate was silent.

"The truth?" he replied. "We pass the days in temple and count the pages until we're done. We buy new outfits, socialize with friends, have a terrific break-fast, and say goodbye till next time."

Without knowledge of traditions and of our past, lacking inspiration, children have no idea who they are. When we have strong roots, we create an identity. We know where we have come from and where we are going.

"It's still not too late," I urged. "Discover your roots, create family traditions, and forge a link back to Sinai. The future of our people depends on you."

He promised, and I hope he took our conversation to heart.

Minhagim and joyful traditions help us develop a sense of unity and purpose as families. When we make our *Yamim Tovim* and holidays meaningful and memorable, we create a legacy for the next generation to embrace. We can draw our children closer to Judaism and to our people. We can transmit a genuine and lasting identity.

We have the power to inspire and to ignite passion and soul within our children.

ENGAGING OUR KIDS

Children are naturally curious. They love to explore, to hear, and to ask questions. When Jewish life becomes stale, our kids shut off and feel that their *Yiddishkeit* and Judaism is boring. There is nothing further from the truth. But the inspiration must begin with us. If we approach the *Yamim Nora'im* with dread or indifference, how can we expect joy and excitement from our children?

Here is the problem: too many of us feel disconnected. We think of the

Yamim Tovim as same old, same old. We cannot outsource excitement for our Judaism to yeshivas, teachers, or a synagogue experience. For inspiration to be transmitted, the flames of passion need to be ignited within us and then kindled within our children's *neshamos*.

We must take responsibility and transmit the beauty of our heritage to our sons and daughters. We need to engage our children. We are the ones who have been given the awesome privilege of bringing these souls into this world; now, let us nourish them with enthusiasm, faith, and traditions. How can we make Judaism come alive for the next generation?

KEEP GROWING SPIRITUALLY

We can reignite passion by learning more ourselves and not stagnating when it comes to our Judaism. I still feel excitement every time I study and encounter deep spiritual wisdom or a teaching that moves me. I love to then share my thoughts with my family. Don't allow the *Yamim Tovim* to pass you by without learning something new. Search for articles, attend a workshop or *shiur*, listen to a class—there are tremendous opportunities for us to study today. Challenge your family with a deep question you've learned, give over a story that touched your heart, and bring color to your table.

If we repeat the same messages each year and if our conversation remains speaking about the mundane and material, then our children feel as if their Judaism has grown stale. And we, ourselves, are not motivated to grow. We become spiritually frozen in time.

FAMILY ACTIVITIES

When we join together, we bond as a family. We maximize our days and increase our connection. Holidays allow us to enjoy our time as one while strengthening the *mikdash me'at*, the miniature sanctuary, that every Jewish home has the potential to become.

Here are a few ideas for children of all ages:

1. Create Yom Tov Cards for Friends and Family

Our world is so used to emails and texts, no one really takes the time out to write a special message anymore. Imagine the joy that you would bring to grandparents, neighbors, friends, and relatives who would appreciate a personal connection. COVID has brought tremendous isolation and sadness to countless individuals. A warm wish for blessings on a homemade card would bring sunshine into the lives of so many.

2. Think of Goals Your Family Can Strive For

Elul, Rosh Hashanah, and Yom Kippur are a good time for self-reflection. In our fast-paced culture, many of us do not take the time to stop and think. We can brainstorm ways that would help us grow more connected to each other. When COVID hit and we were unable to see our children who lived across the border in Toronto, my son began a tradition of FaceTiming us with our grandchildren every night. How sweet to hear their good night wishes, share stories, and say the *Shema* prayer together with the little ones.

3. Create Small Mitzvah Goals

We can create mitzvah goals, such as working on remembering to say our berachos before we eat, responding *amen* to blessings heard, or reciting the bedtime *Shema* prayer before we go to sleep. We can work on trying to banish *lashon hara*, gossip, from our meals and trying to become more sensitive to the many times that we put others down without realizing the tremendous hurt that we are causing.

4. Establish a Tradition of *Chessed*

Establish a tradition of *chessed*, kindness, for your family to do this year. Perhaps you have a neighbor who lives alone. Maybe you have friends or acquaintances who have not yet discovered the beauty of Shabbos. There might be people in your life who are undergoing financial or emotional stress. Wouldn't an invitation to your Shabbos table or dropping off of challah, grape juice, and cookies on a Friday make a world of a difference?

5. Create an Erev Shabbos Phone Call Routine

Create a routine of Erev Shabbos calls to grandparents to wish them a good Shabbos. Include relatives or family friends whom you know live on their own or do not get to see many people in the course of their day.

Open your children's eyes to the potential they have to change lives by simply giving another person a good Shabbos call.

6. Design Tzedakah Boxes

Every home should possess a tzedakah box. Children can decorate their boxes if they wish. Some families have a tradition of placing eighteen pennies in the tzedakah box each Friday before candle lighting. Discuss which organizations and to whom you would like to distribute your tzedakah when the box is full. Speak about the mitzvah of taking from one's earnings and bar/bas mitzvah money and giving to those in need. We must never grow arrogant and forget others in need.

7. Seek Out Forgiveness

As we approach the High Holidays, it is a custom to seek out forgiveness from those we may have slighted, with verbal apologies. Do not allow siblings to bear grudges and hold onto anger. This is not the Torah way. Be sure to have children observe parents who begin the year with peace in their hearts. If you have had difficulties with a child this past year, explain that just as we ask Hashem to forgive and allow us to start fresh, we do the same. Bless your children. You will find the parent's blessing in a siddur or *machzor*, a special holiday prayer book.

WHEN I WAS A CHILD, we would always visit my maternal grandparents, Mama and Zaydah, before Rosh Hashanah and Yom Kippur. I remember walking through the door and seeing their faces light up. My mother would bend, take her parents' hands to her lips, and kiss them, as a sign of *derech eretz*, respect. We would follow and do the same. She would ask *mechilah*, forgiveness, for any hurts caused. I watched as tears flowed freely. We felt the awesome presence of the High Holidays approaching.

The mood would grow solemn as we would line up in age order so that my grandparents could bless each of us. Zaydah would place his hands upon my lowered head, and I would feel his hot tears as he whispered the words. Under his white flowing beard, I felt safe. I knew that I was standing under the shelter of incredible holiness. Then I would find Mama and she, too, would bless me as her eyes filled.

These are the memories that remain embedded within my soul. Many years have passed; I was just a little girl. But I close my eyes, and I can still hear the voices of my Mama and Zaydah. I can feel their tears. I can see my parents lowering their heads as they received their own berachos—the love in their eyes and the trepidation, as well. Yom HaDin was coming.

I know how blessed I am to have been touched by these giants of spirits, my "chariots of fire." The faith and love of my parents and grandparents have carried me, uplifted me, and continue to give me direction for life. I am often asked how one can create such powerful memories if they did not grow up with similar recollections.

Each of us, in our own unique way, has the power to create remembrances for the next generation. We have the potential to mold souls, to create a ladder for our children between heaven and earth and then help them climb.

The question is, when your children look back, what image will they see when Rosh Hashanah and Yom Kippur appear?

A High Holiday Reflection: A Young Girl's Plea

The days between Rosh Hashanah and Yom Kippur are a time of deep reflection and introspection. We review our past year, examine our deeds, and think about how we'd like to grow this year. Whom did I hurt? How can I become a better person? What can I do differently to be my best self? Introspection takes honest and real work. Change is hard. How are we supposed to gather the strength and transform ourselves? Where do we begin?

Sometimes it takes a child to nudge us out of complacency, a young soul whose innocence begs us to listen.

I gave a Zoom talk about our mindset as we approach Rosh Hashanah and Yom Kippur. That evening, I read an email from a participant that made me stop and think. I would like to share this mother's words with you so that we may all take a moment and contemplate the gift of life we have been given.

> *Today is the sixth yahrzeit of my daughter Kayla, of blessed memory, who was diagnosed at the age of fourteen with a rare and aggressive cancer. As a little girl, Kayla loved to make everyone laugh and was always dancing. After she was diagnosed, she always carried herself with the knowledge that she was a special daughter of Hashem...She always thanked everyone with whom she came into contact, even wishing the doorman at the lab to have a nice day. She never lost her faith, and when she found out that there was nothing more the doctors could do, she said, "If Hashem wants to take me, He can take me, but I think I want just one more Shabbos."*

Here is a young girl whose final wish before she leaves this world was "just one more Shabbos."

And we, who have the ability to bring Shabbos into our lives, what do we say? What do we wish for?

As we set aside time for reflection, let us think about this young girl's desire to have just one more Shabbos. Let us try not to take our light of Shabbos for granted. And let us think about the gift we have been given of time, of family, and of life.

If these past pandemic months that turned into years have taught us anything, it is that no one knows what the day holds. We are not in control. Whether it is COVID, the tragic collapse of a building, or the onset of an unexpected war, there is so much that is not in our hands. But we do have the ability to make each day count. Every week brings incredible potential. And every Shabbos allows us to soar above the mundane and plug into the spiritual.

After a class, I asked a listener if she thinks the people around her have changed since COVID hit.

"At first, for sure. We all changed. Scary stories made us appreciate every breath. We were more grateful for our families and for time together. But when all this became the new normal, we forgot. We moved on and stopped appreciating each other. We're back to the same old petty arguments and losing it over the little things. It's sad but true."

When Yom Kippur approaches, we must take a few moments of quiet. Let us think about creating a life filled with purpose. Let us contemplate building bridges of love with our words. Let us ask ourselves how we can make each day count.

And let us take the words of one young girl into our hearts so that when we stand on Yom Kippur we can say, "This year I will try to live higher. God, please bless me with the gift of life."

Sukkos: The Antidote to Our Entitled Generation

Sukkos is the holiday Jewish families need

How can we infuse our children with *emunah*?

We cannot remain at peace as their sense of entitlement and appetite for materialism grows. The holiday of Sukkos brings the wisdom that Jewish families everywhere so desperately need to touch the hearts of our children.

The lesson of the *sukkah* resonates. Most people feel safe while living in the comfort of their own homes. When all is familiar and we sit within the rooms of our house, we do not feel vulnerable.

During Sukkos, we embrace the shelter of faith. We exit the walls of our home and sit beneath the stars. Each time we enter the *sukkah*, we declare our eternal trust in God. We leave all that is familiar and dwell in temporary residences so that we don't grow arrogant and think we will find our happiness within our material possessions. We feel protected and joyous in the sanctuary of the *Shechinah*, the Divine Presence.

Security comes with the knowledge that Hashem is watching over us, surrounding us with His *ananei kavod*, His clouds of glory. This message has become our truth from the time that our forefathers traveled in the wilderness of the desert. Study the long history of our people and discover the *hashgachah pratis*, God's personal hand in our lives, that has accompanied our nation until today. See Hashem's open hand in guiding our daily life.

Knowledge of God's watchful eye and eternal presence builds our faith muscle and becomes our real security—to know that life and all that matters is not about wealth, brand names, or technology. Everything that counts in life is right here, in our *sukkah*, beneath the open sky. Our families, our loved ones, time shared together, all within the walls of this temporary hut.

The *sukkah* allows us to transmit this life-changing belief to the next generation. We are asked to stop focusing on the confines of the material and experience a deeper joy. To realize that, despite our hardest efforts, we cannot guarantee anything in life. Experience the joy of the moment. Reach out to those you love. Reach up beyond the stars to your Creator.

THE SUKKAH'S HUG TO EVERY JEW

According to Jewish law, our *sukkah* must have at least three walls. Put your arm out, as if to embrace someone. Look at it carefully: the upper arm, the forearm, and the hand. With the *sukkah*'s three walls, it is as if God is wrapping his arm around us, welcoming us with His embrace. Come, step out of your home and all the anxiety that lies within. Never stop believing. Never give up hope. You are here for a reason. Think about your legacy, the purpose of your moments here on earth.

We enter the *sukkah* and ask Hashem, "*V'tifrosh aleinu sukkas shelomechah*—Spread over us the *sukkah* of Your peace."[1]

Sukkos provides a tangible experience to connect to spirituality and to the source of genuine security. Our *sukkah* becomes our place of peace.

Bring the *sukkah* home. Sheltered under the wings of the Divine, show your children the everlasting joy within our faith.

---

1 Prayer of the *Ushpizin*.

Every Child Needs to Hear Stories about the Holocaust

We cannot allow our nation's story to be forgotten

Sometimes, it is the small moments that make the greatest impression on children.

One Sunday, I met my daughter and her children at my Uncle Yanky's house. Uncle Yanky is my mother's eldest brother. He was born the day that Hitler, *yemach shemo*, came to power. Full of life and blessed with a sharp memory, our time spent together is always vivid and powerful. But I didn't really expect the children to absorb much. After all, they were young. As the adults sat around the table and talked, I thought that the children would keep themselves busy, running and playing. But what happened taught me an incredible parenting lesson.

The children hovered and then pulled chairs over. They wanted to listen and be part of the conversation.

"Uncle Yanky lived through the Holocaust," I said. "Don't be shy if you want to ask any questions."

It didn't take long.

"Were you ever hurt? What did you eat?"

"How did you get out?"

"Why didn't you just call the police to help you?"

I asked my uncle to begin at the very start of his life. He spoke about walking to school when he was six years old and being spit at, chased after, and called dirty Jew. The children's eyes opened wide.

"Can you imagine?" I looked at my grandchildren. "Six years old, all alone, and having to hear these hateful words."

"Weren't you scared?" one child questioned.

"Yes, of course. But what could I do? I had to walk to school. And this is how life was for the Jews."

We spoke about how my grandparents welcomed fleeing refugees into their home. My grandfather was the Chief Rabbi of Szeged, Hungary. Jews from other countries were trying to escape the round-ups and the looming destiny with death. Hungary would be the last to fall. Each night, desperate, frightened Jews would knock on the door. Uncle Yanky never knew where he would sleep or how many people would be packed into the rooms. The door was always open.

I watched as the children imagined the scene. They understood that no matter what, there was always space for these strangers, because, really, they were not strangers; they were our brothers and sisters. They were family. Am Yisrael is one *mishpachah*.

"Uncle Yanky, can you describe the deportation from the ghetto?" I asked.

The children were riveted.

They heard what it was like to be tightly packed into cattle cars meant for animals, with no water and no bathrooms. No air to breathe. The Nazis, *yemach shemam*, with their fierce German shepherds barking ferociously, as they were shouting orders. "*Schnell* [Quickly]!!!"

Where are we going? What will be with us?

No, it was not too much for my grandchildren to hear. Do we not gather around our Seder table and speak of back-breaking slavery in Egypt? "*V'higadeta l'vincha*—And you shall tell it to your children." We are commanded to communicate to our children about the Jewish babies thrown into the Nile—the harshness, the rising evil of every generation who want to destroy us and throw us into the sea. Still today, they seek to snuff the life out of us. We eat *marror*, bitter herbs, as we recall the Egyptians who embittered our lives. We dip into salt water to remind us of our endless tears. This is our story. It is our reality. And it is our responsibility as parents and grandparents to "tell your children."

So no, I did not hold back, and I did not ask my dear uncle to withhold or protect. Our children must know. They need to understand what anti-Semitism looks like. They need to comprehend that there are those who are rabid and vicious, who detest us more than they love life itself.

They need to know how to stare this monster in the face and stand strong as loyal Jews. Whether facing those who are anti-Semitic or claiming to be "only" anti-Israel, our children will confront those who distort and destroy through their hatred. We must teach our children.

Because, through it all, we have held onto our faith. This is the key to our survival. Hearing and seeing this imprinted within these children's souls that, despite all the suffering, we are still standing strong. A Jew never gives up. Our nation will never disappear. We are a nation born of miracles.

The children sat for three hours! They heard stories of Shabbos in Bergen-Belsen, of the blowing of the shofar despite being beaten to the ground, of the daily roll calls while standing frozen, starving, and covered with sores, and yet, how the faith of our people was not crushed.

Even there, in the darkest abyss on earth, we refused to cower. We would not relinquish our light.

As our time together came to a close, I asked Uncle Yanky to relate the story of his bar mitzvah in the D.P. camp, where the family was taken after the war ended. Awaiting visas, not allowed to enter the Land of Israel, my grandparents and their children were stuck in a displaced person's camp in Switzerland. After going through the indescribable suffering of the Holocaust, there was still no peace to be had. But my uncle was becoming a bar mitzvah.

"Children, do you know what we served at my bar mitzvah?"

My grandchildren leaned forward, wanting to hear.

My uncle looked at them and said, "Water! There was nothing else."

"Then my friends did something I will never forget. You see, staying in the D.P. camps, we children all became friends. They brought a huge box to me, as my present. I could not believe it! I opened the box and inside was another smaller box. Then another. And another. Until the smallest box came out. And you wouldn't believe what was inside. A banana!"

The children's mouths opened wide.

"Yes," my uncle continued. "A banana for my bar mitzvah present. I had never seen a banana before in my life, so I started to eat the peel. One of the other children showed me what to do. I had no idea. And then I cut it into a hundred tiny pieces so everyone could share."

We laughed together and said our goodbyes.

All the way home, the children were filled with awe.

"Bubby, how strong is our Uncle Yanky! And I don't mean muscles...you know what I mean Bubby?"

And then—

"I can't believe it, Bubby. A banana for a bar mitzvah!"

I had silent tears as I drove.

I do not know what our children will face in the future. The world is spinning beyond control.

We must teach our children well. My parent's world, my uncle's world, was not so long ago. Yet, we are once again confronting troubling hatred. It is masked, but it is real.

If we do not know where we've come from, we do not know what we are made of, and we do not know where we are going.

Let us ignite the spark within our children's soul. It is our sacred mission.

The Best Chanukah Gifts to Give to Your Children

This year, give the greatest gifts that money can't buy

Chanukah is the time of year that we shower our children with gifts. Many end up lost, pieces are quickly broken, and toys forgotten. This year, let's take a few moments to focus on the greatest gifts that money cannot buy.

1. Time

Children crave time together with loved ones. They're hungry for positive attention. They seek some type of affirmation of love when we spend time with them. We mistakenly throw toys and gadgets at them, thinking that will make them happy, and then we wonder why they're whining minutes later.

It's not the things that matter; it's what we do with them that counts.

I recall arriving in Israel, when I traveled to visit my children who lived in Yerushalayim and had young children. I schlepped a huge box containing a kitchen play set inside. I couldn't wait to see their faces as they played with my big surprise. It was not easy. I had to have the taxi driver tie the gigantic package to the roof of his car. Together we maneuvered the oversized box up the narrow staircase. Sweat was dripping down our faces in the heat of the day. After finally assembling the kitchen set, I noticed my grandchildren on all fours, crawling on the floor. "Bubby, we love the box! Come play hide and go seek with us!" I had to laugh. After all the hard work and *shvitzing*, all they really wanted was that I play with them and the big box.

Time together is the one gift that can never be replaced Ask your child what he would like to do with you this Chanukah. Some children would love to play a game of ball, others to go ice skating, paint pottery, experience rock climbing, or even build a model airplane together. Whatever it is, when you give the gift of time, be sure you give with all your heart. Don't seem disinterested. Turn off your phone. Don't go grudgingly. You will never regret time spent together. The memory will remain with your child forever.

2. Smile

Sometimes, the easiest gifts are the ones that we find most difficult. We smile when we cradle a newborn in our arms or when we're having a fun night out. But parenting brings challenges. As our children grow, we are stressed and pulled in so many directions and we forget to smile. The joy is missing.

Even if you don't really feel it, give your child a smile. Smile when you see him in the morning and when he comes home from school. Brighten your home, radiate your light.

A smile means "I am happy to be here. I want to spend time with you."

My mother would often describe arriving as a small child to the terrifying darkness of Bergen-Belsen. "*Lichtige kindt*, my precious light," my Zaydah said. "Here you have a *groisse avodah*, a most important mission."

"Here, Tatty?' my mother asked. "What can I possibly do here? I am just a child. What can I possibly do here?"

"Here, you can give people a smile," my grandfather responded, "because when you smile, you give people hope."

My Zaydah's wise words speak to us all. If a child's smile could bring light to such a terribly dark world, imagine the joy that each of us can create today.

3. Identity

Children need roots. They need to feel that they belong. When we give our children an identity, we give them a solid sense of self. Much of future mental health hinges on the self-image that a child has.

Our culture conditions us to forge an identity based on the brands that we wear, the type of sneakers on our feet, and the cars that we drive. When our children feel that they are not keeping up with the Goldstein's, there's a sense of inferiority. Sadly, their self-confidence suffers.

Traditions, joyful rituals, and pride in our legacy and heritage teach children the true source of a greater self. There are incredible stories of our people, courageous giants of spirit, who can infuse our children with spiritual wealth. Communicate these stories as your children grow. Shabbos and *Yamim Tovim* give children time together as a family as well as a positive connection to their roots. Acknowledging values reinforces convictions that we hold dear.

4. Safe Spaces

Family means loyalty, kindness, sacrifice, and giving. Our children feel loved when they feel safe. Homes where sarcasm, unkindness, selfishness, and criticism flourish do not allow our sons and daughters to connect. We must live love. Bonding between siblings, between parents and children, cannot happen if children feel shamed or disparaged. Constant criticism tears children down.

As parents, one of the greatest gifts that we can give is creating a home filled with compassion and gratitude, forgiveness and connection, peace and holiness.

This Chanukah, give your family the greatest gifts. The gifts of your heart will speak to them long past this holiday season.

Queen Esther's Lessons for Today

Timeless messages from the Megillah
for every man, woman, and child to hear

MASTER SILENCE

The key to Esther remaining in the palace of Achashveirosh was her keeping a secret. Mordechai told Esther not to reveal her origins, that she was a Jew. The time was not yet ripe. Esther was required to master the quality of silence.

There are times in life that we must guard our privacy or someone's confidence. How many relationships have been harmed and friendships broken because we could not keep silent? We were given a trust to keep and couldn't contain ourselves. Or we overshared and exposed intimate details of our life. In our world of phones and social media, we are privy to many photos and conversations that should really be kept hidden. Modesty isn't just about dress. It's about living with dignity and self-respect, knowing when to share, and what and when to keep private.

LIVE WITH COURAGE AND COMPASSION

After accepting her mission, Esther says, "*U'vechein avo el ha'melech... v'chaasher avadeti, avadeti*—I will go to the king...and if I die, I die."[2]

I will give it my all. I will muster the courage to do my best.

As seasons of life pass, many people are left with regrets. *If only*...but the moment is lost.

Esther is telling us to seize courage, step up to the plate, and at least know forever that you tried to make a difference.

In one of my mother's final interviews, she was asked what I found to be a most painful question.

"Rebbetzin, what would you like it to say on your gravestone?"

My mother replied, "I want just two words written: 'I cared.'"

---

2 *Megillas Esther*-Scroll of Esther 4:16.

LOOK FOR HASHEM'S HIDDEN HAND

In the entire *Megillas Esther* there is no clear mention of Hashem's name. Amazingly, there is no reference to God. The name "Esther" means hidden. *Megillah* means revelation. Esther is revealing a most powerful hidden truth.

How easy it is to think that life is a series of random events. The story of Purim could seem to be a natural story that took place over the course of many years.

The king just happened to choose this sweet, innocent Jewish woman, Mordechai just happened to hear a plot against the king, the king just happened to suffer from a bout of insomnia, and all the pieces then fell into place.

Esther is calling out to us, urging us to wake up: see Hashem's hidden hand in your life, in your every day. It's not only about the big miracles, like the splitting of the sea—it's about the little moments. God is in every sunrise, every soul, and every success or disappointment that life brings.

The pandemic and all that we have gone through is no coincidence. Hashem is banging on our door.

The question is, do we hear, do we see, and do we open our eyes to what is happening before us?

God's presence is here, even now, amidst the most challenging time that our world is facing.

Esther refused to lose hope even when it felt as if she was lost in a thick fog. "*Keli, Keli, lamah azavtani?... V'atah Hashem al tirchak; eyalusi l'ezrasi chushah*—My God, my God, why have you abandoned me?... So, God, do not be distant. You are my strength, hurry to help me."[3]

UNITY BRINGS STRENGTH

Haman describes the Jewish People as a "dispersed and divided" nation to the king. His words are jolting. These people are constantly bickering and quarreling with each other. Don't worry about them joining together

---

3 *Tehillim*-Psalms 22:2, 20.

and mounting a united offensive—they can't agree on anything. No one will come to their defense because they are hated. Get rid of them.

Esther succeeds in her mission to save her people by uniting the Jews and bringing them together in prayer and fasting. She leaves direction for us, her children. Esther asks that we celebrate this day together with joy, join together for a *seudah*, festive meal, give charity, and send *mishloach manos*, portions of food to one another. Esther is requesting that we create an atmosphere of unity and peace. The antidote to all the infighting and bickering, to all the *sinas chinam*, the senseless hatred between a Jew and his brother, is reaching out to one another with friendship. Unity brings strength.

Our enemies never asked, "What type of Jew are you?" No one was spared the gas chambers based on their observance or the type of yarmulka that covered their head.

We don't all have to be the same. We must know that we are united "*k'ish echad b'lev echad*—like one person with one heart" beating within.

Pesach and COVID: A Message of Hope

Pesach brings us a powerful message that speaks to us today.

We were plunged into a world we could never have imagined. The unknown is frightening. Parents were distressed for their children and children distressed for their parents.

In a world filled with chaos, we yearn for security and stability. The definition of "*seder*" is "order." Herein lies the message of the *chag*: knowing without a doubt that we are not alone in this world. Just as our people wondered in Egypt if they would ever get out of that awful darkness they were suffering, so too, we may wonder, "Will we ever see the light again?"

The Seder comes to teach us perspective for life. True, there are moments of *marror*. Our forefathers suffered deeply. There were times that they were anguished and felt as if they'd lost their spirit. But they did not allow the *marror* moments to overcome them. We dip the *marror* into *charoses*, a delicious mixture of apples, nuts, wine, and honey, to teach us that even in the most difficult of times we must see the sweetness that imbues our life: the friendships, the love, the resilience, and the kindness that surrounds us. Hashem took us out of Mitzrayim, and we will be taken out of this *galus* as well.

At our Seder we make a sandwich of matzah and *marror* with a bit of *charoses*, for such is life. Sandwiched between the hardships are flashes of joy. Grab onto them! Seize the moment.

RABBI AKIVA'S OPTIMISM

Our Haggadah speaks of a famous Seder that took place in Bnei Brak. There were many great rabbis sitting together. One who is mentioned is Rabbi Akiva, who was actually the younger scholar hosting the elders. The rabbis spoke about *yetzias Mitzrayim*, the Exodus from Egypt, until their students came in to say, "Rabbis, it is time to recite the morning *Shema* prayer!"

Rabbi Akiva lived in the darkest of times: The holy Temple in Jerusalem had been destroyed. He saw *churban* before his eyes. The Romans had conquered the land. The spirit of the Jewish nation had been crushed—their soul trampled upon. Studying Torah and doing mitzvos were met with imprisonment, torture, and death. Soon the long and bitter exile would begin. The Jews would be put into chains and sold in the Roman slave market. Who could think about joining a Seder in such darkness? Who could feel inspired and speak about the Exodus from Egypt when despair was in the air?

This is exactly why the sages met in the home of Rabbi Akiva.

Rabbi Akiva was the eternal optimist. He refused to surrender to depression. Where others saw the end of the road, he saw the beginning of the journey. His eye was always on the future. His heart was eternally filled with faith.

We meet Rabbi Akiva once again, walking with his peers to Yerushalayim.

When they reached Har Hatzofim, Mount Scopus, they tore their garments from grief at the sight of devastation. As they reached Har

Hamoriah, the Temple Mount, a fox emerged from the place of the *Kodesh Hakodashim*, the Holy of Holies. The rabbis started to weep. Rabbi Akiva laughed. "Why are you laughing?" they asked. He explained that while they see the destruction of the sacred, he sees the fulfillment of the prophecy. Just as the first part of prophecy had been fulfilled, that the Beis Hamikdash, the holy Temple, would be destroyed, now we must look forward to the second part of the prophecy—the rebuilding of our Beis Hamikdash and return of our people.

We must gather now round the table of Rabbi Akiva. It takes courage to keep a positive spirit. The sages assembled by Rabbi Akiva, the one who would keep hope and faith alive. On Seder night, we must tap into the eternal optimism of Rabbi Akiva.

THE POWER OF THE MORNING SHEMA

When the students came in to say it was time to recite the morning *Shema*, they were transmitting a message, even to us, today: Don't give up! Don't fall into despair!

You are going through most difficult times—it is true. But you must remember this truth: the darkest part of the night comes right before dawn. The morning *Shema* is a prayer of clear-cut faith. There are no shadows lurking and no hazy doubts.

We proclaim our unwavering *emunah* with one voice, when loud and clear we declare: "*Shema Yisrael. Hashem Elokeinu, Hashem Echad.*"

Making Tishah B'Av Relevant

Bringing Eichah, the Book of Lamentations, to life for our children

I made a promise.

I gave my word to my dear Uncle Yanky, Rabbi Jacob Jungreis, that I would not allow his story to be forgotten. So I am sitting at the table of my beloved mother's brother with notebook and pen in hand. We sit for hours.

> *I am the man who has seen affliction…My soul remembers well (Eichah-Lamentations 3:1).*

When I leave his home, I am holding my own "book of lamentations." Each page cries out to be shared and remembered. We dare not forget. I will do my best to bring justice to the sacred memories he entrusted to me. They haunt my soul.

There are not many souls remaining in the world who can give testimony to the evil that threatened to destroy our people.

Listen well.

MY UNCLE'S VOICE

> *As a five-year-old child walking to school in Szeged, Hungary, in 1938, I would be yelled at, "Bidosh Zsido! Dirty Jew! You killed god!"*
>
> *Every day the taunts and screams were thrown at me, and I never understood what that meant. I was always a frightened little boy. But this was my life. We did not know anything different or how terrible things would become.*
>
> *One day in 1943, I was standing next to my father, your Zaydah, who was the Chief Rabbi of Szeged, in the room filled with his holy books. A man came in. Mama, your grandmother, invited him to eat with us. We always had a house filled with people.*
>
> *I will never forget the moment. His eyes were hollow and dark. He said that he had escaped a concentration camp.*
>
> *"Rabbi! You know they are making soap out of our people?"*
>
> *Zaydah's hat fell off as his head slumped down onto the table. Mama cried out. "That cannot be!"*
>
> *No one believed it. It could not happen here. Hungary was a cultured country. Szeged was a civilized city. We had colleges, universities, plumbing, and electricity. There was art and music, museums, and concerts.*
>
> *We didn't comprehend the truth. The carnage was being*

covered up. There were wild rumors flying. We could not fathom that such atrocities existed. We couldn't believe it could happen in our Hungary. Those who dared talk about death camps were shouted down or called alarmists. There were no news stories or radio shows revealing the murder of the Jews. Many who had been taken away were forced to send postcards back saying that they were fine, that they were being taught a trade because Jews were lazy, and that they would soon be home. "Arbeit macht frei—Work will set you free" was the sign greeting those who entered the extermination camps.

Later when we wanted to leave Hungary there was no getting out. Even if we could, no country in the world wanted us. There was no spot on earth for a Jew to find shelter.

Soon after, people started arriving during all hours of the night. They were running across the border smuggling themselves into Szeged.

At 2:00 a.m. we would hear a frantic knock.

"Ver iz dus? Who is it?"

"A Yid."

A Yid? We must open the door. I never knew where I would be sleeping. Mama spread sheets in the corner of every room. Fifty people crammed into our home looking for a place to breathe.

In time, Szeged would become a stifling ghetto.

> Young men drag the millstone and youths stumble under the wood. Gone is the joy from our hearts, our dancing has turned into mourning (*Eichah*-Lamentations 5:13).

Young Jewish boys were forced to join work brigades and slave labor camps. They were brought to our city because we were near the Tisza River, a hub for travel. Once a month, a boat would take three hundred of our finest boys to Bor, where they were forced into backbreaking labor. There, many were cruelly shot, sent on death marches, and slaughtered.

Zaydah and Mama were anguished. These beautiful Jewish young men were here in our city. They were being sent to their death. We could not turn our backs on our brothers, but how could we possibly help them?

Zaydah and Mama spoke to the Jewish doctors of the city. "How can we get these boys to miss the boat and escape their death sentence? How can we help them be sick enough but then get well?"

In Mama's kitchen, concoctions were made. One with unpasteurized milk, another with soybeans crushed into powder. If injected, one would get high fever for forty-eight hours and miss the boat. If the paste was put onto the eyelids, it mimicked trachoma. But how to get these vials to the boys?

Zaydah would take along my little sister, your beloved mother, Rebbetzin Esther Jungreis, of blessed memory, to visit these young men while they were being held. Since he was the Chief Rabbi, Zaydah was given some precious time with the prisoners. He blessed each one with his tears, lovingly embraced them and prayed with them. Mama sewed the poisonous vials into my sister's coat lining. While no one was looking, the vials were given over and countless lives were saved.[4]

There was never a doubt that we had to do whatever we could to save lives. From the earliest age we were given this understanding: Feel the pain of your brothers and sisters. Never look away at the suffering of your people.

> My eyes shed streams of water at the shattering of our people (*Eichah*-Lamentations 3:48).

June 1944, at midnight: there was a knock at the door. "Pack up! You will need to leave your house!"

---

4 Years later, while speaking across the world, my mother met some of these very boys, now grown men, who had survived through these dangerous encounters. Their reunion was incredibly emotional.

Mama woke us up and bathed us one last time. We spent three days at the railroad station. Zaydah took only the handwritten Torah notes of his illustrious ancestor, Rabbi Modche Benet, and the holy tefillin given to him by his Zaydah. Throughout our days in the concentration camps these were never lost and imbued us with continuous faith.

We were kept in pop-up tents. There was a torrential downpour. We were freezing, hungry and frightened. In middle of the night my sister, your precious mother, developed a high fever. Zaydah went to search for an aspirin. Three hours later he returned. There was no aspirin. Zaydah and Mama held your mother in their arms, rocking her while they were crying. I was sitting across from them silent. I couldn't bear to watch my parents suffering. But when I looked away, I felt guilty.

I was eleven years old.

They pushed us into cattle cars. There were barking German shepherds and rifles. Ninety people were jammed on top of one another. We were suffocating. All around people screaming, "I have no air! I have no air!" We didn't know it at the time but we were being taken into the valley of death, Bergen-Belsen.

MOURN FOR YOUR PEOPLE

> *Over these things I weep; my eyes run with water because a comforter to revive my spirit is far from me (Eichah-Lamentations 1:16).*

I pray that I have given life to the memories that have lied dormant within my uncle's soul. I hope that through my words, we can revive the light of those whom the world believed they had extinguished.

This Tishah B'Av, take a moment and mourn for your people. For a world that was. Teach your children. Do not allow them to forget. Dare not remain silent when you witness the suffering of your nation.

Too Many Jewish Kids Think Judaism Is Irrelevant

Speaking to Jewish high school students, I was alarmed by their ignorance and indifference to Judaism.

How do you take the pulse of a nation? Get into the classrooms and speak to the kids. Have some conversations and see what they are thinking and feeling.

While on an international speaking tour, standing in front of an assembly of high school children, I was confronted with the spiritual malaise that is taking place amongst our children. They lack the backbone to stand strong for our people. Too many don't know enough about their purpose, their mission, and their reason for being.

Indifferent or ignorant—take your pick.

Concluding a talk on Jewish pride, I offered to take questions. A hand shot up in the front.

"You speak about our heritage and what it means to be a Jew. So many around us are clueless when it comes to Judaism. So many Jews in my neighborhood don't even know what it means to celebrate Shabbos. How can we share with others and teach more?"

"What an awesome question!" I responded. "Begin with your Shabbos table. Invite neighbors and friends who have not yet discovered the beauty of Shabbos. There is so much for you to do!"

Another hand shot up in the back. The young boy stood up and called out loudly, "That's racist!"

"Excuse me?" I countered.

"To speak up and think that you have what to teach the world about your Judaism means that you think you are better than everyone else. That's racist!" he replied.

A wave of tension swept through the auditorium. I had just a few moments to respond before my time with these teenagers was up. Here before me sat the future fathers and mothers of our people. These souls would soon be asked to lead, commit, create, and cry out for Israel and the Jewish People. How tragic to believe that knowing our holy mission in this world and understanding that we are to be a "light amongst the nations" is considered to be a "racist" idea.

In those few minutes, I explained that striving to share our legacy of wisdom and justice is far from being prejudiced against others. It means that we are obligated to know who we are; how we have the ability to sanctify and make this world into a better place as we tenaciously hold onto the truth and values of the Torah. Like Avraham and Sarah, we are charged to go out and make a difference in the world, to be a moral and spiritual compass. That's not racist. It is a life of purpose. Kindle the light of Shabbos, banish the darkness, and bring illumination to the world. Be a blessing.

Another student raised his hand. "Why do you think most kids my age find Judaism to be irrelevant?"

I threw the question back. I was curious. "Why do you think they do?"

"Because," he responded flippantly, "it is."

"Yes," another student added. "It's archaic. How can you tell me how to live? I resent that."

It is difficult for me to describe the sadness that I felt at that moment. "I am sorry for you," I responded. "I am sorry for you because that's not my Torah that you are describing. And it is not the Torah of my children. Torah is my oxygen; it is our oxygen. My Judaism carries me day and night, through light and through darkness, through every life challenge and situation."

We spoke about Torah's relevance in this world. I shared how Torah is alive and gave examples from the harm of oversharing on social media to protecting the dignity of women. Judaism is current and viable. One just needs to know where to look and how to study.

I was grateful for the questions. I touched a nerve. But this was only the beginning. Obviously, we have a problem here, and I don't pretend to have all the solutions.

There are some glaring issues though that we, the parents and grandparents, the educators and laypeople, must confront.

First, the passion is missing. What are we willing to sweat for, sacrifice for, and stand up for? When have our children felt *mesirus nefesh*, sacrifice, sincerely giving of heart and soul for our nation?

As a child, I remember standing hours in the cold and marching for the freedom of Soviet Jewry, who were stuck behind the Iron Curtain. I recall being in shul when the Yom Kippur War broke out. I saw real tears being shed; worry and grief etched on the faces around me. It had nothing to do with being religious or not. At that moment, we were a family of Jews, united. I felt part of a people, a nation that stood together because we were bound together as one family.

Somehow, we've lost that connection. When asked what they are willing to sacrifice for, what will our children say? Most will respond making money, becoming famous, acquiring gadgets or things. The bond that once held us together as we were scattered throughout the four corners of the earth has frayed, weakened. The eyes that once searched for Yerushalayim now seek the next best app.

I cannot help myself from believing that we have lost something most precious through these decades of comfort. We have lost the passion and spirit born upon the birthing stone of suffering.

For millions of Jews, Judaism has become irrelevant. What can we do?

Let's recognize that we must put our hearts and heads together and think hard about the Jewish education, in school and at home, that our children are getting. It's time for a detox. All the excess that we've thought to be religious values—but which are really spiritual junk food—should be let go: the meaningless, over-the-top bar and bas mitzvah parties that have become the defining moment of our children's Judaism with an open bar that has nothing to do with any mitzvah, the over-the-top pursuit of the material, and the desire to blend in more as "citizens of the world" have all contributed to our children's disconnect.

We must look at ourselves in the mirror. Upon what do we reflect when we greet the Shabbos Queen, when we sit at our Yom Tov table, when we speak about our faith and our values? Are Jewish holidays simply about buying new clothing, matching the kids, and making the latest gourmet roast recipe? How do we pray? Our children see it all, watch it all, and take it all in. Do we make Judaism come alive each day? Do our children ever hear us stop to make a berachah, to express gratitude to God, to study Jewish wisdom steadily no matter the daily pressures we face, or to embrace a mitzvah mindfully? And, if they do, do they see passion and fire in our eyes?

Finally, when it comes to Eretz Yisrael and Yerushalayim, we have come to take our gift for granted. The world slammed its doors on us. No country wanted us even after we were shoved into cattle cars and taken to be gassed in the ovens. Miraculously, we witnessed Hashem's mighty hand from above. From a nation of skeletons, we fought the vast Arab armies who surrounded us and pierced the sky above Yerushalayim with the sound of the shofar. After thousands of years, we once again touched the ancient stones of the Kosel and wept.

"*Sha'alu shalom Yerushalayim*—Pray for the peace of Jerusalem," David HaMelech implores.[5] How many of our children have seen us shed a tear for Yerushalayim?

We conclude our Seder with the words "*L'shanah ha'baah b'Yerushalayim*." We break a glass at every *chuppah* to recall the shattered Temple that once stood in glory, because our joy is not complete. We dip eggs into ashes and mourn on the floor every Tishah B'Av for the majesty of our people that was lost.

Are these simply acts done by rote? Do we yearn for the rebuilding of Yerushalayim?

"*Im eshkacheich Yerushalayim tishchach yemini*—If I forget Jerusalem..." must be more than a beautiful melody sung under the *chuppah*.

Teaching a group of high school girls about the loss we must feel for *churban Yerushalayim* and the hole in the heart that *galus* has brought, one student raised her hand.

"But how can we mourn what we do not know?"

We, the parents, must contemplate the truth in this question.

How do we keep the dream of Yerushalayim alive? How can our children long for that which they have never truly tasted?

It is our mission to give our children a soul connection to Eretz Yisrael, to the sanctity that every stone holds, to the vision of returning one

---

5 *Tehillim*-Psalms 122:6.

day to our land as one nation, and to the devastating loss that *galus* has brought.

I remember being a little girl, watching in wonder as my parents cried and laughed out loud, simultaneously. The voice on the radio filled our kitchen: "*Yerushalayim shelanu*—Jerusalem is ours again!" We went on a trip of a lifetime to rediscover the land of Israel, the Kosel, and Yerushalayim. Every step was magical.

My mother describes the scene in her first book, *The Jewish Soul on Fire*.

> *We stood there as if in a trance, my husband, my children, and I. We could not speak. There were only tears. For two thousand years, we waited for this moment. Our ancestors had prayed for this day. What they would not have given to stand here, even for a fleeting second, and yet they were denied the privilege. How strange that we who were unworthy, we, who were wanting in faith, were the ones to stand here in the presence of sanctity! How dare we approach this place?*
>
> *I looked up at the heavens and searched for my grandfather. Surely the angels had gathered his ashes from Auschwitz and brought them as an offering to this very spot.*
>
> *"Zaydah, Zaydah," I cried into the night, my voice merging with the sound of a million other voices, "please walk with me, for I cannot stand alone!"*

Somehow, our sons and daughters are clueless. We have traveled the four corners of this earth and gone through every type of persecution. The earth is drenched with our blood. But our story remains blank. There is no memory. It is up to us to educate, to teach, to speak out, and to speak up.

We have much work to do. Let us strengthen ourselves and touch the hearts of the next generation. The future of our people is in our hands.

CHAPTER 5

Strengthening Our Children, Strengthening Ourselves

Communicating and Connecting

Speak Up

What comes out of our children's mouths is just as important as what goes in

"Can I have that, Mommy?"

You hold up the bag of chips and check the *hechsher*, kosher supervision. You check the ingredients. You deliberate what your child puts in his mouth, wanting him to eat healthy. But did you ever think about what comes *out* of your child's mouth?

What comes out of his mouth should be wholesome and good too.

God created us with two eyes, two ears, two nostrils, but only one mouth. We do not have one mouth for prayers and moments of holiness, and a second for eating and speaking the mundane. We can't close one and then open the other. Everything that exists within us must be imbued with some sense of sanctity. Our food nourishes our body; our words nourish our souls.

When God breathed life into Adam, a soul was breathed in through his nostrils and he was granted the gift of speech. What separates man from animal is the power of our words. My words reveal my inner thoughts.

Think about Yom Kippur, the holiest day of the year. Jews from every walk of life gather together to chant the *Kol Nidrei* prayer. "Forgive me, God, if I have broken my vows; not kept my promises." Because who am I if my word is not my word?

OUR WORDS ARE POWERFUL

Words can build, words can destroy. Words can heal, words can hurt. And using profanity or harsh language deadens the sense of self respect and dignity that lies within one's soul.

Our children are often left to view online clips and play video games that casually introduce unacceptable language into their vocabulary. Even in their classrooms, there are students who backtalk, are rude to, and even express contempt for their teachers and classmates. Children then come to believe that this is OK and even normal.

"Come on, everyone talks like that," they vehemently protest. "What's the big deal?"

We cannot simply sit back and throw our hands up in disgust as we listen to our children's words. It's easy to nod sadly and blame our children's language and disrespect on our loose culture. But society is not parenting our children, we are. Or, at least, we should be. No, it doesn't take a village; it just takes a parent—one who is connected and concerned with his or her child's character, one who is attuned to the power of one's own words, as children absorb the way that we speak. After all, if Mommy or Daddy can talk "like that," why can't I?

A KOSHER MOUTH

Jill has attended my parenting classes from the time that her children were infants. In one series, we focused on the power of our words. We spoke about teaching our children to speak with respect and sensitivity. She sent me this email:

> *I walked past my son while he was looking through his baseball cards. He was tossing the ones that he didn't like and, to my surprise, repeating over and over again, "This one ____!" as he tossed them. It was a less desirable word than "stinks." Not a curse, but a clear indication that his exposure to first-grade language had left my once-pure little toddler forever changed.*
>
> *It is so casual, this disconcerting change, that it leaves a mother frozen in her tracks. I thought of all my years of Jewish parenting with you and wanted to let him see now at six that he could have a higher standard than what he sees around him. He should know that he is different than the status quo. How could I be angry when he is learning from his environment? This is, unfortunately, what surrounds him each and every day.*
>
> *I said to him, "Zack, honey, I am surprised to hear you use that word over and over again while you play. That language is not for you, Zack. You're holy."*
>
> *With that Zack looked up and took a quick moment. He then thoughtfully asked, "What does that mean?"*
>
> *I was so happy he cared. "Zack, you are a mensch, a Jewish boy, and God placed a very special soul inside of you. Your mouth is kosher, and you are an example for others."*
>
> *Suddenly, His face was different. My words got through. I knew it. He thought about what I'd said; he really took a good look. He went back to his cards differently, and I was so happy that I hadn't missed the moment.*

BRINGING GOOD SPEECH HOME

How can we parents help our children maintain higher levels of communication as they grow?

1. Be Involved

Too often, we take a *laissez faire* attitude or unknowingly allow our children to set their own standards. We frequently have no idea which clips they've watched. Many fall into trouble with devices and gadgets. But we are here for a reason. We have a right and responsibility to see what our children see, to hear what they are listening to, and, if we don't approve, we cannot be afraid to say "No, that's not OK."

When my son was growing up, I took him to buy a game for his Gameboy. We showed the salesman two games and asked him to explain why one was rated "T" (for teen) if they both seemed similar.

"Oh," he replied, "the teen one has better graphics and curse words in the background."

"Then, of course, we'll take the other," I said.

The salesman looked at me. "What's the big deal? It's only in the background. It's so low you hardly hear it."

"Well, why do you think it's there?" I asked. "It must be doing something. It obviously enters your head as you play, and that is not for us."

I was glad that my son was able to learn the effect of even subtle background noise that we often ignore or just accept as a sign of the times.

2. Hear Yourself

We often set higher standards for our children than we do for ourselves. We expect greatness from them, yet lower the bar as we live our daily lives.

A mother asked me why I think her family's Sunday dinner outings always ended in disaster. No one was ever happy, and she found herself wishing that she'd never taken her children out.

"When you and your husband sit down at the table, what do your children hear? Are you putting down the menu, criticizing the food, belittling the service? Are you waiting impatiently and griping about it?"

"How did you know?" she asked. "That's exactly my husband. Nothing is ever good enough."

And here lies our answer. Children mimic all that they hear. They pick up our language, our attitude, and our tone. If we desire children who speak respectfully, who are kind with their words, then we must first hear ourselves.

Let us teach each child to speak "up." Raise your voice, my child, not in anger or debasement, but rather through speaking with self-respect and graciousness. You will then "raise yourself" as you take the higher road. Speak up for truth and compassion. Reflect sanctity even as you talk. See the power of your words as they touch those around you. Speak up and allow your words to create a better world.

TTYL

Connecting with spouses and children in a world gone texting

While driving the other night, I noticed a couple in the distance. They were taking a relaxing evening stroll. *How great that this couple took the time and decided to enjoy each other's company*, I thought to myself. Then as I drove by, I noticed that both of them were on their phones, texting away.

Today, we can live next to each other, occupy the very same space, but manage to reside, each of us, in our very own world.

There have been countless articles discussing the impact of cell phones and texting on our children's lives. Concerned parents attend workshops where we are taught how to monitor access to the internet and clips on our kids' phones. There are worries about compromising pictures that are sent and the effects of constant texting.

The problem is much greater than filtering your child's gadgets.

I believe we need to be just as concerned about the family environment that we're creating as we, parents, become attached to our phones and devices.

How often do we pick up our children from school holding our phones in one hand and greeting our children with a distracted hello as we finish our conversation? If we are so fortunate to have children who want to tell us about their day, how can we blow it by texting and talking to those who are not even with us?

How many times do we go to a restaurant and believe that we're spending great family time? But if you look closely, you'll find parents and children alike with their eyes engrossed as they stare downward.

Unknowingly, we have built invisible barriers that obstruct our connections with the ones whom we are supposed to love most.

The *New York Times* reported on a study observing the effects of technology on parents and children for the past five years. It was found that feelings of jealousy, hurt, and competition are common in many homes as children and spouses vie for attention that is being given to technology instead.

Children spoke about feeling hurt at mealtime, sports events, or pickup times, when they found parents more interested in their phones than in them.

"There's something so engrossing about the kind of interactions people do with screens that they wall out the world," the researcher said. "I've talked to children who try to get their parents to stop texting while driving and they got resistance, 'Oh, just one more quick one, honey.' It's like saying one more drink."

A parent I know was taking a summer hike with his wife and children in the mountains of Vermont. The scenery was breathtaking, the air delicious. The father's phone unbelievably had service despite the high altitude. Every few minutes, his office was calling. He was walking while looking at his screen, which constantly buzzed with another email message. Finally, his six-year-old daughter called out to him.

"Daddy," she said, "can I have your phone for a minute?"

"Why?" he asked.

"So that I can throw it down the mountain and have you be a part of the family."

That moment was his personal wake-up call.

He decided to turn off his device and try to make up for the lost time.

CAN WE TALK?

Talking to our spouses and children is more than having a conversation. We are demonstrating to our families that we are interested in their lives and care about their words, thoughts, and feelings. When we look at our wife instead of our screen, we are showing that we are not bored of or apathetic toward her. If a wife greets her husband as he comes through the door at the end of the day with a half-hearted welcome as she is busily finishing her latest text, what is a husband to feel?

If this is the effect on marriages and spousal relationships, imagine the effect that we are having on our children!

Young children need verbal interactions with parents in order to learn about the world and develop their vocabulary. They come to feel secure knowing that their parents are tuned in to their concerns and questions.

Children need to see an array of emotions in order to read faces. Sparkling eyes, or sadness that comes through without saying a word, both communicate messages. Children who do not learn how to interpret silent facial messages lack necessary emotional skills to navigate relationships as they mature.

A grandmother told me that she watched her daughter give a bottle to her baby, and what she saw broke her heart. The infant kept cooing and peering up, but her mother was scrolling and looking at her screen. After a while, the baby was quiet. She just gave up.

As children grow, they need to feel that parents are engaged and attentive to their lives. This is the bedrock of family life, the glue that holds us all together. If children feel that we listen with half an ear, they will come to perceive our connection to our "technological other" as an aloofness and lack of caring.

Husbands and wives also need to feel that they are not invisible. If you cannot seem to look at me while I am speaking, what does that tell me about my words? Do I even matter to you?

WHY YOUR SON DOESN'T TALK TO YOU AND WHY HE PROBABLY WON'T TALK TO HIS CHILDREN EITHER

Many parents have been made to feel as if they don't count in their children's lives. Perhaps this has always been a parenting issue, but it is now way too easy to disconnect from the ones who wish to love us and to feel our love most.

A couple approached me to speak about their fourteen-year-old son.

"I try so hard, but my son just won't talk to me," the father said. "It's not like he sits there talking with my wife all day long, but to me, he is a total zombie. I even offered to take him to a basketball game with his favorite team—best seats in the house. The entire time he just sat texting on his phone. Not a word between us, except when he wanted to get a Coke. I can't understand it."

I told this father that I don't mean to be hurtful or blaming, but I just have one question: "All these years when you would drive your son's carpool, when he would ask you to play with him or read a book, even while you were out catching a bite together, were you checking your phone? If that's the behavior he saw, he is simply doing what you did with him. He thinks it's perfectly normal."

The parents looked at each other and, from their faces, I saw that there was nothing left to say. Regret is a most painful emotion for us to carry.

And how are these sons and daughters going to relate to their own children and spouses? What does the future hold for families down the road?

Love and affection are displayed not only through saying "I love you," but through eye contact, attentiveness, and being able to disentangle oneself from outside distractions.

FIVE QUESTIONS FOR EVERY HOME

Ask yourself these questions:

- Do you constantly check your cell/device after you return from work at the expense of having an uninterrupted conversation with your family?
- Are you on the cell/device when your spouse or children come home at the end of the day?
- Have you created an environment where spouses and children feel that you are an interested and active listener?
- Do you make eye contact with your spouse and children when they speak to you?
- Do you generate feelings of belongingness and attachment within your family?

Family is more important today than it has ever been. We have been witness to a breakdown of marriages and parent-child relationships at an alarming rate. Even families that remain intact have parents and children who have stopped speaking to each other, as they are constantly engaged with those who are not physically present. We cannot afford to lose our connection with our children. We need to make our families our priority.

The Power of Positive Communication

Using positive communication with our children

A parent relayed a conversation that her husband had with her teenaged son, after he brought home a disappointing report card. Besides doing poorly in various subjects, her son, Benjamin, failed an elective class.

"Listen, Benjamin," her husband said. "You failed. Your report card is awful, and I think you should immediately drop this course."

Her son replied, "But, Daddy, I really tried. Let me try again."

"Why? So, you'll fail again? You'll just end up showing Mom and me exactly what you can't do. What's the point?"

Dejected, Benjamin lowered his face as his cheeks grew bright red.

"Prove me wrong, Benjamin, prove me wrong!" her husband shouted as he stormed out of the room.

After she related her experience, I spoke with the mother about what had occurred.

"Tell your husband," I said, "that instead of saying, 'Benjamin, prove me wrong,' he should say, 'Benjamin, prove me right! I know you can do better. I believe in you. Prove me right!'"

THE POWER OF POSITIVE WORDS

Hashem used positive language in the Torah to drive the lesson of positive language home. When describing the sense of aloneness that Adam felt before the creation of his *ezer k'negdo*, his helpmate, Hashem could have said, "It is bad that Adam is all alone." Instead of using negative language such as ***ra***, "bad," Hashem used the words ***lo tov***, "it is not good," not wanting to even mention the word *ra*. And so, the words used are "***lo tov*** *heyos ha'adam levado*—***lo tov***—it is **not good** that man is alone."[1]

Let's take our cue from the Torah. When we communicate with our children, we should try to express ourselves using positive language. Positivity sets a tone. We relay optimistic expectations. This can be done even when we are disciplining.

For example, instead of saying, "You're always fighting with your sister!" try, "I know that you can get along much better with your sister."

Instead of, "I've never seen such a mess! Your room is a disaster!" try, "You can be neater. Your room needs to be put in order."

At the end of one parenting session that I gave, Danielle, a mother of three approached me. "I realized something today. My six-year-old wakes up in the morning and it takes him forever to get ready. I'm embarrassed to tell you that I've even called him 'turtle' a few times. I decided today that I am going to make a change. I am going to try using positive words with him."

After the next class, Danielle told me that she could not believe the difference in her son that accompanied her new attitude. Instead of dragging his feet, he's the one who tries to be down first in the morning. One night, as he was going up to bed, he gave his mother a kiss and whispered in her ear, "Mommy, thank you for not calling me a turtle anymore."

We have the ability to help lift our children's spirits and help them soar higher.

When Moshe was commanded to take a census of the Jewish nation, he was told, "***Ki sisa*** *es rosh Bnei Yisrael*—When you count the Jewish People"[2]—literally, "***ki sisa*—lift up**" the heads of the people. Our mission as parents is the same; to elevate our children, to make every child feel that they count. Don't ever push a child's head down in shame or

1 *Bereishis*-Genesis 2:18.

2 *Shemos*-Exodus 30:1.

negativity. Each day, we have limitless opportunities to help our children grow and believe in themselves and to help them reach higher.

Let us try to lift up our children's heads, to give our children ideals to aspire to instead of digging deep holes into which they may descend.

After all, we don't call it "*raising* children" for nothing!

How to Talk to Your Teen

The art of keeping connected to teens

Just when you thought that you've got parenting covered, your child becomes a teen. Now it's a whole new world to deal with. Gone are the sweet hugs and goodnights, the little hand grasping yours, and the giggles at your jokes while driving carpool. In their place enters moodiness, sulking, emotional conversations, and testing limits.

To be a teen is to be called a "*naar*," which is defined in *lashon hakodesh* as "shaking off." Rabbi S.R. Hirsch expounds that "self-control and obedience to duty appears burdensome to them. In their quest for independence, they seek to 'shake off' this burden."

How can we best keep connected to our teens while they navigate these challenging years and inner conflicts?

A parent asked me how to deal with her fifteen-year-old daughter who wanted to go on a summer trip with friends, but it just did not "feel right." Every day became the same complaining and nagging discussion. "Why can't I? Everyone else is going. Why does everyone else get to do fun stuff but me?" The teen retreated to her room and gave one-word answers when spoken to.

What's a parent to do?

When there is constant bickering, the arguments can overtake your conversations. There is no time or energy remaining to have easy, flowing conversation.

There is an art to keeping connected to teens.

The key to connection is good communication. When Hashem created the world, there was emptiness and darkness until Hashem said,

"*Yehi ohr*—Let there be light." Through speech, Hashem created light in a world that had none: "*Vayehi ohr*—And there was light."[3] Hashem's words were required before every creation, teaching us the great power we hold in our mouths. The word for speech in *lashon hakodesh* is *dibbur*, which is made up of the same letters that are used to spell the word *davar*, a thing. Jewish wisdom is clear: Know that every time you use your power of speech you are creating something. With your words you can create connection and love, or you can create distance and animosity.

Throughout the world, there is one common expression used by magicians: "Abracadabra." Think about it. Abracadabra can be read as *abarei kedabarei*, meaning, "I will create as I speak." We can generate greatness and joy just by opening our mouths. This is the magic that lies within each and every one of us: the *ko'ach* of *dibbur*. Our words can bring us closer to our children, especially to our teens. If we know how to focus on good conversational skills, we too, can create light in our homes.

LOVE LANGUAGES

Adolescents are grappling with the changes that their age brings (physical, hormonal, and emotional). They sometimes question their place in the family as well as their parents' love, causing them to feel insecure and vulnerable. You may think your children feel confident in your love for them, but they may not be. Children have various languages of love, and it is important to identify your child's lingo. Languages that relay love include physical touch, words of affirmation, quality time, gifts, and acts of service. For example, if you realize that your child's primary language of love is quality time, then look for enjoyable ways to spend time together, just the two of you, even if it's simply chatting comfortably before your child goes to sleep. When your child feels secure in your love, he will better be able to deal with the emotions and challenges of being a teenager.

FINDING SOLUTIONS

When faced with a child like this fifteen-year-old who keeps nagging about the trip, believing that she will wear her parents down, we should

---

3 *Bereishis*-Genesis 1:3.

first ask ourselves if she is correct. Children who detect weakness, observing that parents are not firm in their values or decisions, who hesitate while sharing their rules or limits, will keep at it until a parent gives in. If this is your pattern, you now know why your teen does not stop asking for the same thing over and over. She knows that she is a battering ram who will soon break through the wall. Enough sullenness, push-back, and badgering will get her to attain her desires. The faster this pattern stops, the stronger a parent you will be.

BUILDING BETTER COMMUNICATION SKILLS

Recognize, too, that the more time we spend talking and listening to our children when they are young, the better chance we will have of communicating with them as they grow up. It is hard to start a relationship when kids and parents live parallel, silent lives. If you can, begin *today*.

Talk at dinner time; share a funny story or interesting incident that happened throughout your day. Here are some pointers to build good communication with your child: Look at your child when you speak. Don't seem rushed or impatient when he is talking to you. Show interest in your child's stories. Be curious about what he is saying. Maintain eye contact with your child—not your screen. Offer reassuring words instead of jumping in with negative judgments. Reflect your child's feelings to show that you get him.

Your tone and your body language are also tools to foster goodwill with your teen. Coming off as "shrieky," nervous, or condescending can impede even the best-intentioned conversation and impact your child's reaction to what is being said. Teens will often ask, "Why are you screaming at me?" and parents respond, exasperated, "I'm not screaming!" They interpret your talking quickly or going on and on about the same thing, as screaming. Take a pause and listen to yourself as you speak. Check that your body language does not convey anger, disgust, or frustration as you are trying to communicate a positive message. Watch your volume, tone, and pitch as you continue your discussion. Don't give long monologues or bring hurtful things up from past years, saying, "You always..." or "You never..."

These are all simple approaches that we can work on to help ourselves sustain a strong relationship with our children while navigating through difficulties and stressful situations.

KEEPING CONNECTED WHILE SAYING "NO"

How can we maintain a good relationship when we want to say no without losing ourselves and our teens to negative emotions?

The key is not in always saying yes, but in how we say no.

Teens who feel that we are constantly shutting them down will move away from expressing themselves. They stop confiding, sharing, or asking. They know that they will not be heard anyway, so what's the point? Feeling misunderstood, they seek out others whom they know will listen to their voice. Or they withdraw within themselves.

The main ingredient for parents to think about is: How can I give my child a sense that I am listening even if I do not acquiesce to his request?

- Tell your child that you would like to hear what he has to say in a private, quiet time. Do not speak with other children in the room who will be distracting, chiming in, and voicing their opinions. Preferably both parents should be available for the conversation. Parents need to be on the same page. Remind your child that you can only hear him when he speaks with respectful words and tone.
- Don't mock or shame your child for his ideas. You may not agree, but that is not a reason to put him down.
- Keep the tone even and calm. Control your temper. Remember that you are the parent, and you are the adult. Recognize the feeling when you begin to lose your cool so that you can gain self-control. Some people feel their cheeks turning red or heart pounding as rage begins to take over their emotions. Know yourself so that you can maintain your calm before the situation explodes. Speak to your child the way you would like them to speak with you. Respect breeds respect.
- Take notice of your child's thoughts and emotions. Ask relevant questions to show that you are taking him seriously. Maintain eye contact. Don't interrupt your child as he is speaking.

- Be solution oriented. Instead of just rehashing the problem, tell your teen that you would like to find viable alternatives. For example, maybe this trip won't work out, but you are open to planning another and hearing suggestions.
- Do not debate, defend yourself, or get into an argument. Once the tone turns disrespectful, simply say, "When you are ready to speak respectfully and in a considerate tone, I will be happy to continue this conversation."
- Don't belittle your child's friends or their families. You want to transmit your values and priorities, not put others down. Be careful not to be drawn into a heated discussion, arguing about the standards and morals of other families. Your child will be pulled and feel the need to defend his friends. It's not about the other families—it's about creating a spiritual and moral compass for our own.
- If you see that the conversation is going in circles or getting too intense, it's OK to say, "I hear you. We need time to think about this and get back to you." Hit the pause button if you must gather your thoughts. It is also perfectly fine to say, "I know that you really want to do this, but we are just not comfortable. It's isn't about not trusting you—it's about not trusting the situation."

Listening to our teens upholds the parent-child connection as they move on to discover this new phase of life. It is exciting and fearful at the same time. Our children need to know that they are loved, valued, and cherished. They also require boundaries and limits because they are not yet ready to tackle the world on their own.

Offer timeless wisdom and values that you have learned. Offer your heart, your voice, and your listening ear.

Kids and Stress

Stressful times produce stressful kids.
What can we, as parents, do?

The kids are not all right.

I met Miri, a sweet eleven year old, who came to speak with me in anticipation of her bas mitzvah. After talking together for a few minutes, Miri's sparkling eyes grew serious. "Slovie, can I tell you something?"

"Sure, sweetie, what is it?"

"I'm really scared. There are people that I know who are sick, and I'm afraid that someone I love will get sick or get into a car accident or something. And some kids in my class, well, their parents lost their jobs, and they have to sell their house and move now. They're really sad. I stay up at night thinking about all this, and I get a scary feeling inside."

We live in challenging times. Our world is changing drastically and there are moments when we all feel vulnerable. We stress about our families, our future, and our children feel our strain.

Children sense their parents' pressures. They feel worried, sad, and frustrated.

It becomes easy for children to feel our tensions and grow tense themselves.

Life is filled with struggles. There are times that we must confront frightening health issues, relationship problems, tension with children, or financial challenges. Some parents try to guard their children from the storm, but kids know that something is going on. They see past the masquerade of frozen smiles and overly cheerful voices. They grow even more frightened as they imagine the worst and try to overhear hushed conversations.

While we do not have to give our children inappropriate details, we must acknowledge our children's fears.

Storms will rage. One day our children will be forced to face their own struggles.

The way to protect our children is not by trying to outwit tomorrow, but rather, by giving them tools and values for today. If we can teach our children how to handle stress without falling apart and how to grow resilient, we have given them the ability to attain *menuchas hanefesh*, a life filled with inner peace and calm, despite it all.

How can we strengthen our children as we strengthen ourselves?

1. Don't Allow "Trickle-Down Stress"

Our children know that we are stressed even if we think they don't. If the mood in the house is tense, you sense it the minute you walk in. When we are overwhelmed, it becomes easy to snap, as our patience is short.

"Mommy, can you help me with homework?"

"Daddy, can you play a game of catch with me?"

"LATER! I'M BUSY!"

You didn't mean to answer with that harsh tone. You feel awful when you see your child's face react to your sharp response. But what could you do? You were overloaded and short on time and patience.

Take a breath. Concede to yourself that you are going through challenging times. Be sure to take some quiet time out for yourself each day, even if it's just for a short walk or a thoughtful prayer.

Resolve that you will not allow your stress to impact your children. Your short-temperedness will only upset your children as you diminish yourself.

Your children are seeking answers. Reassure them that despite the hardships faced, your love is unconditional and forever. You are here for them. Tell them that you are doing your best and that, ultimately, things will be OK.

2. Parental Peace Brings Calm

Before takeoff, flight attendants instruct you that in times of emergency, you must put on your own oxygen mask first, begin to breathe, and only then should you attempt to help your children.

The same holds true in life. We can only help our children deal with fears if we live with the confidence that we can overcome obstacles. When children detect that parents are panicking, they grow fearful themselves.

Parents who transmit a sense of calm, despite the turbulence, provide their children with serenity.

Husbands and wives in stressful situations should speak privately to resolve the issues in order to create a haven within their home. This means that we need to watch our tone, our language, and try hard to communicate patience and understanding. We shouldn't react sharply or flick our loved ones aside with a dismissive word or gesture because we are under pressure. I know this is not easy for parents, especially in demanding times. But there are no winners when there is constant tension in a home.

Shalom bayis, peace in the home, becomes the antidote to stress that can wear us down. When children feel that their parents are kind to each other and at peace, they feel confident in their home and family life. Domestic harmony anchors the family, giving children (and parents) the strength to withstand challenges and stress.

3. Peace Within: Recharging with Faith

Drawing upon one's *emunah* also provides families with a sense of security in difficult times. When we reinforce our family values and find solace in prayer, we are showing our children that we live with clear and established beliefs despite the turbulence. It is not a matter of convenience, dependent on moods or feel-good emotions. Our faith is our bedrock of strength, independent of turmoil and challenge. We are standing on a solid spiritual foundation.

Each week we are given the heavenly gift of recharging our faith. "The Holy Blessed One said to Moshe, 'I have a precious gift in my treasure house called Shabbos.'"[4] Shabbos is our opportunity to infuse our family with spiritual serenity. No matter how difficult the week has been, my Shabbos candles bring light into my home. We join together at our Shabbos table, creating beauty, goodness, and love. As we tell our stories, share *divrei Torah*, thoughts, and sing *zemiros*, we use the time to grow closer. Shabbos is our means of nourishing spiritual and emotional connection.

---

4 *Shabbos* 10b.

Be careful not to fall into the trap of having your Shabbos table become a painful memory as you send children to their rooms, speak harshly when upset, and lose yourself in exasperation while children bicker. Every moment does not have to be picture-perfect. Children will be children. Instead, realize that these are potential moments to build family togetherness, create childhood remembrances, and infuse *emunah* and joy each week.

Tefillah, prayer, too, brings us to a place of peace and security. We can help our children counter stress when we construct a ladder between heaven and earth.

After 9/11, many of the couples I teach communicated to me that their children were frightened and afraid to go to sleep at night. I shared with these parents the power of prayer to bring us calm—especially the *tefillos* of *Ha'malach Ha'goel*, the angel who redeems me, and *B'shem Hashem*, the blessing of the angels who surround me. I relayed my own childhood memories, then watched a new generation gain comfort and strength from these beautiful prayers.

I told these couples that, though I am a *bubby* today, if I close my eyes, I can still hear my father's soothing voice, reciting the *Shema* with me as a child. His singing of *Ha'malach Ha'goel* and *B'shem Hashem* brought me to a place of peace. I learned that I was surrounded by Hashem's *malachim*. When my children grew, the tradition continued each time my father would visit. Today, it is they who sing these same songs of the *malachim* to their own children and bring them tranquility in an unsettled world.

My entire life, I knew that no matter the time, day or night, I could call my mother and ask her to daven for me and for our children. I recall once telling my mother how badly I felt, burdening her with my worries as I asked her to daven.

"Slova Channalah," she said, "this is what we do. When I was a young mother, I remember calling Zaydah Eintz (as we called my great-grandfather) and asking him to daven for me. I had tears and was worried about something at the time. '*Mein lichtige kindt*,' Zaydah Eintz said lovingly, '*yeder Shemoneh Esreh hab ich dir in zinnen*—My precious child, I have you in mind at every *Shemoneh Esreh*. I am your *zaydah* and I *must* daven for you.' Always know that just like my *zaydahs* and *bubbas* davened for me, I am davening for you, all the time."

A sense of relief spread within me. I felt stronger, not alone.

My mother's *Tehillim* is with me today. The pages, tattered and worn, are stained with her tears. Now it is my children's turn to see me open my mother's book of *Tehillim* and continue her path of prayer. Prayers of parents and grandparents are precious. We can never know the full impact, but we do recognize that every single one of our *tefillos* counts, protecting and bringing blessings to our generations to come.

We are never too weary to utter a *tefillah* as we try to pierce the gates of heaven.

In a broken world, we parents are here to bring wholeness and healing.

Maintaining a Positive Attitude in an Anxious World

How to help our children combat anxiety

Anxiety has become overwhelming for too many children. What can we do to ease their load?

When my daughter, who was living in Israel at the time, returned from a trip to the United States, she was greeted with a "Welcome Home" sign on her front door. There had been a number of tragic terrorist attacks that year. Her six-year-old daughter colored a picture of an El Al plane, with a bright yellow sun. Behind the windows of the plane, she drew her mommy's smiling face along with other passengers, and parallel to her mommy were the faces of terrorists, each with a fist raised holding sharp daggers.

Is this how our children see the world?

It's not only in places where children have heard of or seen images of fearful attacks that they've grown frightened. I have spoken with children who confided that they often feel scared or anxious. Add to that the distress of a pandemic, natural disasters, and war, and the world easily feels overwhelming.

It can be distressing for children to deal with so much chaos. In addition, they are handling the burdens of family situations, school, and social pressures.

How can we keep our children grounded and maintain a positive outlook in life?

1. Carve Out Time with Children

Spending time with children shows them that we love them, that we are here for them, and that we enjoy their company. Activities, conversations, and moments of laughter build memories of joy. We cannot always choose the circumstances, but whether we infuse our home with a positive or negative energy is up to us.

2. Model an "Up" Attitude

Your children hear your words, observe your actions, and watch your reactions. If you do not allow challenges to get you down, your kids will pick up on your upbeat attitude. Make a point of sharing your efforts in being more resilient, even the small moments. A flat tire, a burned Shabbos kugel, or a stuffed-up sink are all learning opportunities. When you handle disappointments without falling apart, children learn the power of grit.

3. Teach Children That They Can Make a Difference

When a child feels anxious because someone they love is sick or in pain, we can teach our children to reach out to Hashem. *Re'eh na v'anyeinu. Refaeinu. Shema koleinu.* We ask Hashem to see **our** pain, heal **us** and hear **our** voices—all in the plural. Teaching children that they can pray for others allows children to experience the knowledge that they can make a difference. Every prayer has an address. No prayer goes to waste. Even if we do not see immediate results or even if we feel disappointed, children should know that they have contributed to the spiritual account of another in the heavens above.

After my father left this world, I felt crushed, wondering about all our prayers and the mitzvos that we had taken upon ourselves. We had tried so hard. How could this happen? My mother offered words of comfort. "You should know that Abba went up to *Shamayim* on the wings of your prayers. You, children, gave Abba the greatest gift!"

We have within us the ability to make this world a little bit better, to help dissolve some of the pain through our prayers and deeds. In times of challenge, this is most empowering for a child, and for us all, to remember.

4. Be a Force of Light

We can take this sense of participation a step further as we encourage our sons and daughters to create a force of light in this world and actively do something that will make a difference. Instead of being lost in anxiety and worry, they can take positive action.

After Hurricane Sandy's devastation became apparent, I spoke to the many wonderful couples whom I teach. I described the unbelievable situation with which many were faced. Homes were filled with sewage and salt water that destroyed literally everything—cribs, linens, clothing, furniture, strollers, bikes, washers, dryers, boilers—you name it, it was all gone.

And then, an incredible thing happened. I saw dazzling points of light being created. Mothers and fathers arrived with their children, their cars loaded with "wish lists" that had been filled and now ready to be delivered. Boys and girls carried toys, bikes, and clothing to children who had none. I was asked to deliver babysitting money, allowance dollars, and notes that said, "Instead of a Chanukah present this year, I want to give this gift to a child my age."

Instead of being helpless, these children became helpful. Feelings of powerlessness were replaced with emotions of being powerful. They realized that, despite all that is beyond us, there is much that we can do to make a difference in this world.

One mother wrote to me after her visit:

> *This Chanukah we decided to take the money that we would have spent on each other and instead help a family with which you matched us up: a mother and father and their eight children, the youngest born just before this horrific storm. They lost their entire first floor. Their children lost everything that was in their rooms and basement.*

> *This is a family so unlike my family. Our customs and lifestyles are completely different. Our paths probably wouldn't have ever crossed. Our one connection is being Jewish. We are one family.*
>
> *As we pulled onto the block, we could see the devastation immediately. We spent time talking and getting to know each other a bit. I noticed how all the children were taking care of each other. They were all in good spirits, thankful for what they had, and not focused on what they had lost. I honestly don't know how we would have fared if that had happened to our home. This was such a joy to experience, and this has made such a difference in our lives, one that we will remember forever.*

We can help our children make it through challenging times and grow with new understanding that it takes just a little bit of light to push away the darkness. Help your child discover his or her inner force of light. Together you will triumph.

5. Help Children Cope

How can we help our children better cope with anxiety in everyday situations? (Of course, we are not speaking about childhood trauma that must be addressed professionally.)

- Recognize that your child's distress is real.
- Don't ignore your child's fears. Children become afraid of different situations at different ages. Apprehension, worry, and feeling frightened are genuine concerns.
- Validate the emotions. Show understanding.
- Allow your children to share their fears. Talk to them and permit them to communicate their feelings.
- Don't make fun of or belittle their worries.
- A child shouldn't feel as if he or she is bad or babyish for expressing worry. Be careful to avoid saying things like, "A girl your age shouldn't be afraid," "That's just silly," or "Stop being such a crybaby." That only knocks your child's self-esteem and will discourage them from sharing in the future.

- Show empathy but be careful not to fall apart each time your child tells you that he is afraid. When kids hear us talking about them and telling spouses and grandmothers that they are scared and anxious, we are adding drama to the situation. Find a balance between the emotions you display.
- Teach coping strategies. Ask: How can I self-calm? Some children do well with music, others with art, journaling, bike riding, or having a calm corner where they can sit for a bit, in quiet, until they become more composed.
- Help your child work through the challenge. Positive self-statements like, "I can do this," or, "I will be OK," can help children navigate moments when they feel anxious. Some kids are empowered when they draw upon words of a prayer, others when they envision a happy memory. Some children who are afraid of the dark can be pacified and calmed with a nightlight. Get to know your child and find the strategy that works for them.
- Sharing stories of your own fears and how you overcame them can be an incredible source of comfort to a child.
- Model being brave in your own life.

6. A Parent's Mission

Adults who lose it will raise children who lose it. Whether it is a fear of cockroaches, flying, blood tests, or unseen dangers from the world in which you live, you cannot afford to lose control. Children who view their parents as in control feel secure in a world gone mad.

To be a parent means that we cannot allow ourselves to crumble. We keep on walking even if we stumble and fall. We pick ourselves up because that's what a parent does. I have been asked, "What if my childhood was difficult? Can I still be a good parent?"

If you come from a dysfunctional home where your parents let you down, that does not mean that you are weak. God told Avraham and Sarah, "*Lech lecha*"—go from your land, your birthplace, your father's home. You have the power to write your own story. Leave the dysfunction and the deficiencies behind. Live tenaciously. Become a force of blessing in this world.

And if you are thinking, *I just don't have the strength. I am too tired*, then remember this beautiful piece of Jewish wisdom. The Hebrew word for "test" is *nisayon*. Contained in this Hebrew word is the word "*nes*," which means both a banner and a miracle. When you go through this challenge of a lifetime and feel as if you are barely holding on, but you keep on going, then you have created the most magnificent banner. This banner proclaims your life force, your personal miracle. No one can deny it or take it away from you. Ever.

No matter how chaotic things get, our mission as parents is to guide our children through the darkness. Creating a pocket of peace will become part of our lifelong legacy.

CHAPTER 6

Challenges of Technology

How to Raise Kids in a Digital World

Parents must tune in as kids tune out

The digital world is taking our children away from us.

Most parents agree that our children are excessively plugged into their devices. The average eight-to-ten-year-old spends nearly eight hours a day engaged in different forms of digital media, and older children and teenagers spend more than eleven hours per day. Texting may become the next behavioral obsession with which parents must contend. Teenagers send sixty or more texts a day, and one in three send more than one hundred. These are alarming statistics that are only increasing.

In an article in *The Atlantic*, Derek Thompson describes how screen time is replacing leisure time and physical activities for kids. He writes how compared with the early 2000s, teenagers are less likely to go out with their friends or play sports. They are also less likely to get a good night's sleep. The National Recreation and Park Association reports that children today spend less time outdoors than any generation. They would rather use their time sitting in front of a screen.

Parents and educators have noticed that children's attention spans have grown shorter. There's often a struggle to sit through finishing homework or focus on real conversation. Dr. Michael Manos, clinical director of the Center for Attention and Learning at Cleveland Clinic Children's Hospital explains that the ever-changing environment of fast-paced technology doesn't require sustained attention. "If kids' brains become accustomed to constant change, the brain finds it difficult to adapt to non-digital activities where things don't move quite as fast." Our children are more distracted. It is more difficult to keep their attention.

What can we do to prevent our relationship with our children from disintegrating?

PARENTS MUST TAKE CHARGE

For parents to make a difference, we must focus on both our own behavior as well as that of our children. When we want time to ourselves or just want the kids to keep quiet and not bother one other, we use technology as a convenient babysitter. But we don't stop to think about the potential harm that we are causing. Conversation ceases. Carpools, dining out, and relaxed leisure time are spent in silence. Families stop sharing thoughts, interactions, and laughter.

These are important bonding moments. Even siblings' bickering becomes an opportunity to navigate relationships and learn how to speak and listen to one another. But playing video games, looking downward at a screen, and constantly checking phones prevents kids from staying focused on family.

They miss out on nonverbal cues, which is how we learn to communicate and read people's emotions. And when parents were absorbed in their devices, researchers found children more likely to act out as they attempted to get attention.

We encourage this behavior because we are not contemplating the impact of our actions.

Few parents have set rules for their children and teens when it comes to tech and phone use. Even if they did so in the beginning, with time, many of the guidelines vanish. Kids left to their own devices neglect homework, remain sedentary, are sleep deprived, and become easily pulled into the addictive nature of the online world. Add to that the dangers that unknown sites and chats pose, and we realize that we need to rectify this situation before it's too late.

Children often have technological skills that surpass their parents. In an annual study from Ofcom, the UK's authority for analyzing media habits, one in twenty children circumvented parental controls put into place to stop them from visiting certain sites and apps. This included younger children whose parents had no idea that they had obtained access to social media.

Parents need to be educated and attentive. Especially, when it comes to teenagers, there is much to learn. Even if a phone is filtered, tech experts warn that there is still a danger zone to be aware of. Innocent apps, such as WhatsApp, can also be a source of sending pictures and videos that are far from innocent.

In her best-selling book, *The Big Disconnect: Protecting Childhood and Family Relationships in the Digital Age*, Dr. Steiner-Adair recommends the following steps:

- Parents should think twice before using a mobile device when they're with their children.
- Check emails and texts before interacting with children in the morning, during school hours, and after kids' bedtime in the evening.
- When parents come home from work, they should walk through the door unplugged. The first hour home should be used to reconnect with family. Children have said that they despise their parents using the phrase "just checking" as their parents look at their devices and check emails and messages.
- Establish "cell free zones" for both parents and kids. Critical moments like pickup from school are crucial transitional times for children to talk about their day. Parents should not be saying things like, "Just a minute; I need to finish this call." Homework should be done without phones in hand. Dinner time, both at home and in a restaurant, should be another "device-free zone." We nourish not only bodies, but souls too, when we join together at a table.
- Young children should not have their own devices.

- Be wary of devices and where they are used. Computers and laptops should be used in a family room where others are present and not taken into a child's bedroom.
- Technology requires limits and filters. It is not too late to set them. Don't be afraid of taking charge and enforcing appropriate rules. Phones should not be left in a child's bedroom to be used all night while parents are sleeping.
- Caretakers should also be made aware of the dangers of not paying full attention to the children in their charge. There has been a recent 20 percent increase in accidental injuries seen in pediatric emergency rooms attributed to caretakers' texting or talking on their phones and not properly watching children while the children were in the bath or on the jungle gym.
- The negative effect on our relationship with our children is best seen through the words of a girl interviewed for Dr. Steiner-Adair's book. She said, "I feel like I'm just boring. I'm boring my dad because he will take any text, any call, any time, even on a ski lift."
- We must take the time to disengage from the world of technology and nourish our relationships. Heartache comes when we realize we have wasted years looking down, missing out on connecting with those we love who are sitting right in front of us, waiting to look into our eyes. Our children need to feel that we value our time together. They deserve our full attention, and we will never regret time spent together.

New Hazards Your Kids Are Facing Online

Awareness that Games Hold Hidden Harm

Parents are aware of the typical dangers that kids face online. We know about cyber bullying and have been given tools to watch over our children's phones and devices.

But there are new hazards threatening our children, and we must arm ourselves with knowledge. I have spoken with parents who believe that they are providing their children with the best education (both religious and secular), vigilant about what their children see and hear, but they are clueless as to the possible devastation being caused by seemingly innocent video games. Even the most basic handheld video games have the potential to chat with strangers, online. Many parents remain clueless that this is even possible. We need to become educated about the damaging risks that are seemingly innocent and unlikely.

Video games, when deemed appropriate and non-violent, appear to be fun for kids whose parents are OK with them. But parents have been horrified to discover popups of conversations filled with graphic language and imagery. Children are being lured by predators who pose as other kids their age, meet them online through multiplayer video games and chat apps, and then interact with them.

These criminals confide in their victims with invented stories of hardships or lack of self-worth, and slowly build trust. Their goal is to eventually have the child share compromising images of himself which will then be used as blackmail unless more graphics are sent. The child is told that the predator knows their family and that the pictures will be posted everywhere if there is a lack of cooperation. There have even been threats where the child is told, "I know where you live. Here's your address, and I'm coming to harm you if you don't send more pics."

The *New York Times* describes these crimes,[1] and they are growing. In children's own homes, the threat is lurking. The problem is that the games and technology have made it simpler to connect with strangers, and we have no idea who they really are. Some parents of children as young as six admitted that they had no idea that their children were even capable of chatting on their games. The predators will send gaming currency to the child and, in this way, build a connection. So many kids play these games, it becomes a perfect avenue to send the child "v-bucks." Next, the child is sent imagery that gradually becomes more

---

1 "While They Play Online, Children May Be the Prey," December 7, 2019.

graphic. They are asked to send images of themselves, which many do. This has happened on commonly played games. Those arrested included people from all walks of life: police officers, teachers, ministers, nurses, mechanics, dental hygienists, delivery men, and college students. Social media and video streaming platforms also snared children, some as young as eight.

WHAT CAN PARENTS DO?

Being literate in your child's online life is a must.

Parents need to know what their children are playing. They need to teach children how to recognize inappropriate messages, block users, and shut off chat functions.

It is not only about spending too much time playing games online but also about being sure that the content is appropriate and knowing that having access online is a privilege and not a right. Parents must create real standards and have access and control online in order for children to stay safe.

The following are tips for online safety:

1. Spend Time with Your Child on New Games and Apps

When you share time with your children and see what they see, you are going to gain their trust as well as information. You will be better able to discuss with your children the risks and hazards that you have found.

2. Talk to Your Child about Online Safety and Listen

Groomers and abusers count on children remaining silent. Give children the understanding that they may always come to you with concerns. Give ideas of ways a child can stay safe and out of trouble online. This is an important conversation to have with children about life and their safety, regardless of engaging in games.

3. Encourage Your Child to Raise Any Concerns with a Trusted Adult

Children need to be told that they may never send compromising photos of themselves to anyone. Too many kids have ended up in horrifying situations because this first rule was never set or ignored.

Here's a rule: If it makes you feel uncomfortable, listen to your feelings. Don't do it.

Kids should also be taught to recognize red flags showing that there is a dangerous situation ahead, for example: they're told to keep the relationship secret, they're asked for a lot of personal information, they're promised gifts or game currency, and there are discussions about their appearance or a request to meet in person. Tell children that they should never be afraid to speak to an adult whom they trust to share their concerns. These are vital guidelines for all children to be cognizant of in everyday life, as well.

They do not have to be embarrassed or ashamed. They do have to stay safe.

4. Be on the Lookout for Warning Signs of Abuse

Parents should pay attention to excessive periods of time that kids are spending online or angry reactions when parents say, "No more." Parents can detect a problem in teens who seem to be excessively fatigued, have drastic mood changes, and a sudden obsession with protecting their privacy.

Children should beware of requests for inappropriate behavior. For example, anyone who says, "Don't tell your parents," is a danger.

5. Don't Blame Your Child

Groomers and predators know that many children are afraid to share embarrassment with their parents. Kids are scared of getting into trouble. Reassure your child that you are not angry at them. Don't judge your child and blow your top. Your child needs to feel safe confiding in you.

6. Take Charge as Your Child's Online Protector

As a child guardian, it is up to parents to take control. You cannot buy these games and then expect a child to stay safe on his own. Just as you would never hand over the keys and say "drive," you need to be watching and guiding.

Parenting in a tech world is opening us up to new challenges. We are digital foreigners in a new land. We don't speak the language. Our children are the digital natives. We must remain informed so that we can give our children the tools to feel safe and strengthened.

Kids Are Out of Control and What You Can Do about It

The pandemic has brought out risky behavior in our children

The conversation I had with a child healthcare professional as the pandemic was unfolding was disturbing.

"You cannot imagine what I am seeing," he said. "Kids who never got into any trouble before are taking all types of risks, and parents don't know what to do. These are good kids from good homes in good schools. The kids are out of control."

A few discussions with parents and educators confirmed what I was hearing. We are talking about behaviors that compromise values and character. Kids who are sneaking out of the house while parents are sleeping, testing boundaries, chatting inappropriately on social media platforms, and experimenting with substance abuse. Many are grappling with their faith.

Children are losing their souls.

Why now?

VULNERABILITY

The pandemic has caused teens and preteens to deal with months of uncertainty. Do we have in-school learning or remote? Many activities once taken for granted were canceled or changed: graduation ceremonies, senior year, bar and bas mitzvah celebrations, family gatherings, Shabbos and Yom Tov with grandparents and friends, summer camp, school trips, and team sports, just to name a few. Kids have been dealing with fear of the unknown unlike anything they have ever experienced before.

Stories of pandemic-related illness, death, and the sense of living in a world out of control overtake a child's being. There is a huge sense of feeling vulnerable.

And even as the COVID world begins to ease its restrictions, all that which children have gone through—the emotions, anxieties, and fears—remain within their memories.

LESS ROUTINE

The pandemic brought children less routine, and less routine means that there is a void in a child's day. Left with emptiness, many kids have discovered that the solution to boredom and a lack of schedule is risky behavior. What do you do when you have extra time on your hands and nothing to do? Kids have tried out activities that would not normally enter their sphere or have seemed possible in their mind.

Remote learning is lonely. Being home for extended time is tiresome. Some kids were sitting alone in their rooms while parents were working or occupied with other children. Kids need friends and in-person contact. Solitude means seeking more online connections. Social media and being online is the virtual door out. Many kids have found themselves jeopardized after sending inappropriate photos, texts, or having engaged in improper conversations, the result of unfilled hours in the day. Boredom leads to trouble.

FOMO

The fear of missing out (FOMO) can drive a child to behave in ways he never could have imagined. If everyone's out socializing, then why shouldn't I be? If my classmates are breaking curfews, rules, and hanging out, I can't be the only one staying home and out of it.

There is also a sense of entitlement that has taken hold. "This was supposed to be my graduation year." "We were supposed to have our family trip that you promised me." Feeling shortchanged, like they need to make up for things that they've missed out on and do something exciting, can cause children to make huge mistakes.

WHAT CAN WE DO?

Parents are exhausted and burned out. I know how difficult it is. But now is not the time to give up. We are living the true definition of being a parent—to guide and inspire the next generation. Our children need us to be the captain of our ships. In times of challenge and chaos, they must see that we are present in both body and soul and that we care.

Begin with a conversation. Don't wait for the situation to unravel in your home. I've spoken to parents who have been shocked with the behavior their "good kids" have gotten into. Communicate in a non-threatening way. Acknowledge the challenges your child is facing. Don't be busy with everything and everyone else and then be forced to confront the damage done.

Speak about the loneliness, the vulnerability, the boredom, the sadness, and the frustration from losing out on life events that just happened.

Be prepared to limit screen time. Pay attention to your child's online hours. They can easily run from morning to evening, if unwatched. Don't let days and nights go unsupervised even if you are beyond exhausted. See to it that if your child is home, you check in with him and that he takes healthy breaks throughout the day.

We don't know what the future holds. The pandemic has taught us many parenting lessons. Here's one: If your child is spending a lot of time indoors and school is sporadic, stay engaged. Be informed. Ask yourself: With whom is my child spending his waking hours? What is he doing all day? Think about filling the empty time with more engaging activities.

Confusion and fear bring kids to seek out new ways to deal with the chaos confronting them. They grasp for whatever will bring them a sense of calm. Uncertainty can bring a child to experiment with vaping, smoking, drinking, or using nonprescription drugs. Stay alert. Don't be that home where parents are caught snoozing while their children are raiding the liquor cabinets or making bad choices that cause devastation and harm.

When children go through turbulence and stress, we parents tend to feel sorry for them. That's normal. We open our hearts to our children's fear and pain. Children need to feel that we hear them, that we understand them. But we can't feel so badly that we ignore their responsibility to live with character. That would mean living with misplaced compassion. We cannot allow a pandemic to strip our children of the morals and wisdom for which we've sacrificed so much and for so long. This challenge becomes one of our greatest missions.

Every generation has its test; the pandemic has become ours. And parents, be sure to tell your children that you believe in them, you love them, and that we will get through this together.

CHAPTER 7

Nurturing Our Children's Greatness

Helping Children Thrive

Better or Bitter?

Five-year-old Lily shows us how to get through life's challenges

"Sometimes, it really hurts when the doctor puts a needle in my arm."

I am visiting five-year-old Lily, whose mother attends my parenting classes. During the summer, Lily had some awful headaches. One night, they became so terrible that Lily woke up her parents in the middle of the night. The shock upon receiving a diagnosis of a brain tumor was beyond words.

Lily's initial treatments included six weeks of radiation and chemotherapy, and then some more chemotherapy. Besides treatment days, Lily never complained or even missed a day of school. Lily was put on a clinical drug trial.

Allow me to share a memory with you.

We, beautiful Lily, her incredibly gracious mother, Felicia, and I, are sitting at Lily's little play table as she colors a tzedakah box that I had brought over. Lily carefully peels off the Hebrew stickers that spell her name and decorates the box. She chooses the most vibrant colors that she can find. It is obviously hard for her, as she is in pain, but she giggles her sweet little giggle with each colorful stroke. Then she asks her mother if she could fill her tzedakah box. Only the shiniest and most beautiful pennies will do. Carefully, Lily counts each coin as it clinks inside.

"One...two...three..." Her face fills with delight as she drops each bright penny.

Lily stops for a moment. Her soft voice grows serious. "Sometimes it really hurts, you know. And I get scared."

Felicia leans toward Lily. "That's OK, sweetie. We all get scared sometimes. I'm scared of spiders, did you know that?"

Lily's eyes open wide.

"And I'm scared of big bugs," I add. "Not only that, but one of my children jumps from loud thunder and lightning. It's OK to be afraid sometimes."

Lily giggles. I want to scoop this precious child up into my arms and kiss all her fears away.

While we were spending time together, Felicia told me that Lily's preschool class embarked upon a tzedakah project. After collecting coins, the class discussed where the charity should go. Lily's teacher called to say that Lily raised her hand and expressed her wish. She described going to the doctor and finding children in the office who had just a few toys and crayons to play with as they waited. Some toys were broken and old.

"Can we give the tzedakah to my doctor's office, to buy new toys and arts and crafts supplies for all the children?" she asked.

The class voted. The decision was unanimous.

Driving home, I cannot get Lily out of my mind. I am trying hard to decipher the day. I feel as if I've been privy to a sacred moment in time. I am awed by this child and her sweet innocence as she confronts a most difficult and terrifying challenge.

OUR CHOICE

When I returned home, I was inspired to write. *How could this be,* I thought to myself, *that this child, who must be so frightened and pained, can rise above it all and feel the pain of another*? So often, we adults are stressed or wounded, and we cannot see beyond our own reflection. We cannot feel beyond the throbbing aches that beat within ourselves. Whether emotional or physical, it doesn't really matter. **The test of life is this: When I go through my challenge, when I confront my mountain, will I grow better or bitter?** This beautiful child taught me the way to go.

There is no life that will be spared adversity. True, some challenges are more arduous than others, but for each person, his challenge is an uphill battle. Health issues, financial problems, marital stability, and difficulties while raising children are just a few of the struggles that may come our way. We cannot choose our life challenge, but we can choose how to get through those challenges.

Despite her constant trials and difficult tests, Lily grew kinder and sweeter with each day. She wrapped herself in pink ribbons, purple dress-up feathers, shiny jeweled necklaces, and happily insisted on getting to school on time even though she was having difficult chemotherapy treatments. She called her father "my cheerleader" and swallowed her awful medications just to see her daddy smile.

Each week Lily embraced the mitzvah of Shabbos with heart and soul. She'd count the days till it was time for the whole family to sit together and bask in the comfort of the Shabbos candles. As the candles danced, she'd proudly sing her Shabbos songs and twirl beside them. She'd love the feeling of being blessed by her mother at the Shabbos table. Lily's fifth birthday was celebrated in school as the special "Shabbos Girl," with a crown on her head. What a great day, Shabbos and a birthday combined!

Every sunrise would bring Lily another day, another opportunity to love life and teach us adults how to live with joy despite it all.

Weeks after my visit with Lily, I traveled to Silver Spring, Maryland, to speak about parenting. As I stood at the podium, a woman approached me.

"I saw your article about Lily on Aish.com," she said. "My children and I were so inspired. This child has real courage, and my daughters want to be a part of her tzedakah."

She handed me an envelope that had been decorated with bright red magic markers. I could feel the coins and dollars inside. There were hearts colored all around and in the middle of the envelope in huge letters was written, "LILY'S TZEDAKAH." And at the bottom in children's scrawl: "Naomi and Rachel, Silver Spring, Maryland," along with more red hearts.

Here I was about to start speaking, and I found myself speechless. How incredible is the power of our children? Two children inspired to bring goodness into this world through a little girl that they only read about but never met! Isn't this all that we pray for and try to bequeath to our children: to feel for others, think about others, do well for others, and rise above ourselves.

TOUCHED BY AN ANGEL

Early Thursday morning, I returned home from my lecture. I must have just walked through the door when I received the painful news. Lily, our sweet, beautiful Leah Chana, returned her soul to the heavens above. I gave out a gasp and realized that I was crying.

This past summer, I was touched by an angel...

So began my words about Lily at her funeral. I described Lily's tzedakah project and her ability to rise above her challenges by growing better instead of bitter. I then held up the envelope with "Lily's Tzedakah" written boldly across the center and told the story behind the bright red hearts.

I wanted to share this message with Lily's parents and family. I wanted to convey this thought to the hundreds and hundreds of people who filled the room that morning. And I want to share my words from that day with you:

> *As Lily was taking her last breaths, we could not imagine what this child was still accomplishing in this world. Though it was her final day here on earth, she was still inspiring others and making a difference in this world. Unbelievably, she was*

bringing mitzvos and good deeds into this universe. This is the magic of our sweet Lily.

For the past sixteen months, hundreds of women have kindled their Shabbos candles with a prayer for Lily on their lips. We have taken this mitzvah upon ourselves as Felicia's friend, Jennifer, sent out countless emails each Friday that were then forwarded to even more women. Some of these women never lit Shabbos candles before. Many never knew Lily but were praying for her and kindling their "Shabbos lights for Lily" with great love.

I can tell you this: When Lily's soul returned to Shamayim, to the heavens above, she was surrounded by thousands of magnificent lights that had been kindled in her honor. Lily was lifted upon the wings of thousands of prayers. We will continue to light our Shabbos candles and through our mitzvahs, honor our precious Leah Chana.

Felicia and Greg, it is written that in the heavens, God has a treasure house of souls. The purest of souls are kept beneath the throne of God. These are the holiest of souls. These are God's diamonds. They must only come into this world for a short amount of time before they complete their mission. They then return to the heavens above.

To whom should God entrust His most precious jewels?

Only to the kindest and most trustworthy parents. Only to those parents who safeguard this diamond, watch over it, and guard it well. Parents like you who have been chosen to watch over God's jewel and, though it is incredibly painful, to return the diamond when it is time.

I know that I speak for countless people when I tell you that it has been our privilege to be a part of this beautiful child's life. In her five years, she has accomplished and taught us more life lessons than some adults do with their long years. She is our pure soul, our treasured jewel, and her radiant light will live on in our hearts.

After hearing about Lily's glorious life on that very painful day, many people who had never studied Torah before asked how they could begin to learn about Jewish wisdom. In my heart, I know that Lily is still working her magic.

How to Help Your Homesick Child: "I Want to Come Home"

Preparing your child for a successful camp experience

Camp season is here. The trunks are loaded, the lists checked off, and it's time to board the bus.

You talked about it all year, but now there's this pit in your child's stomach. You encourage, you wave goodbye, and the tears begin. What do you do when you receive the call, "Mommy, I want to come home!" or when the camp mother is on the phone telling you that your child is homesick?

Do you bring him home? Do you promise presents and bribes?

Before we speak about handling the situation let's be aware of two points.

First, understand that feeling homesick or anxious is normal. It does not mean that something is wrong with your child. Being away from home in a new environment can be tough, especially after dealing with COVID, which brought school closures and more time with parents and family members indoors. Children of all ages can be feeling homesick, but it is especially common amongst younger kids or those who have not really ever spent time away from home.

Second, it is best to deal with the problem **before** it occurs. Some children are genuinely not ready for camp. They cry and show anxiety just thinking about it and find it difficult to go on sleepovers. Research has shown that it is healthier to think about prevention. Parents who work on their children's worries and fears before the child is in the bunkhouse will be more successful than those who simply ship their kids off. Believing that your child will just tough it out is not the answer. Understand that the child who is not adjusted is different than the child who is emotionally and physically ready to go but will be homesick at times. We are describing the typical camper who is set but may need some help adapting to the camp experience.

Here are three ways to help your child prepare for overnight summer camp throughout the year:

1. Communicate

Tell your child what camp life is like. Describe a typical day along with which sports and activities to expect. Explain what happens at mealtimes and in the dining room. If possible, show photos of the grounds and bunkhouses. The unknown creates fear. Helping your child feel familiar allows for a feeling of safety. Talk with your child about his concerns and identify emotions. Reassure him that being scared or worried is normal. He will be OK.

2. Don't Berate

Never make a child feel badly for expressing fears and emotions. Don't say things like, "Stop being such a baby" or "Come on, this is ridiculous!" Not only will you shut your child down, but he will think twice before sharing with you in the future. Listen well to what your child has to say and don't belittle his feelings. Convey a sense of understanding.

3. Practice

It is important to help your child graduate to independence by experiencing small moments throughout the year. Sleepovers in the homes of trusted friends, grandparents, and family members are a good way to begin. Help your child ease into the idea that "I can spend time away from home, even if I'm nervous. I can do this." It is better not to wait for camp to be the first time a child is truly sleeping out of the house for an extended time.

GOING OFF TO CAMP with good friends can help your child feel more secure. Some parents want their children to meet new kids from different backgrounds and communities. That is a wonderful idea, but not every child can acclimate while knowing absolutely no one. When a child feels isolated, sad, and lonely, it becomes difficult to make friends. It may even create a situation where a child is easily bullied. It is best to put thought into who your child will be spending his summer with and not assume that it will just work out.

How can you best help the adjustment?

1. Bring a Bit of Home with You

Nighttime can be the hardest time for your child. It helps to have something from home—either visual, a scent, or a sound. A favorite stuffed animal, family photos, or linen or a pillow from home, can all help create a feeling of security.

2. Create a Toolbox of Coping Skills

To help your child be prepared, give tools for better coping. Some days in camp will be difficult. There will be sport games lost, tension with bunkmates, and food that will not be to your liking. Trips and experiences may bring disappointment. Sometimes you will feel lonely and sad.

3. Teach Self-Care Skills

What should you do when you feel alone? What is the best reaction when a bunkmate makes you feel bad? How can you calm yourself when feeling anxious? What is a good way to make new friends?

4. Teach Positive Self-Talk

Guide your child to think positively when he or she starts to view camp with a negative eye. A great way to help oneself is by combating "down thoughts" with upbeat reflections. I call this skill "brainwork"—the art of deliberate thinking. It is really a wonderful life skill that will bring peace of mind beyond summer camp. The moment he starts feeling badly, teach him to switch gears and think to himself, "I am safe even though I am not at home." Or compose a positive sentence together for your child to draw upon whenever he begins to feel homesick.

5. Empathize

Empathy is not the same as sympathy. You do not want to have your child feel as if you are commiserating with him. No pity party. Get rid of the sensationalism.

Empathy means that you are warm, interested, and paying attention to feelings. Tell your child that you understand it is difficult and offer reassurance. Daily calls will not help the situation. It is best for your child to be busy and active. Boredom reinforces feelings of homesickness.

DO NOT OFFER PRIZES AND BRIBES. Do not offer to bring him home. Instead offer support and encouragement.

One of the greatest gifts you can give your child is the knowledge that you believe in him. Write a note for your child to see your words and become strengthened whenever he is feeling homesick.

Tell your child: I believe in you. Even if you are feeling scared, even if sometimes you are feeling nervous, it's OK. I am confident in you. I know that you've "got this." You can climb this mountain. I love you.

Battling Sibling Rivalry

Can the war between siblings ever be won?

Dear Slovie,

I have a nine-year-old son and a seven-year-old daughter. It was her birthday smack in the middle of Chanukah, and my son could not let go of the fact that her birthday gift was bigger than the one he received on his birthday a few years ago. He "lost it" from the moment that she opened her gift, and the next night of Chanukah was no better. I like to think that I approach Chanukah correctly. We do give a gift from each child to an organization for children in need, and some small trinkets the other nights. Well, the next night my son got a huge box compared to his sister, and while hers was a small painting set, he got a tabletop hockey/football set. Not only did he not like it, but he did not even acknowledge when we pointed out that his sister never compared sizes of gifts! His reaction to what we thought would have been a great surprise was quite a disappointment to us.

I am frustrated and sad. What should I do?

One of the greatest joys of parenting is watching our children get along. "*Hinei mah tov u'mah na'im sheves achim gam yachad*—How good and how pleasant for brothers and sisters to dwell together in unity."[1] And one of the greatest pains of parenting is hearing our children fight and knock each other down verbally, sometimes even physically. How many vacations, car rides, weekends off from school, and mealtimes have been ruined all because of ugly fighting between siblings? Brothers and sisters who send verbal zingers across the room or who cannot handle each other's good fortune destroy peace within the home.

Must sibling rivalry be a part of our growing up as brothers and sisters?

LIFE AS A TUG OF WAR

Parents should know that there is a major difference between sibling rivalry and common children's disagreements. Kids who get along learn to resolve their disputes and problem-solve together. They may sometimes fight and have conflicts, but there are also times that they are able to communicate and enjoy each other's company.

Sibling rivalry, on the other hand, is a whole other story. Rivalry is defined as a contest, competition, or conflict. We are talking about brothers and sisters who are constantly competing against each other. Life is one big tug-of-war, each side pulling against the other.

These children are constantly measuring and comparing:

"Hey! Why did she get a bigger piece of cake than me?"

"When I was his age, you never let me stay up so late!"

"Why does he get an electric scooter for his birthday? You never bought a gift like that for me!"

Sibling rivalry can grow uglier with time. Imagine the scene in this family's home next year when Chanukah arrives. Parents are holding their breath waiting for the explosive tantrum as their daughter opens

---

1 *Tehillim*-Psalms 133:1.

up her gift, while their son rants and feels forever neglected. No matter what they do, it will never be good enough.

Even as grown adults, these feelings surface. We all know men and women who, in their mind's eye, are constantly being treated unfairly. Somehow, everyone else always has it better.

"I should've gotten that raise!"

"Why does my sister have such a great life?"

"How did my brother ever get that job? I am so much smarter than he is!"

Such individuals never feel at peace. They are forever comparing and don't know how to be content with what they have.

THE GREEN-EYED MONSTER

How do children come to sibling rivalry? The bottom line is jealousy. Children who envy each other become rivals. They cannot handle the fact that their sibling has something and they do not. It may not be something they need or even like. But jealousy eats away within and pushes a person to grow into a green-eyed monster.

Children who view life through an envious lens need their parents' help so that they can redefine their very nature. An envious child grows into a spiteful character who spews forth resentment and begrudging remarks.

We often mistakenly feed the jealousy as we attempt to even out our children's lives.

Thinking that we are helping them, we give in to the tantrums. We try to measure out the pieces of cake, compare cups of juice, buy toys at the same time for each child, and struggle to give each child everything "the same."

What a blunder! There is no life that can ever be the same. The contest between siblings only grows uglier.

OVERCOMING JEALOUSY

We need to help our children overcome jealousy. Teach them that there are no two people in this world who are exactly the same. We each have our own birthdays, talents, likes, and dislikes. And just as we each have our own unique set of fingerprints, so too, we are each born with our own particular mission in life, our "spiritual fingerprints." As parents, our goal should be to help each child shine in his own particular way so that he feels fulfilled enough as an individual and will not cast a malicious eye on his brother's (or anyone else's) blessings. My focus with my children is not on being "equal" but rather, it is "individual." Why would he need to knock his brother if he feels self-satisfied and complete within himself?

When I was a little girl, I was taught that being jealous is like eying someone else's gorgeous piece of luggage. You lug it home excitedly, open it up, and realize too late that nothing fits. Besides, half the stuff inside isn't even your taste. What are you left with?

Parents should teach children to avoid casting their eyes on the lives of others. Kids should know that every child in the family is appreciated for his individuality. Stop comparing lives. We also should not encourage tantrums and discontent by striving to make each situation equal.

Yaakov Avinu paved this parenting *derech* when he gave his final berachos to his sons. "He blessed each man according to his particular blessing."[2] Each son was given an individual berachah in line with his ability and character, so that he would know what his unique mission was. It is crucial to recognize that Yaakov Avinu did not praise one path over another. He never implied that one particular track is better. Each child's uniqueness became his life's blessing. As Rabbi S.R. Hirsch says, "And each was in need of a special blessing because Hashem cannot make a person happy against his will and without his cooperation." In other words, each human being has a sole, singular mission to bring to this world. But if a child does not want to be happy with who he is and what he has been given, no one—not even a parent—can make that child happy. Happiness must come from within. As parents, we ignite the desire to live with joy and not jealousy through helping each child discover their exclusive purpose. We grow each child's self-awareness. There is no "thing" that can replace positive self-identity.

The goal is to help our children transform the way they see themselves and their lives. We want them to know that they are valuable,

---

2 *Bereishis*-Genesis 49:28.

resilient, and purposeful. We call this "inner wealth." When we believe in our greatness, we live inspired to accomplish greatness.

On a Shabbos walk, I once asked my mother why a child I know was being bullied. It seemed to me that the bullies "had it all." What would drive them to be so mean? What were they lacking?

"*Sheifele*," my mother replied, "you *think* they have it all. They are missing the most important ingredient, though, that every person needs. '*Eizehu ashir ha'same'ach* ***b'chelko***—Who is wealthy? He who is happy with **his portion**.'[3] But they have no ***cheilek***, no inner wealth, and no sense of identity or purpose. Despite all that they've been given, they feel empty inside. In order for them to feel good about themselves they need to push another person down."

I understood then how crucial it is for each child to realize their distinct contribution to their circle of life. This is indeed the key to self-confidence, to *fargining*, being happy for another's success, especially a sibling, and wishing others well. This is the ability to say to oneself: "I count. I matter. I am happy with my portion and who I am. I make a difference in this family and in this world."

We cannot give in to jealous tantrums nor should we attempt to justify ourselves as fair parents to our children. What we can do is help our children discover the potential for greatness that lies inside of them. Each child does not need the same blessing. They need to grow aware of their own **unique** blessing.

Indulging their jealous eyes will only make it more difficult for them to overcome their envious nature. Part of being a mensch in this world is being able to look at others without malice.

---

3 *Pirkei Avos*-Ethics of the Fathers 4:1.

Raising Confident Children

We cannot shield our children from hard work and eventual disappointments—and the same goes for parenting

Sometimes, we think that we're helping our children when, in fact, we are impeding them.

An article that I read describes a latest parenting trend. Mothers are hiring personal organizers to pack their kids up for summer camp. Despite their mature age and abilities, the children can't manage to pack their own trunks. Other mothers arrive on visiting day and spend their time together organizing their children's cubbies and personal stuff.

I recall those days of getting ready for camp. I would go through the camp list, take clothing out of closets and drawers, label, and make piles for hours. My parents were available if I needed help. But it was up to us to carry things in and out of our trunks, load our stuff, try to zip it all closed, and, finally, schlep it to the front hall. And at the end of the day, we felt as if we had accomplished something great.

It wasn't just packing a summer trunk. It was the knowledge that I was on the road to independence. I could do for myself. I would arrive at a bunkhouse far from home. There were new surroundings and faces, so much was unfamiliar, and it was OK. While unpacking each item into my cubby, I would recognize all the hours of hard work that I had put into packing myself up. I was given a feeling of satisfaction, an understanding that I had this ability to accomplish independently. Although there were those tough days of bunk politics and losing color war, I never felt like giving up. Confidence had grown within, along with responsibility.

If we want to raise a child who grows to become self-sufficient, we must provide opportunities for that to happen. We cannot be fearful of new surroundings. We cannot shield our children from hard work and eventual disappointments. There is no substitute for toiling over a project and seeing the results firsthand. There are no shortcuts when it comes to developing character. Integrity, diligence, and responsibility are all traits intertwined with striving and accomplishing. We are selling a whole generation of children short when we do not hold them accountable for even the simplest tasks.

HELPING CHILDREN SOAR THROUGH REFLECTIVE LANGUAGE

When we notice a child attempting to do for himself, acting responsibly, or overcoming a difficulty, instead of simply saying "great job," or "awesome," we should utilize language that reinforces the positive character trait we perceive. Reflect back through your words the light that you see.

Just as our eyes are opened when we make specific blessings for various types of foods, scents, and experiences, and we don't simply utter a universal berachah, saying "Thank You, Hashem," so too, we should be specific in communicating our children's good qualities. Instead of giving indistinct blanket praise, plant seeds of greatness by verbalizing defined character acknowledgment. Our children will grow toward the energizing language we use to describe them.

Here are some examples of words to boost self-confidence and self-awareness: responsible, sensitive, brave, considerate, forgiving, thoughtful, tenacious, kind, respectful, curious, and understanding. We can pinpoint moments of *middos* coming alive by articulating and using language such as *vatranus*, letting go of hurts; *zerizus*, diligence; *savlanus*, patience; *chessed*, compassion; *emes*, honesty; *simchah*, happiness; and *gevurah*, strength. Of course, there are many more character traits; it is up to us to identify, express ourselves, and deepen our children's confident spirit. Another way to help a child grow is to mention a specific action that conveys your belief in his capabilities. Saying "I'm so impressed with the way you set the Shabbos table without me asking," instead of "thank you" or "super job," tells a child that you notice his efforts.

Children's entire mindset will be transformed as they come to recognize the potential that lies within. That recognition begins with us parents, and our ability to identify the good that we are seeing.

BEING PRESENT

Many parents have forgotten that raising confident children means that we are required to toil as well.

I recently spoke to a couple who are preparing for their son's bar mitzvah. They told me that they had spent hours in meetings with event planners. They wanted their son's bar mitzvah party to be over the top, making sure that the night would be the best that money could buy.

"This would be a sure way for our son to know that we love him," they explained to me.

"You are equating things with love," I said. "Whenever I give a parenting class and ask for the happiest childhood memories that come to mind, no one has ever described a thing they had been given. It is always remembering getting together with cousins by Bubby's house, biking with Daddy, story time with Mommy, or trips with parents and siblings that come to mind. All the toys, gifts, and money spent fade away. Our children need us to stop hiring others and start spending time together as a family."

It may be difficult to set aside our stress and listen to our children with both hearts and minds. There are days we want to scream. There are nights that we do not believe that we can sing bedtime lullabies, sit over math problems, or give one more good night kiss. We are simply depleted. *But we do it because we love them*. These are the moments that build an unshakable bond between parents and children. These are the moments that our children grow confident in their parent's constant love and presence.

When we teach our children that we believe in their ability to accomplish and to strive, we give them the greatest tools for life. But we cannot transmit this lesson by having others step in for them or by handing them lots of "things."

When our children see us parent lovingly through our very own pressures, they come to understand that, despite challenges, we work hard to create strong homes. It is the day-to-day interactions—the power of our smile, the encouraging words, the belief in their ability to rise above, and the time that we take to listen and manage our day-to-day parental responsibilities—that transform a child from helpless and weak to helpful and strong.

V'NAFSHO KESHURAH V'NAFSHO

A parent who transmits love, no matter what is happening in life, provides a child with a confidence unlike any other. This child is certain that "no matter what, I am not alone. I am loved. I am cherished. I do not have to be afraid."

After going through the horrors of Bergen-Belsen, my mother and her family were taken to the D.P. camps in Switzerland. Somehow, even there, she was separated from her parents, once again. Each night, as evening would descend, the darkness in the room brought nightmares and cries amongst the children. The dresser in the corner, the chair by the window, all became shadows of Nazis coming to take the children away. Their petrified screams brought fear into each child's heart. My mother would describe sitting up in her bed, terrified.

And then a figure would enter the room. My gentle Zaydah, a *malach* here on earth. He would gather the children and gently sing the *Shema*. His voice brought solace to each broken heart. Many children were left as orphans, losing both their fathers and mothers, as well as their entire families. They were completely alone in this world. Zaydah felt their pain and would not leave before being sure that each child felt his calm presence and love. He would then tuck my mother in and whisper into her ear: "*V'nafsho keshurah v'nafsho*—And his soul was bound with his soul,"[4] the words that Yehudah used to describe the boundless love between Yaakov and Binyamin.

These words became our family's code for everlasting love. Each time my mother signed a card or message to us, she would inscribe "*V'nafsho keshurah v'nafsho*."

I knew growing up that this love never fades. Confidence in a parent's love allows a child to thrive.

When You and the Teacher Disagree

Dear Slovie,

We are a group of mothers working in the same office who recently had a heated discussion about how to deal with situations when we don't agree with our children's teachers. We wanted to hear your opinion on this matter.

4 *Bereishis*-Genesis 44:30.

Here are some of our stories.

"My daughter is in the eighth grade. The other day, her teacher gave an assignment to memorize a bunch of Rashis. Of course, she was very frustrated and kvetched about it. My husband was fuming, and he told my daughter that her teacher is ridiculous, and she should just make sure she doesn't fail. My daughter wanted to know what I thought about it. I was very torn. I agreed with my husband, but I didn't think it was a good idea to tell my daughter that her teacher was wrong. I just told her it doesn't matter what I think because it's an assignment that I can't change, and she should just try her best. I still wonder, what is the right thing to say to our children when the teacher gives too much homework but won't listen to the parents when we call to tell her to ease up."

"My daughter's school has a million rules about their dress code. Now, I'm certainly one for tznius, but I find some of these rules to be overbearing. What do I tell my daughter when she complains to me that these rules are ridiculous? Should I tell her my real opinion about chinuch and education with too many rules?"

The bottom line of this letter is: What should we do when we disagree with our children's teachers or school rules?

Thank you,

Concerned Mothers

Dear Concerned Mothers,

Your questions are both crucial and timely.

You describe a heated office discussion. This type of conversation can easily become emotional and turn into a "blame game." What I would like us to do through this exchange is disentangle from the fiery sentiments and discover a path through which we can navigate these chinuch challenges.

Our schools are crucial to the building of the next generation. We realize this from the moment that Yaakov Avinu sent Yehudah down to Goshen first, "l'horos l'fanav,"[5] *to establish a beis midrash and place of learning. This set the precedent for us to know, forever, that the soul of Am Yisrael is the study of Torah.*

I mention this because we must first ask ourselves: What is our goal here?

Our mission is to inspire our children, both spiritually and emotionally, so that they can discover the potential that lies within. Together with the school, we want to strengthen their mental health, emotional health, sense of security, and connection with Hashem. We want to imbue middos, resilience, compassion, and derech eretz. And of course, we want our children to accomplish and achieve as they learn in an environment of stability, consistency, and tenderness. These are lofty goals to strive for in the limited time that we have with them. Impediments such as social and learning difficulties, family and financial stress, trauma, and health issues can set children off track. We see how important it is that the parents and the school work well together so that children find success.

What happens when a troublesome situation occurs in the classroom or parents find schoolwork to be "ridiculous" or the rules to be overbearing? Do you tell your child that you are not in agreement and that the school/teacher/policy is crazy?

The goal we need to contemplate here is way beyond the Rashis memorized (or not), or the dress code required. It is about the alignment between school and home so that children grow up in a secure environment based on respect.

Let us first speak about the parent-school relationship and then we will discuss the situations presented.

Rabbi S.R. Hirsch writes, "As with a husband and wife, as with a father and mother, the school and home must stand side by side, working together for a common goal. Offhand remarks

---

5 *Bereishis*-Genesis 46:28.

in the presence of the child can cause great damage. Granted, no teacher is perfect, and no school is perfect. Every school is founded and operated by human beings with human weaknesses, so parents will always be able to find faults that might prompt them to make disparaging and disrespectful remarks. It must be kept in mind, however, that a child who hears such remarks will lose respect for the school and its teachers, which undoubtedly will undermine the school's efforts to educate him."

A supreme value of chinuch is not to denigrate or mock anyone but to be especially sensitive about the way we speak about mechanchim, educators, spouses, and grandparents. Ridicule and put-downs will breed incredible chutzpah that will eventually trickle down and be used against you. If you do not respect or listen to one another, why would your child bother to listen to you? There will come the day when he, too, will mock your thinking, values, and rules. Unfortunately, he will have learned this behavior from you.

Once your child is enrolled in a school, your allegiance and loyalty mean that you believe in the chinuch that your child is receiving. You have decided to place your most precious possession in the hands of those who are educating your child. Your support assures your child that he can rely on and trust your decision making for him, and that he can trust those whom you choose to guide him.

Does that mean that you must remain silent when you are troubled by something happening in his school? Does that mean that you will always see eye to eye with the teacher and the school? Of course not. But just as in marriage, our goal is shalom bayis and a solid foundation. There is a dignified way to disagree.

I suggest that you put your kochos and energy into strengthening and raising your children higher, instead of putting down the teacher or school. There will always be situations where we will find ourselves disagreeing with someone who matters in our lives. One day your child will have to navigate a relationship and deal with discomfort. Whether it is a spouse, in-law, boss, or coworker, he will need the skills to manage that challenge with grace and maintain shalom in the relationship. Look at this as an incredible teaching opportunity.

When we find ourselves in choppy waters, we are given a life vest to remain afloat. Your daughters now find themselves in choppy waters. Obviously, you don't want to take them out of the school at this point, nor do you want to submerge them in waters of rebellion by ridiculing the mechanchim who teach them. We want our children to remain afloat despite stress. I propose a "life vest" to help them get through this time successfully, with middos intact.

Remember ***VEST****:* ***v****alidate,* ***e****ncourage,* ***s****afety,* ***t****ime.*

V: Validate*—In order to validate your child's feelings, don't brush aside her concerns. Give verbal responses and use body language to show that you are listening. Try to talk less and listen more. When we receive this type of validation, we feel not only that our emotions are heard, but that we are also accepted.*

For example, after your daughter expresses her feelings, you can say, "Wow, this must be so frustrating for you" or "That must be really hard" or "I see you're upset. I'm here for you."

The point is that we do not want our child to feel isolated or rejected. Children need to experience connection with us. Validation strengthens our bond and gives the message, "You are important to me." By listening and being present, we can also lessen the intense emotion that accompanies distressing situations. Of course, throughout our conversation, tone and words must remain respectful.

E: Encourage*—When we encourage our children, we provide them with an ayin tovah. We show that we believe in them and are optimistic that they can climb this mountain. Whether it is memorizing Rashi, struggling with math equations, or respecting school rules, we support their hard work. We want to inspire our children to accomplish, to try to do and be their* *best. Encouragement comes not only with energizing words, but with loving gestures as well. Bringing them a yummy hot cocoa while studying, writing a supportive note, or going out together for special time because you noticed their effort are all ways of showing encouragement. We want to reinforce our children whenever we see them strive.*

S: Safety—*Children pick up their parents' attitudes. Showing anxiety about grades or ridiculing the school's chinuch and educational approach does not offer our children the safe space that is required for them to thrive. Regarding homework and tests, it is OK to say, "Try your best. I love you no matter what." Unconditional love means that you are not being judged by your marks, looks, talents, or trophies. Wildly successful or not, you are loved for who you are. Period.*

If you feel the homework load is indeed too heavy and you haven't yet spoken to your child's teacher, then take that step. (Older children should be encouraged to speak to the teacher privately and with derech eretz.) Most teachers want to work together with parents and students and see success and joy in their classrooms. The point is how you convey your message as well as not breeding disrespect within your child.

You can also offer your child a feeling of safety by saying, "I know how overwhelming this feels, and I'm here for you. What can I do to help you study better?" or "I can see that you're feeling a lot of pressure this week. If you'd like, I'll drive you to school so you have some extra time in the morning."

When it comes to the school's rules, whether we are dealing with dress code or smartphones, the message to our children must be that we respect and uphold the guidelines that are set in place by the school we have chosen. Safety means less friction and more mutual appreciation between home and school. A child is assured that the alignment is intact. When there are open clashes of hashkafah, spiritual outlook, and obvious discord with the school, the entire foundation of chinuch is affected.

Rav Mattisyahu Salomon writes, "There is a direct correlation between kavod and hashpaah, respect and influence, on one's character. The more we honor and respect the people from whom we need to learn and derive inspiration, the more we will be receptive to what they have given us. We need to respect our rabbis because we need to be guided by their leadership. We need to respect our parents because we need to be molded by their loving and devoted chinuch."

Safety comes along with the sense of security and stability that we convey to our children.

T: Time—*Wise parenting takes a tremendous amount of time (and of course tefillah). Children who grow up knowing that their parents have a positive presence in their lives discover the magic of family. Even when school seems overwhelming, home remains a haven of love. In years to come, it will not be the homework, reports, or tests that will be remembered. It will be your reaction to times of challenge and stress. Beyond the myriad of rules that your daughter's school has, the question for you to ask is: What has my child learned from my attitude toward discipline and established boundaries?*

Think about how much you can accomplish through guiding your child positively throughout this time.

I conclude with the image in my mind of receiving a berachah from my parents each Leil Shabbos. No matter how difficult the week, those were the moments that sustained me, inspired me, and keep me connected until today. The hands on my head, the glistening in my parents' eyes, and the whispered words of love nourished my soul. No matter how pressured or chaotic our children's world becomes, let us resolve to be the lighthouse of their lives.

Let us all, parents and educators, come together b'shalom and explore how to ignite the pintele Yid in all our children.[6]

---

6 Adapted from article published in *Ami Magazine*.

CHAPTER 8

The Road to Respect

Disciplining without the Tzaros

Leave the aggravation behind

Relationships don't just happen. We need to work on bonding with our children. From the moment that a child is born, we are here to nurture and cultivate. Sing to your babies. Read to your toddlers. Play ball and ride bikes with your tweens. Find out what your teen loves to do—and then find the time to do it with him. Even if it's not something you enjoy doing, just taking an interest means that it's important to you because it's important to him. That's how we forge relationships. Once children learn to trust us and feel connected, it is easier for them to accept our "no." Especially if they don't like what we have to say, they appreciate our love and do not want to disappoint us.

Discipline takes work. Having high expectations and handing over responsibilities is not enough. If you want to successfully teach boundaries and self-control, you must commit to building a relationship with your child and acquiring the skills and insights needed to raise children with standards of behavior, values, and respect.

A child who feels wanted feels the warmth of your love and that you are looking out for his best interests—even in moments of discipline.

When a child perceives that a parent only cares about his own needs, his own name, or what the neighbors will talk about, he will automatically put up a wall. Saying things like "You're killing me" or "What will people think about us?" will backfire. Is our reaction all about others or about what is best for you, our child?

There are times when it takes more than love and good thoughts to make it through a tough situation. We are faced with a child who just pushes our buttons. It seems as if every day brings more explosive confrontation. Life becomes chaotic. There are emotional head-on collisions. Drama lurks behind every doorway.

You, the parent, feel drained. Now what?

STRATEGIES FOR EFFECTIVE DISCIPLINE

Some children seek power through misbehavior. They feel validated when they are noticed; negative attention makes them feel important. Too many rules frustrate them and are disregarded.

Challenging kids and parents who are overly forceful clash. They don't know how to work together and find solutions. They are too busy waging war. You will find that the more you demand, the more the child pushes back. Days together are spent arguing. We want to break this cycle.

How can we discipline effectively?

- Don't engage in hostile exchanges.
- Don't give angry ultimatums.
- Don't lecture, go on and on, and talk about "when I was your age."
- Do choose your battles wisely. If you do not have to say no, then say yes. But if you do choose the no, then believe in your decision and be consistent.
- Do take time to listen.
- Do reflect your child's words and emotions so that he sees that you hear him.
- Do speak calmly, but firmly.
- Do find opportunities to bond and spend enjoyable time together.
- Do give clear and direct discipline.

Hear your child. If he has something to say, don't make him feel afraid to voice his ideas and thoughts, as long as he speaks respectfully. Children with strong natures enjoy leadership roles. If you can give this child some opportunities to shine, he will feel greater self-worth and be more comfortable with himself. You will find it easier to discipline as you build a rapport and mutual respect. Also, keep in mind that when your child thinks that something was his own idea, he will want to make it work.

For example, instead of simply telling a teen what time his bedtime is, you can discuss real options along with the responsibilities and natural consequences that come with a later bedtime. When your child sees that you consider his opinion and that he has a part in the conversation, he becomes invested in a positive outcome. He feels more in control because he was given a voice. He will be making the natural choice to follow through successfully.

FOCUS ON BEHAVIOR INSTEAD OF CRITICIZING

The point of discipline is to improve/correct behavior and teach right from wrong. Parents often mistake criticism for discipline, and then wonder why nothing has changed. Giving criticism just makes a child feel badly about himself. Successful discipline happens when parents focus on the behavior they'd like to improve. Instead of making a child think that he is the definition of bad, they point out bad behavior that needs fixing. They also communicate confidence in the child's ability to do better in the future.

DON'T GIVE IN TO TANTRUMS

I recently attended a child's birthday party. It was a festive event with decorated cookies and donuts piled high. One three-year-old began to screech. His grandmother tried to calm him to no avail. The screeching became louder. The child dropped to the floor and began to kick his legs.

"What does he want? Why is he screaming like that?" I heard the *bubby* ask her children.

"They ran out of the blue frosted donuts. There are only vanilla ones left. And he only wants blue."

The father joined his son on the floor.

"Would you like me to take you to the bakery and see if they have blue donuts for you?"

Still wailing, the child nodded. Daddy scooped up his child, carried him on his shoulders, and off they went to find a bakery with blue donuts.

Now I ask you: When will this child learn that sometimes we must deal with a situation, and the answer may not be the one we want to hear? As a child grows, it is crucial that he learns how to handle frustration. Today it is blue frosted donuts, but who knows what disappointments tomorrow will bring? The solution cannot be that parents always step in and make it all better.

Of course, we don't relish times when children feel bad. But this moment presented a perfect opportunity for teaching a life lesson and self-discipline.

Instead, these parents used it to create an entitled child who can't deal with disappointment. Rewarding tantrums is a sure way to reinforce bad behavior.

The same goes for older children who cause grief and pain, yet they are never asked to be responsible for their actions.

Eventually, the behavior catches up. Parents who have shielded their children from limits and responsibility scratch their hands wondering why they can't seem to get their children to listen to their rules. The answer is: Because they have lived a life lacking rules. Boundaries are not respected.

Here are some crucial parenting questions:

- Do I allow my child to experience limits?
- Do I give empty threats? Do I follow through?
- Do I hold my child accountable for his actions?
- Do I allow misbehavior to slide?

Positive actions you take are deposits in your parental "bank account." Moments and gestures of trust help your account grow, so that when there must be a withdrawal—such as consequences and discipline—your account is never depleted.

Discipline 911

Don't be afraid to discipline your child

"What do you say to a four-year-old boy who wakes up in the middle of the night and refuses to go back to sleep?"

It was at the end of a parenting lecture, as I was putting on my coat getting ready to leave. A husband and wife approached me with their question.

"Well, what do you do when he wakes up?" I asked.

"I cover him with a special blanket, turn on a video, and bring him a cup of hot cocoa," the father replied.

"You're kidding, right?"

The couple looked at each other sheepishly.

"No, I'm not kidding."

"Of course, he won't go to sleep, why should he?" I asked. "You're treating him like a king for waking up at 2 a.m. Why are you doing this? Let me ask you something. How do you get him to go to sleep at night?"

"We wait for him to tell us that he's tired."

I paused for a moment before I spoke.

"How old are you?"

"We're both thirty-two."

"Are you telling me that a four-year-old is telling two thirty-two-year-olds, when he thinks that his bedtime should be? Why do you allow this?"

Husband and wife shuffled uncomfortably. "We're scared."

"You're what?"

"We're scared to tell him what to do."

"What do you mean you're scared?"

The father glanced around to be sure that no one was listening to our conversation. He then rolled up his shirt sleeve. I noticed long, red marks all over his arm.

"What's this?" I asked.

"That's my son scratching me when we tell him to do something he doesn't want to do, like going to sleep."

I was speechless.

"But really, he's so cute! I know you'd think he's adorable if you'd meet him."

"Cute?" I asked. "What's cute about scratching your father's arm bloody and not listening to your parents? What you think is cute at age four becomes obnoxious before you know it. And what will you do when he's a teen, maybe even stronger than you, and wants the car keys against your wishes? You need to learn how to discipline your child, fast!"

The wife looked at her husband for a moment before speaking.

"I try to tell him that we need to discipline Jack, but he just doesn't listen to me. He's always giving him another chance. Tonight, you spoke about the rules of discipline, but where do we even begin?"

A SPIRITUAL STANDARD OF LIVING

Honor and respect are basic foundations of our home. In Judaism we call this concept *derech eretz*, literally "the way of the land." It means that we must live with a daily spiritual standard of living. Discipline is the thread that ties honor and respect together. It allows *derech eretz* to take form as we mold our children's character.

Too often, we think that our children won't like us if we discipline them. We remember thinking as a child, *I'll never do that to my kids*! So, we hold back on discipline hoping that our children will love us more. We want our children to feel that we are best friends forever and that they can always confide in us.

But discipline doesn't mean that we push our children away. What it does mean is that our children are given boundaries to live by. No scratching. No biting. No hitting. No hurting others, not with your hands nor with your words. Listen and speak with respect. Be truthful. Treat others as you yourself would like to be treated. When you do not listen to the rules, know that there are consequences in this home as well as in life. (Of course, we ourselves must live with the standards that we teach our children).

Children come to appreciate parents' wisdom and guidance and grow to understand that a home built on a foundation of *derech eretz* is a home filled with both respect and love.

WORK AS A TEAM

I told this couple that they should begin by deciding that it is time to bring discipline into their family picture, and they must discipline *together*. Creating your spiritual standard of living is a joint parenting mission. When you are sitting at the dinner table and Ari kicks his sister under the table and then answers you back disrespectfully, how will you handle the situation?

If one parent says, "Apologize and take a time-out until you decide that you can sit here respectfully," and the other says, "Come on, what's the big deal? Give him another chance, he didn't really mean it," you are undermining each other's authority. Your discipline cannot possibly work. Little Ari now knows that you are working against each other. There is no family unity. The parenting team has fallen apart.

The *ben sorer u'moreh*, the rebellious child defined in the Torah, is described as "*Einenu shomeia b'kol aviv u'vekol imo*—He does not listen to the voice of his father nor to the voice of his mother."[1] Our sages teach us that he became defiant because his parents spoke in two separate voices.

So, when a parent says, "Don't tell your mother that I said you can do that..." or, "Be sure not to tell your father what we spent..." the seeds of alienation are planted. Children see parents who oppose each other and disregard one another's opinions. They learn to ignore and look down at their parents.

Wise parents know that they need to show a unified front. When they do disagree, they speak privately to resolve their differences. They hear each other. They listen to their spouse's view and then seek resolution so that they can demonstrate to their children that they're on the same page. When necessary, they have a go-to person whom they both respect (like a trusted educator, rabbi, *rebbetzin*, Torah teacher, or therapist).

We continued our conversation with added insights to help them deal effectively with the lack of discipline in their home.

---

1 *Devarim*-Deuteronomy 21:18.

1. Don't Make Excuses for Bad Behavior

There are times that children will disappoint us. They act out, fail to step up to the plate, and show poor judgment. It does not mean that the child is bad, but it does mean there is bad behavior to confront. Instead of rationalizing, think about the best way to help a child overcome and grow.

It's easy to look away at poor character traits by making excuses. Who wants to deal with discipline, tantrums, back talk, and tears? It's tiring. Parents are pressed for time, stressed out, and dealing with financial, emotional, and familial responsibilities. So we say things like, "She's having a hard day," or, "He's tired." We allow disrespect, entitlement, and meanness. Of course, it is wise to put ourselves in a child's space and try to understand if there is a reason behind the misbehavior or language. But, at the same time, we cannot keep tolerating troublesome character flaws with defenses and excuses.

This behavior will not go away on its own. Children require boundaries. They need to learn natural consequences. They must see the ramifications of their actions. We cannot do this for them and expect character to develop.

Too many times, we say no, but convey "maybe," or "I'm not sure," which breeds confusion. Children read our hesitation and pounce on our doubt. You, as a parent, must believe in yourself and your parenting choices.

If we believe in ourselves, are consistent, clear, and stand firm in our parenting standards, and balance discipline with loving times spent together, our ability to discipline becomes strengthened.

2. Don't Explode in Times of Tension

Life is not perfect. We can never really anticipate the challenges. Children can be moody, irritable, anxious, and difficult. (Teens, especially, do not always clearly see the consequences of their actions.) Effective parents do not fly off the handle or parent from rage. A common mistake parents make is to mirror their child's moodiness. "If you are grumpy and don't respond to me, why should I talk to you?" A wall between parent and child is created.

Good parenting requires calm. Instead of losing it when a child speaks or acts wrongly, say, "Let's try this again." Bring tranquility to counter the turbulence, and parent with wisdom.

3. Say What You Mean and Mean What You Say

One final point to remember is to be consistent. Some parents spend half their life saying, "If you push your brother one more time…" or "If you talk like that to me again…," but nothing changes. The child just does the same action again, because he knows that we simply give empty threats. Some parents blow up, scream, and get enraged. Losing it does not mean that we are being effective. After a while, parents get tuned out.

You must decide what kind of home you'd like to create: a home where children slam doors, raise their voices, ignore you, and hurt their siblings, or a home where parents are united as they teach their children to live with respect and values. The choice is yours.

Why the Chutzpah?

What triggers the disrespect?

"We have a problem."

"Tell me," I say to parents on the phone.

"Our nine-year-old daughter…"

I hear only silence.

"Yes?"

"Well, we want you to know that she is a really special child. We don't want you to think badly of her. She's usually so good. She's great in school, has lots of friends, and her teachers only have the best things to say about her."

"OK," I respond. "So, what's the problem?"

There is an uncomfortable pause on the other end. And then, Malya's mother begins to speak.

"She is so disrespectful; I am sometimes reduced to tears. She erupts in anger and says mean things to us."

Malya's father now adds to the conversation. "Sometimes, I can't believe the behavior I'm watching. I totally don't understand it! She is a doll to everyone else. She gets awards in school. Whenever she has a playdate, her friend's parents cannot stop praising her. But here, she can become nasty and turn this house upside down."

It's quite common for parents to hear glowing reports about their child and yet feel helpless at home as they live on the receiving end of incredible disrespect.

What could be happening to cause such a drastic change in public versus private behavior?

"Let me ask you a few questions. First, can you describe to me some of the chutzpah and then we can figure out if there are any triggers."

Malya's parents tell me about her coming home from school each afternoon and making a big deal about supper. She would rather eat junk food, and so she refuses to eat dinner until she consumes the snacks that she desires. She does her homework, but after she is done, the night becomes an evening without boundaries. She refuses to go to sleep at her set bedtime. She refuses to get into pajamas and brush her teeth when told. Usually, she ends up playing on the computer or reading until she decides it's time to call it a night. When told to go to sleep, Malya ignores her parents and keeps on doing whatever it is she is in the middle of doing. Malya calls the shots.

"This behavior can't be allowed to continue," I tell Malya's parents. "Not only is it destructive to Malya, but her younger siblings are certainly taking this all in and believing that this is permissible. Soon this will be a family based on disrespect.

"We know this is bad," they say, "but what can we do? She just doesn't listen. "

"You and Malya are going to sit down and have a very serious discussion. Both of you need to be there—no cell phones, no siblings, no interruptions. She needs to see that you mean business. I am going to guide you, but I want to know one more thing. When the chutzpah occurs, what do you do?"

Malya's father tells me that the disrespect is often flung toward him. He tells her it's not right to speak this way, and then she answers back that he doesn't know how to handle her.

"You should learn from Mommy! She knows how to handle me."

"What does she mean by that? What exactly does Mommy do?" I ask.

Malya's mom explains to me that she often cajoles her husband to give their daughter another chance. When Malya misbehaves or speaks disrespectfully, her father will get upset and threaten her with a punishment. Malya's mother then asks her husband to look away or let their daughter "have just one more cookie, or five more minutes."

Malya's mother can't stand dealing with the emotions and conflict.

I now have my Aha! moment. This is the information for which I've been waiting.

In many families, there is one parent who tries to be the "nice guy." When there is conflict, this parent wants to restore peace quickly and be surrounded by happy faces.

The first thing I advise Malya's parents to do is to come together and parent with one voice. I ask them to decide how they would like to handle the conflicts and which behaviors would bring consequences. I explain to Malya's mother that she is contributing to her daughter's disrespect every time she asks her husband to look away or give in to bad behavior.

We set six principles of discipline to be followed that I would like to share with you:

1. Remove Unnecessary Sources of Conflict

Just as we remove delicate or dangerous objects from a toddler's reach instead of saying "no" the whole day, it is wise to eliminate any insignificant causes of disagreement. Decide which situations are important and which you can look away from. This way, you do not feel as if your days and nights are spent constantly quarreling. Home should never feel as if it is a battlefield with war raging.

2. Establish Routines

Many conflicts occur when children do not know what to expect or what is permissible. If we sometimes allow children to play ball indoors or nosh before dinner and other times we say no, we cause confusion. Children then test our limits and push until they hear "yes," because they know that we will give in if they push hard enough.

3. Act, Don't React

How often do problems occur because we were not specific with our kids or ignored a situation that got out of hand? Be clear with your child. When children understand what is expected from them, we avoid confrontations and feeling as if we are not being listened to.

For example, a grandmother I know told me that her grandson was visiting her for a long weekend in Florida. She stayed up for hours worrying and waiting for him to return on Friday night. When he finally walked in at 1 a.m., she screamed at him and gave him a speech. The minute Shabbos was over, she called his parents, who yelled at him and gave him a long talking-to. There was a feeling of resentment and anger that enveloped the rest of their time spent together.

When questioned, the grandmother informed me that all she had said to her grandson before he left was, "Don't come home too late." To this teen, no rules were broken. In his mind, 1 a.m. was a normal time to return.

How much pain would have been avoided if the adults (parents, especially) in this family would have *acted* by setting clear limits and times instead of *reacting* to this boy's late return? If only the rules would have been openly explained beforehand, confrontation and hard feelings would never have occurred.

4. Do Not Use the Word "Punishment"

I never use the expression "punishments." A punishment connotes "evil stepmothers" in fairytales and inspires feelings of unfairness, suffering and revenge. Instead, let us consider consequences. We want to help children learn that they are responsible for their behavior—both good and bad. This brings us to number 5.

5. Discuss Privileges and Natural Consequences

Explain to your child that it is a privilege to be in this family. And it is a privilege to play on the computer, have special time to read before bed, as well as toys with which to play, gadgets, scooters, and nights out with the family. If you speak disrespectfully or ignore family rules, you obviously do not appreciate the privileges that you have been given. You cause yourself the natural consequences of losing these privileges.

Children will test you to see if you really mean what you say. Be firm. Believe in yourself. Have the child understand: you choose your actions, and you choose what happens. Always relate the consequence to the action. You did not come to eat dinner until everyone was done? I feel badly for you, but this is what you chose. You missed dinner. There is always cereal or a sandwich. You are responsible for the choices that you make. For older teens, you did not use your phone responsibly? That is a behavior that you chose and now you will deal with the natural consequences that we decide. (I have spoken to parents whose child's phone was confiscated in school because he broke the rules, and then they asked if they should buy a second phone as he is insisting he needs one. What *chinuch* lesson does this child come away with?)

6. Speak with Strength

Be sure that you are not creating a pattern where you need to say the same thing over and over again, or finally scream in order to get your child to listen. If this is what is happening in your home, your voice has become ineffective. It is time to figure out why.

Don't ask your child if he wants to take a bath or is ready to go to bed. Instead, say, "It is time to take a bath" or "It is time for bed." The same goes for ending your sentences with "OK." "We're putting away the Lego now, OK?" or "Let's put on your coat now, OK?" We are not giving a choice here: "It's time to put away the Lego" or "Time to put on your coat."

It is wise to give a heads-up to prepare a child's mindset so that he is ready to go from one activity to another. For example: "In ten minutes we are leaving the park" or "You have fifteen minutes until bedtime."

Do not respond to chutzpah and disrespect. Do not honor a conversation that is filled with arrogance or attitude. Simply say, "When you are ready to speak to me respectfully, I am happy to listen." Often a child will test you, and try to engage you, to see how firm you are and to keep the disrespectful conversation going. Once you engage chutzpah, you are saying, "It's acceptable for you to speak to me like this." It is not. We can teach our children that it is possible to have a meaningful conversation and leave the chutzpah behind.

If both parents support each other as they maintain consistent discipline in the home through these guidelines, they will find that their children respect their unity and leave the chutzpah behind.

Teaching Your Child Derech Eretz

How to build an atmosphere of respect in your home

In a culture that invites disrespect, is it possible for us to teach our children to speak and act with reverence and consideration?

The Torah and our sages offer us tools to help us instill this sense of honor and respect in our children. These guiding principles empower us and help us create an environment in our home that becomes imbued with a spiritual standard of living. There is a direct connection between respect and transmitting our values to our children. When we respect and honor our parents and educators, we honor all that they teach us as well. The spiritual existence of the next generation is contingent upon the *derech eretz* and reverence that we infuse into the very foundation of our homes.

Here are a few of the guidelines:

1. Refer to Parents Respectfully

Children should not call parents (and grandparents) by their first names. This includes toddlers, who we think are adorable, but they can easily cross lines that become unacceptable. When we laugh, children are encouraged to continue their behaviors. It becomes difficult to instill new rules when they are older and we don't find their behavior adorable anymore. Referring to parents as "he" or "she," and saying statements like "Why did he say that?" or "Well, she said I could," is disrespectful and lacking *derech eretz*.

2. Ask Permission to Sit in Parent's Seat

Children should ask permission before sitting in a parent's designated seat. For example, a parent's set seat in the kitchen or dining room cannot be sat on without first asking. If a child is sitting at the computer and a parent is standing as they work or look at a site together, the child should be taught to offer the chair or bring another one so that the parent can sit down.

3. Request with Respect

Children should be taught to request with respect. For example, if your child is playing and you say it's bath time, do not establish a pattern where a child screams, "NO!" and then you negotiate each night. Instead, teach your child that when it's time to move to the next activity, be it bath time, dinner, or homework, and he is in the middle of something, you will consider his request for a few more minutes if he asks in a pleasant and respectful tone. This does not mean that his desires will be granted all the time. And he should understand that when you say no, there will be no stomping feet, slamming doors, screaming, or just plain ignoring you. That is disrespectful. If he cannot ask respectfully, there is certainly no way to consider his request. Give your child examples of how you would expect him to speak and make his request. Often, we get upset in the moment without realizing that we have neglected to give our children good alternative behaviors.

4. A Parent's Things Are Private

It is not OK for kids to go through their parents' wallets and pocketbooks, assuming that it is fine to take cash or use a credit card when needed. It is also not OK to order things online using a parent's credit card without first asking. Wearing Mommy's outfit or using Daddy's things without permission is also showing a lack of consideration and reverence.

5. Think of Others

Encourage children to think of others while thinking of themselves. When a child pours a drink for himself or gets a plate for himself, he should be taught to ask others if they would like some too. When a teen drives and goes out to pick up pizza or ice cream, implant within him the idea that it is considerate and respectful to find out if his parents (and other family members) also would like some. We can teach our children to grow sensitive and more reverent.

6. Greet Those Who Walk through the Door

When parents or grandparents (or guests) walk into the home, *derech eretz* dictates that children do not simply ignore their presence. Even if they are in middle of a game or doing homework, children should be encouraged to stand up, say hello, offer a drink, and give a warm greeting or smile. If there are bags or luggage needing to be carried, respect means that the children do not allow the moment to pass without helping ease the load.

IS THIS REALISTIC?

Some of you may be wondering if all this is really possible. Can children today really live up to our expectations and teachings?

Allow me to share with you a moving encounter that I had with a child.

It was Thursday night and I found myself at my local supermarket for the third time that day. Somehow, the number of guests at my Shabbos table kept growing, and I needed to pick up some more items. The store was packed, and I did not see any free carts. I balanced many items on top of each other and hoped that the heavy glass jars would not come crashing down.

In front of me at the checkout counter stood a young girl and her mother. The child turned around and noticed how difficult it was for me to juggle everything. She asked me why I wasn't using a cart, and I told her that there were none.

"Mommy," I heard her say, "I feel so badly for this lady with all this heavy stuff. I am going to try to find her a basket." As she went off on her search, I told this mother that she has such a special child.

"You don't even know the half of it," she replied. "My daughter was given a most difficult diagnosis this year. Every step is painful. This is not easy for her."

As this little angel walked back carrying a basket, I noticed the braces on her legs for the first time. Every step took effort.

I crouched down so that I could look at this little girl in her eyes as I spoke.

"You are the sweetest child," I said, as her mother stood beside her. "I want you and your mother to know that I speak all over the world about parenting. Parents and grandparents dream of having a child just like you. You should be *gebentched*. May Hashem watch over you always."

This child touched a chord deep within my heart. As I drove home, I wiped away my tears.

Teaching children kindness and compassion coupled with honor and respect paves the road for us to help them discover the greatness that lies within.

Reinforcing Standards

A practical guide to bringing the spirit of kavod into your home

A mother called to tell me that, while on vacation, her husband slipped and ended up in the emergency room. Her teen kept texting—not to inquire about her father, but to say that she's bored and wants to leave the hotel room.

"Can you believe her?" she asked.

When I asked her if she'd confronted her daughter's behavior, the mother sheepishly replied that she had not.

We create a parent-child relationship built on respect by upholding our values and infusing our homes with an atmosphere of *kavod*, the word in *lashon hakodesh* for honor. *Kavod* is related to the word *kaved*, heavy. To have *kavod* means that you live with spiritual weight. Rabbi S.R. Hirsch teaches that *kavod* indicates the magnitude of spiritual and moral essence. Beyond simply teaching good manners, we are talking about transmitting dignity, standards, and strength of character. It describes a respect and reverence that is felt for your parents and those who came before you.

Here are some practical ways we can bring a spirit of *kavod* into our homes every day.

1. Create an Atmosphere of Mutual Respect and Peace in the Home

Children seeing parents speaking and acting respectfully toward one another is the most important way to inculcate respect. Husbands and wives who, despite differences of opinion, maintain their dignity, speak in calm tones, and use words and body language that do not threaten, do more to teach their children the value of respect than any lecture can.

When children witness put-downs, mocking comments and eye rolls, and lack of consideration for each other's thoughts and opinions, they learn to disrespect.

Seek out ways to convey that you hold your spouse in high regard. It is not just about not putting your spouse down in front of the children, but rather, expressing the respect and pride you feel in one another. Show your children acts of kindness that you are happy to do because you love one another. Be positive about your spouse. Express appreciation in front of your children. Tell your kids how special their mother and father are.

When I was a child, I would find a plated grapefruit cut into slices on the table each morning. My father had prepared the fruit for my mother at the crack of dawn, before he left for minyan. This daily gift of love taught me the power of seemingly small gestures that can create a huge impact on the atmosphere in the home.

Children who see honor learn to give honor. They also feel strengthened when the bond between parents is strong.

2. Teach Respect for Others

Expect your children to respect others. And if you see a deficiency, act upon it.

Here are some daily examples that your children can do to treat others with *kavod*:

- When speaking to others, look at them instead of your phone.
- When grandparents come to visit be welcoming. Stand up and greet them; don't wait for them to find you and then grunt your hello.
- Smile. There is a famous teaching in Judaism: "Encounter every individual with a pleasant face." Your smile, or lack of one, has an impact on others.
- Don't interrupt others while they are speaking—even if it is your younger brother and you feel that what you have to say is

more important. When your parent is on the phone, unless it is a real emergency, have the patience and respect to wait without insisting on being heard "right now." And no, wanting to know when supper will be ready is not an emergency.

- Listen and be open to other ideas and opinions. You are not always right, and you do not know it all. Even if you do not agree you can still listen respectfully.
- Teach children to give their chairs or space to elders. I have been to many shuls and events where the children were sitting, while the adults were standing with no place to sit. Parents who do not teach their children to get up and offer their seats are imparting a lack of *kavod* and *derech eretz*. How can we watch a seven-year-old sitting comfortably in shul or at a *kiddush* while an adult has no chair? I was on a crowded stairwell behind a fragile *bubby* who was walking slowly, holding onto the banister. Everyone was headed to the *kiddush*. Two little girls were trying to slide under the elderly woman's arms and almost knocked her over. "Girls," I said, "You need to wait a moment and let this *bubby* go first. This is called *derech eretz*." If we do not teach our children, they will never know.
- Parents, be respectful when you discipline. Humiliating your child will push your child away. Behind most angry children lies pain. Of course, parents must discipline, but be sure that in the process, you do not make your child feel like a zero. Be clear and consistent. Follow through. Don't ruin the teaching moment through shaming and public disgrace.

3. Teach Respect for the World around You

We are given a mitzvah to respect the incredible world that God created and not destroy it pointlessly. In the middle of speaking of warfare, the Torah demands that we remain aware of the fruit trees and not needlessly cut them down. "When you besiege a city for many days to wage war against it, do not destroy its trees…"[2] God is teaching us that

---

2 *Devarim*-Deuteronomy 20:19.

even in the midst of a heavy battle, we must not lose ourselves in the wave of destruction. Value the sanctity of life. Value even a tree that is growing, giving shade, and producing delicious fruits.

Think about it. If we are asked to watch over a tree, how much more so must we guard every creation and every soul that we encounter?

We live in a world where we have been given plenty. In such a society it is easy to waste, to throw away, and destroy unnecessarily.

Teach children to take care of their things. Throwing away plates filled with food because too much was taken mindlessly, carelessly losing headbands and baseball caps, and leaving clothing all over the house are small examples of kids forgetting that everything we have should be valued and cared for.

These standards should be upheld whether we are home or on the road.

At one Pesach program, I watched as a group of children were jumping on the lobby sofas. Their nosh bags were flying in all directions.

A staff member walked by.

"What are you doing? Would you treat your living room at home like this?"

"What's the big deal?" one child retorted. "This isn't our home anyways, so who cares?"

We cannot tolerate this type of talk or behavior. It is not the Torah way.

4. Teach Respect for Heaven, *Kavod Shamayim*

Too many children today feel apathetic toward and disconnected from spirituality. A relationship with God provides our children with an inner strength that cannot be found elsewhere. Challenges come; unexpected disappointments arrive. We cannot shield our children, but we can give them tools to thrive. Spirituality empowers the next generation with an understanding that there is a Higher Being who watches over us. We are not alone. There is a Divine Plan, and *hashgachah pratis* is our truth.

Awareness of Hashem in our lives arrives with *kavod Shamayim*, respect and awe of Hashem. How can we communicate this to our children?

- Model *tefillah*. Try to have a daily *tefillah* routine. For busy mothers, even if it is just a few moments of spiritual connection, children absorb our actions. Greater than any discussion is the modeling that we do. While davening, be aware that children are observing. Don't engage in conversation and don't check your phone. When you are in shul, be sure to reflect the respect and *kavod Torah* that you wish to see in your child. This means that we don't chat during davening or have children run around inside the shul and treat a sacred place of *tefillah* as if it is a playground.

- Maintain proper respect for holy books such as siddurim, *Tehillim*, and *sefarim*. Do not leave them strewn and lying around or casually piled under other books.
- Children should see behavior that reflects *kavod* when we celebrate traditions and are *shomer* our mitzvos. Ask yourself: What is my mood and stress level when I welcome the Shabbos Queen? What is the conversation at my Shabbos table or my Seder table? Do I rush while lighting my Chanukah menorah or do I savor the moment? Do I mumble my berachos mindlessly?
- Think about opportunities to create connection, spiritual awareness, and *yiras Shamayim*. From the time that children are young, show them the gifts of Hashem's handiwork in our world. Stop and be mindful of Hashem's world. Express thankfulness for the vibrant colors of our fruits, the dazzle of the glittering ocean, the glorious pastels as the sun sets, and the exhilaration of watching snowflakes fall from the heavens. Open your children's eyes to the wonder of Hashem's creations. As children grow, they will recognize Hashem's hand in nature and beyond. They will learn the art of living with awe.
- Share stories of *hashgachah pratis* with your family. Tell your children about life happenings and moments in your day where you have seen Hashem's hand and experienced His kindness. When you are fortunate in life, when you experience moments of happiness, when you have family *simchahs*, when you get to travel on a vacation or decorate your home, be sure to say *baruch Hashem*, thank You, Hashem for Your blessings. Create an atmosphere of *emunah* by showing gratitude to Hashem who is the source of all our blessings and spiritual connection in our home.

- The relationship our children have with Hashem is intrinsically connected to their bond with us, their parents. When I first began giving parenting classes, I asked the couples I teach: What do you wake up early in the morning for? What sets your heart on fire? What do you sacrifice for? Because this is how your children learn passion. This is how your children absorb priorities.
- When children see their parents waking up early to daven, engaging in Torah study, embracing Torah and mitzvos with love, they come to a place of *emunah*. Instead of talking about faith—*live* with a legacy of faith.

HONORING PARENTS THROUGH THOUGHTS, words, and deeds are the basics of imparting respect. We have countless opportunities each day to mold our children and help them discover their spiritual essence.

CHAPTER 9

Seasons of Life

Personal Reflections

Walking with My Father

We never walk alone

Parents can get bogged down in carpool schedules, after-school activities, and the stress of homework and tests. The constant hurdles of discipline and scheduling our children's lives can rob us of the bigger picture. We easily forget that our parenting is truly a journey of love.

As I think about my father, I recall him taking my small hand into his larger one, and giving me the gift of his words to carry me throughout the many seasons of my life. Though he is no longer here beside me, the image of him walking next to me and trying to share a life legacy is never lost. These are sweet moments that for me are frozen in time. Though they may have occurred years ago and lasted just a few minutes, the imprint has never left my soul. My father let me know that I never walk alone. Perhaps, we can all take a closer look at the message that we would like our children to recall when they think about us, one day.

SEASON OF LOVE

August, 1984

Soft music was playing in the distance. Before me stood two tall doors that would be opened in just a few minutes. In my tulle wedding gown, veil covering my face, I was about to walk to my chuppah. My parents stood at my side. I was starting a whole new stage of life and excited to begin my married life.

My father motioned to me. He wanted to tell me something. He took my hand, and I saw that his eyes were moist. "*Sheifele*," he whispered. (He always called me *sheifele*, a Yiddish term of endearment.) "As you walk to the chuppah tonight, I want you to know that you are not walking alone. On your sides are all your holy *bubbies* and *zeidies* who walked before you. Their *neshamos* are here, and they are bringing you blessings. They are holy and they are watching over you. Wherever life takes you, never be afraid."

I knew that my father had lost his parents and entire family in the Holocaust. I knew that for him to see life begin anew was a miracle. And I knew that he had inhaled despair but exhaled faith. Now he was sharing this faith with me. As I began my life as a young bride, my father wanted me to always know that my faith would carry me through. He gave me this blessing, this incredible knowledge that we never walk alone.

The doors opened. We began our walk down the aisle, hand in hand.

SEASON OF LIFE

September, 1985

"The doctor says I need to walk."

We were in the hospital, anticipating the birth of our first child. My husband and I had arrived at the light of dawn thinking that I was in heavy labor. Instead, I was informed that I had lots of time to go. My parents arrived, and I related to them the advice that the doctor had given us. He had said that walking would be the best thing for me to do.

Once again, my father took my hand in his. "Come, *sheifele*, let's take a good walk around the block together. When you feel terrible pain, squeeze my hand."

I squeezed my father's hand hard that day. I was afraid that I was hurting him, but he laughed and said, "This is what fathers are for." As we walked, he once again reminded me that I never walk alone.

That night, my husband and I welcomed a precious baby boy into this world. He was named for my father's elder brother who had been taken away by the Nazis. He had left behind a beautiful family who were also never seen or heard from again. My father carried their lives within him. It was a heavy load, though he never allowed himself to grow bitter or become lost in sadness. He never uttered a word of complaint. I knew that we could offer some small solace for all that my father had lost through the naming of our son. And my father offered us great love and patience for all our children who followed.

Watching my father parent my children was a lesson in joy. He would laugh out loud as grandchildren ran through the sprinklers and shared their delight in the splash of water on a hot summer's day. He loved carrying our babies on his shoulder and rocking them to sleep with his kisses. He always had time for another bedtime story or to sing the *Shema* prayer. As the children grew, they relished visits with him because he listened—he really listened. He was never impatient. He never seemed tired or bored. He made us all feel loved unconditionally. I know that he had plenty of pressure. But, somehow, he always pushed the stress to the side, put a magnificent smile on his face, and delighted in us, his children and grandchildren. This is the inspired parenting that I draw upon as I am trying to climb my own ladder in life.

SEASON OF LOSS

January, 1996

"The doctor says that I need to walk."

Once again, I was in a hospital, but this time we were not anticipating the exciting birth of a child. My father was in Memorial Sloan Kettering, a cancer hospital in New York City. I knew that he was very ill, though we only discovered a few weeks before that he was facing the fight of his life. We were shell-shocked. My beautiful six-foot-two towering father, who had always carried us upon his broad shoulders, now lay in a hospital bed. I was spending time with him. My father told me that the doctor said it would be a good idea to take a walk around the corridors. I helped my father up from the bed and we approached the hallway.

My father took my hand in his. We took a few steps, silently. I did not know what to say.

My father stopped walking for a moment.

"*Sheifele*," he turned to look at me. "Do you remember another walk we once took together? Do you remember how you said that the doctor wants you to walk?"

I nodded, not trusting myself to speak.

"This is a different walk, I know. But I am still taking your hand in mine. And you can still squeeze my hand if you feel pain. I want you to know that even here we never walk alone. You never have to be afraid. And when, one day, when I am not here next to you anymore, I want you to know that I am still by your side. Remember that I am walking along with all your *bubbies* and *zeidies*. You will never walk alone."

Not long after that day, my father gave me his final blessing. He left me with a legacy that I try to live up to each day.

As we parent our children, let's try to show them that we enjoy being with them. Let's give them the message that even though there are pressures and moments of stress, we hear their voices and never turn away. And when there are moments of challenge or fear, let us impart a message of faith.

"My sweet child, you will never walk alone. No matter what, I am here beside you. Never be afraid."

Snow Angels

Paving a path for our children

It was snowing again in New York. Outside, a soft white powder blanketed the bare trees and red brick driveway.

"Mommy, can we go outside and play?" my children asked. "Don't worry, the snow is stopping and it's not even deep."

As I sent them out in hats and gloves, boots warming their feet, I was reminded of a story that my mother told me about her childhood.

The winds of war were blowing over Hungary. My grandparents decided that they would take my mother and her two brothers to visit their Bubba and Zaydah one last time before the inevitable Nazi occupation.

The trip, by both trains and horse and carriage, would be a long and dangerous one. My grandfather's noble beard and rabbinical attire could have easily brought on vicious beatings for the entire family. Despite the severe cold and peril, the decision to embark upon this hazardous journey was made.

Hard snow was falling; yet the Bubba and Zaydah stood outside in the freezing cold, waiting anxiously for their children's arrival. Finally, the horse and carriage arrived at the little home in the village of Nadudvar, where my great-grandfather, Rabbi Yisroel HaLevi Jungreis, *H"yd*, was the spiritual leader.

The children were embraced with delighted hugs and warm kisses. Inside, sweet treats and a delicious hot meal were waiting. Considering the poverty and painful events of that time, the beautiful spread was almost an impossible miracle.

Zaydah's study, lined from floor to ceiling with his holy books, was my mother's favorite place to be. My mother would sit on her grandfather's lap as he would immerse himself in the study of Torah. The room would fill with Zaydah's melodious voice, as he would be singing and chanting the words while he learned. There was a warmth felt there, a comfort that touched even a little child's soul.

After spending precious days together, the final day of the visit had arrived. The family was scheduled to return home to the city of Szeged. A sorrowful sadness filled the air. Once again, my mother sat with her Zaydah, neither of them knowing that this would be their last good-bye. As my mother looked up at her grandfather's face, she saw that he was crying.

Frightened, my mother ran to find her father. "Tatty, Tatty! Zaydah is crying! Why is my Zaydah crying?"

Eyes filled with tears, my grandfather took his daughter's small hand into his. "Come," my grandfather said. "Let's take a walk outside and I'll explain to you why Zaydah is crying."

After putting on her boots and gloves, my mother and her father began their walk. The sky was clear, but the ground was packed with deep snow. It was hard to tread and easy to slip.

"I am going to walk a little ahead," he said. "You are going to walk right behind me, my precious child. Be sure to follow in my footsteps."

After walking like this for a short time, my grandfather stopped. He turned so that my mother could see his face and hear his words.

"Do you know why I walked ahead of you?" my grandfather asked, gently.

"Yes, Tatty. You didn't want me to fall down in the snow. You walked in front of me so that I could walk in your footsteps," she replied.

"That's right," my grandfather said. And then my grandfather told my mother a truth that would remain with her long beyond that fateful day.

"When your Zaydah studies the holy Torah, Zaydah is studying not only for himself. He is studying and making a path for you. Zaydah's tears are paving a road for you and your children...a road that you will always find here for you. Soon the snow is going to be very deep. And even if you fall, remember that Zaydah made footsteps for you. You will stand up and remember your Zaydah and his tears, my child. Hashem will give you strength, and you never have to be afraid. Ever."

The last time that my great-grandfather was seen, he was being herded into the gas chambers of Auschwitz, holding a precious grandchild in his arms while crying out the words of the *Shema*.

Though my grandfather did not survive, his tears remained. They created a path so that my mother could find the fortitude to go on, no matter how deep the snow around her fell.

My mother's faith has become her legacy, illuminating our path until today.

Each generation faces its own challenges. The snow feels so deep. It is easy to be afraid and fall. We live in such difficult times. Terrorism. Pandemic. Anti-Semitism. Natural disasters. Financial distress. Marital tensions. Health issues. Unspeakable tragedies. Challenges with our children.

But remember, you are not walking alone. We all have *bubbies* and *zeidies* who walked before us, who paved a road with their tears. Perhaps we never met them, or knew them, perhaps they lived long ago. But they have cried for us, their children. We must only draw upon their strength and prayers. And as we, ourselves, parent, we must create footsteps for the next generation.

Footsteps of courage. Footsteps of compassion. Footsteps of faith.

I was jolted from my thoughts as I heard my children's laughter outside. They waved, and I waved back.

"Look, Mommy!" They were lying on the ground, their arms flapping in the snow. "We made snow angels!"

You are so right, I thought to myself, smiling.

Angels in the snow. May they accompany you wherever you may go.

My Father's Greatest Parenting Advice

One line of wisdom to guide parents through weariness

Despite the passing years, I am still that little girl pining for her father. I take a small box out of my closet. Gingerly, I finger my father's yarmulke, the one I had carefully put away. I lift it up, inhale, and take in my father's familiar scent. I close my eyes and hear my father beside me again. I catch his laugh, his booming voice as we'd enter the house and he'd call out, "Gorgeous children! I'm so happy to see you!" My children would run into his outstretched arms and spend precious time playing together, sharing stories and hugs.

I wish I would have asked the many questions that pop into my mind today. "Abba, how did you lose all those you love in the flames of the Holocaust and still hold onto your fiery faith? How could you have gone through such suffering and pain and yet, you gave us only love?"

I never heard my father raise his voice in anger. I realize now how extraordinary this is. My father had difficult days. He had to begin his life over again as an orphan in a new country. Being a community rabbi, teaching Hebrew school to kids who had no interest in being there, pioneering a traditional synagogue together with my mother in a spiritual wilderness while raising us—all this must have taken incredible mental strength and emotional energy. What was his secret?

The answer came to me, wrapped in a moment of time that speaks to me even today.

We were at a family celebration. The band was playing loudly, and the room was packed with people. One of my children, a toddler at the time, was on the floor crying. I was feeling overwhelmed. My father walked over, scooped my child up and settled him onto his broad shoulders.

"*Sheifele*," my father said to me with his magnificent smile, "Never be so high that you cannot bend down to hear the cry of a child."

It took just a moment. But I realize now the wisdom that my father was trying to teach me. We grow tired. We are stressed or simply not in the mood to hear our children and deal with their tears. No matter their age, whether they express it or not, they need us. And if we are too removed, if we are too weary, we will find ourselves in a place where we have created a distance that makes it difficult to bend down and listen to the cries of our child.

This is true especially now when our world is spinning out of control. Children are losing their emotional balance. They need parents who can extend to them a sense of spirit, the courage to live each day with strength despite the chaos that surrounds us. Instead of raising our hands in exasperation, we need to bend down, look into our children's eyes and put our energy into raising each child up. This means that when our children show us through their actions or words that something is not right, that they are in turbulence or pain, we have the ability to connect to them.

I believe that my father was teaching me the truth of unconditional love. No matter what you've done, my child, no matter how hard the times are, know this for now and forever. I am your mother; I am your father. I am here for you. My love for you does not mean that I will always love your behavior or approve of your actions. But it does mean that I will show my love to you all the time.

Every child has another way of translating the definition of a parent's love. Whether this means that we take the time to hear our child's voice, write an encouraging note, give a warm hug, or spend more time together, know that we are here for you.

Let us remember that children will act like children. If we love them only when they please us and meet our expectations, they will not feel genuinely loved. They will come to feel they can never be good enough or smart enough for our hearts to be open to them. This does not mean that we do not discipline or give consequences when needed. It does mean that our children's greatest emotional need is the knowledge that we are never too high to bend down and listen to their cries.

Gifts My Mother, Rebbetzin Esther Jungreis, Gave Me

How to live an empowered life

In this difficult time, how can we gather our inner strength and get through this world crisis?

Many have asked me: What would your mother say? I know that her life speaks her response.

How did my mother bear the burden of suffering that weighed heavily on her shoulders? What about the moments of pain, of struggle, and of unbearable hurt that sears within the deepest crevices of one's soul?

If we could once again have a precious few moments together so that I could gain perspective and strength, what would my mother relay?

Sometimes, life brings us to places that we never imagined possible. But here is what you must do, my mother would tell me. "When faced with darkness, you have a choice. You can either grow angry or depressed. Or you can light a candle and illuminate the darkness. Slovie, never sit in darkness. Always ask yourself, 'How can I grow from this? How can I find purpose in the pain? It is not about *lamah*, why, but *lemah*, for what reason, am I going through this ache in my soul?' Don't agonize and say '*Madua*?' Instead, the question is '*Mah de'ah*? What can I learn from this difficult experience?'"

My mother's wisdom has sustained me throughout my life. And though she has left this world, her legacy remains my spiritual lighthouse. I'd like to share with you three gifts (among the many) that my mother gave me. I take these gifts with me and carry them in my heart. They embolden me as the world around us is filled with untold tragedies, pain, and fear.

1. Live with Passion and Meaning

I will never forget sitting front row in Madison Square Garden, November 18, 1973. There were thousands of Jews from every walk of life—some even sitting on the floor because there were no more seats. The room was pitch black. Suddenly the spotlight beamed brightly onto the stage. There standing bravely was my mother. "You are a Jew," she proclaimed. She spoke with power and passion. That night was magical. At the end of the evening, thousands rose to their feet, danced, sang the words of the *Shema* together, and knew that their souls had been touched and changed forever.

Sometimes, I wondered and asked my mother, how did you, a child of Bergen-Belsen, ever think this was possible? How did you arrive in this country barely speaking English and then speak to presidents and prime ministers, to the Israeli army, the American army, and across the world to thousands upon thousands of people? How did you declare your faith and never feel afraid? How did you rise from the ashes and start a worldwide movement called Hineni to bring Jews back to their roots?

My mother told me that when she arrived at America after suffering through the Holocaust, she saw a spiritual holocaust happening before her eyes. She dared not remain silent. She never lived a day without being cognizant of her responsibility to make a difference for her people. I believe that the words of Mordechai to Queen Esther constantly echoed in my mother's mind. "*Ki im hacharesh tacharishi*—If you remain silent at a time like this…*revach v'hatzalah yaamod la'yehudim mi'makom acher*—the rescue of the Jewish nation will come from another place…

u'mi yode'a im l'eis k'zos higaat la'malchus—and who knows? It might be for this moment that you were made queen!"[1]

My mother believed with her heart and soul that each of us has our life mission, our moment. One day we will be asked, "What did you do with the life that you were given? How did you use your gifts to make this world a better place, to bring light to your people?"

How could my mother have survived the flames of death and *not* give her life to the survival of her people?

"Live with passion" my mother would say. "But make it meaningful. If you believe in your mission, you can accomplish anything."

2. Never Give Up on a Soul

I watched my mother connect with every type of person. What was her secret?

My mother believed that within us all is a soul waiting to be ignited. I can still hear the concluding words she cried out that night, in Madison Square Garden. "It is a flicker of a light, a tiny flame. But if you will it, that tiny flame can become a great fire, from which the words '*Hineni*, here am I, my God,' shall emerge!" I witnessed the awakening of souls that had lain dormant, the explosion of the *pintele Yid* before my eyes.

In 1982, I traveled with my mother to war-torn Lebanon, where she spoke with battling Israeli troops, giving them words of *chizuk*, and then to a meeting with the Prime Minister of Israel, Menachem Begin, in Jerusalem. From Lebanon to Yerushalayim, we were greeted with incredible respect and graciousness.

My mother received a call to address the women prisoners incarcerated in Ramle prison. I listened as some who were privy to the call tried to dissuade my mother. "Rebbetzin, you are coming from the office of the Prime Minister. These are just women sitting in jail. Why speak to them?"

To this day I recall my mother's reply.

"These women are daughters of our people. How can I ignore them?"

---

1 *Megillas Esther*-Scroll of Esther 4:13–14.

She gave the imprisoned women who exuded despair, rays of hope. My mother saw beyond clothing, beyond the body, and found instead the sacred spark that lies beneath.

Each one of these encounters I had witnessed—whether a battalion of *chayalim*, the Prime Minister of Israel, or Jewish women in prison—was precious to her.

I remember one Yom Kippur in NYC, where we held our yearly Hineni davening in the Essex House Hotel. Besides those who were part of our "Hineni family," all were invited to join gratis. We never knew exactly who would show up. At the conclusion of the davening, my mother would give a heartfelt berachah to all who attended.

A woman dressed in white walked up to the front of the room, wrapped her arms around my mother, and embraced her. She was wearing flip flops; her hair was matted, and her clothing looked worn. "Rebbetzin, give me your blessing. I have not been at a Yom Kippur service since I was a little girl. I am all alone in this world." The woman began to cry. It was clear that she was homeless and had somehow wandered in from the street.

"Uch!" the girl standing next to me said. "How does your mother do it? That lady must stink!"

I thought for a moment and responded. "The truth is, if you think about it, we all must stink a bit right now before God. We all have a little *lashon hara*, a little jealousy, a little moment of unkindness, along with other sins, staining our *neshamos*. And don't we all say 'Hashem, please! Hug me. Love me. Give me Your blessing.' My mother sees the beautiful soul that we all wish God sees when He looks at us."

The struggles of our people became my mother's struggles. She channeled her own pain into feeling the pain of others. And the *pintele Yid* that lay hidden was never too concealed to be unearthed and discovered.

3. Know Where You've Come From

My full name is Slova Channah. I was named for my *bubby* who was last seen together with her husband, Rabbi Yisroel HaLevi Jungreis, *Hy"d*, holding their youngest grandchildren in line at the gas chambers of Auschwitz.

I grew up cognizant of the story of my name. People have asked me, "When did you find out about your family and how they perished and suffered in the Holocaust?"

There was never a time that I did not know.

We were given the names of our *bubbies* and *zeidies* so that we would live as strong Jews because they could not. We continue to give the very same names to our children and grandchildren so that our descendants know forever from whence we have come and the potential that lies within us.

One of the greatest gifts that we can give our children is solid *shoresh*, roots. When we know where we've come from, we have direction in life and know where we are going. We understand what we are capable of and plug into the spiritual DNA that lies within. We dig deep, realizing with wonder that we are a nation of miracles. We survive against the odds, resilient and strong. Growing up, I had no doubt that indeed, I, too, was given a mission. I carried my *bubby*'s name and through me, she has remained alive. It's not about Jewish guilt. It is about Jewish pride and responsibility.

During the start of COVID, my husband and I participated in the *bris* of our grandson over Zoom. We were in New York, and our children were in Toronto. As the baby's name, Asher Anschil, was pronounced, I gave a gasp. Sparks of the soul of our holy Zaydah, the *Menuchas Asher*, known as the Csenger Tzaddik, the Miracle Rabbi, would once again be revived. My children had held on tight to our glorious roots, to our teachings, and to the majesty of our *zeidies* and *bubbies*. A new generation would bear witness, and with God's help, sprout greatness, nourished through the life-giving waters of yesterday.

My son held his baby, looked into the screen, and gave me a smile. I cried tears that only a mother can comprehend.

Our children must know that they are put onto this earth for a reason. Those who came before them struggled mightily. The sacrifice was great. But with each new link in the chain back to Sinai, a connection has been born to those who walked before us.

Parents: It is now your turn to inspire and guide your children. Teach your child the meaning of their Jewish name. Tell them stories about the greatness of our people. Help your children carry the sacred legacy of our nation.

Mama's Secret Language of Love

Discover how to communicate your everlasting love

My grandmother, Mama, loved life with a passion. Despite surviving the anguished suffering of Bergen-Belsen, Mama never lost her fire. I often wonder how she, as a young mother, was able to hold on while watching her little children shoved into cattle cars, starving, shivering, terrified, and surrounded by the stench of death.

Arriving in this country brought more pain. How does one begin life again?

My grandparents, Mama and Zaydah, decided that they would somehow build a Jewish day school as testimony to the eternal spirit of our people. We may go through darkness, but we kindle a light and illuminate the world around us. We never give up.

The neighborhood had many Jewish children who were unaware of their legacy. Shabbos, Jewish holidays, the stories of our people, were all a mystery. Even knowing one's Jewish name was hidden in a cloud of uncertainty.

I recall sleeping over at Mama and Zaydah's tiny house. At the crack of dawn, I would get woken up by the sound of clanging pots. Mama would be baking her delicious Hungarian cakes and cookies for the students in her yeshiva. She would then fill her impossibly huge bag with treats and *kippahs*. Off we would walk the long blocks together in time for the buses to arrive.

Mama stood at the school doorway being sure to not miss one child. Despite being under five feet, her spirit reached the heavens. No one would ever dare start up with my Mama.

"*Boker Tov*, good morning!" Mama would greet each and every student before they'd step foot into the building. She would then say their name and kiss each child's head. Only after they would respond with their own "*Boker Tov*, Mama," would she reach into her bag and hand them one of her homemade delicacies. "Now let's make a berachah, a blessing, together." Mama would patiently utter each word and then wish the child *hatzlachah* and a wonderful day.

I didn't realize it at the time, but I was learning one of the greatest lessons of love.

Use a child's name. Look at them. Make them feel wanted. Show them that you care.

To this day I meet adults who can't help but smile as they remember Mama. Somehow the image of the tiny woman with sparkling eyes and a huge heart remains. They recall the warm greetings, the sound of their Hebrew names, the undefeatable spirit, and the blessings they made together.

"You can't imagine what those mornings meant to me," I am told, over and over again.

"I remember my Jewish name only because of Mama. Mama was the *bubby* that I never had. She made me love being Jewish."

I have the privilege of teaching young women in Manhattan High School for Girls. I leave my home before the sun rises and sometimes arrive a bit early, depending on the traffic I encounter. Standing on the stairs, I watch a figure greet each girl by name with a warm "good morning."

For a moment I am back with Mama.

I call out to the woman on the staircase.

"Mrs. Rottenberg, I must tell you that you remind me of my grandmother, Mama." As I begin to describe my grandmother's language of love, Mrs. Rottenberg smiles. "Where do you think I learned this from? I used to work with Mama every day in the yeshiva! I'll never forget how Mama greeted every child by name."

I am floored.

"You know," she adds, "my father was in the concentration camps. He told me that the first thing the Nazis did was strip him of his identity. They took away his name and reduced him to a number. My father always told us how we must value and cherish our Jewish names."

Our names hold incredible *ko'ach*.

When Hashem spoke to Yaakov Avinu in a vision of the night, implying the impending darkness of a long exile, He called out, "Yaakov, Yaakov." *Rashi* comments on Hashem's repetition of Yaakov's name as *lashon chibah*, a language of love. At this moment that Yaakov was facing his greatest fears for his family and future descendants' survival, Hashem sent him a gift of love. Yaakov Avinu's name became a symbol of Hashem's eternal love.

"Yaakov, Yaakov! Though you may find yourself in exile, know that you will never be exiled from your God forever. I love you and will love your children no matter where they may be."

We have the opportunity to give our children the greatest gift of their lifetime. Each and every day. Call your child by their name. Look them in the eye. Give warmth. Show them that you love them.

Mama's Lullaby

Creating a forever bond with our children

When I was a young mother, my husband and I decided to go on vacation to the island of St. Martin. With a newborn and active toddler, I wanted to have an extra pair of hands on the trip. But who?

And then it hit me. Mama! My grandmother who loved life and never lost her spirit was beyond excited to join us. Mama had gone through incredible pain and suffering. As a young mother, she was forced onto the cattle cars together with my Zaydah and their children. In Bergen-Belsen she never knew if the dawn of each terrifying new day would bring death to her and her loved ones.

Despite her tiny stature and the horrors she experienced, Mama had an indefatigable life force that refused to be extinguished. *Everyone* affectionately called her "Mama." She was the perfect person to be part of our vacation.

The first morning, my newborn woke as the sun began to rise.

Mama was thrilled to take a walk exploring the island with the baby's carriage in hand. As she strolled, she would sing to our baby the Yiddish lullaby that her mother, and her mother before her, used to sing, "*Shluffy, shluffy meidele*—Sleep, sleep my girl [or boy], you will study Torah and grow great and righteous."

Each morning Mama would return from her early walk with a smile on her face. "What a gorgeous world God created!"

One morning, Mama returned, and her eyes were sparkling. "You'll never believe what happened to me this morning!" she said.

I couldn't imagine what could possibly have happened at 6 a.m. on a small quiet island with almost everyone still sleeping.

"I was walking with the stroller, singing to the baby. There was a tall guy ahead of me, he must've been six feet tall. He was jogging with a girl and suddenly he stopped and looked at me.

"Excuse me, can I ask you something?"

"Sure, of course you can," I said.

"Is that a Yiddish lullaby you are singing?"

"Yes, it is."

"I can't believe it! That was the lullaby my *bubby* used to sing for me every night before I'd go to sleep. I haven't heard these words for twenty years! Wow! I have a question for you. Do you think you could sing me my *bubby*'s lullaby?"

The girl next to him got upset. "Are you nuts?" she said to him.

He looked at me and said in a low voice, "She never had a *bubby*. She can't understand. But I am asking you. Can you sing my *bubby*'s lullaby for me?"

"Yes, on one condition," Mama replied.

"What's that?"

"Only if you call me Mama."

The young man smiled. "Mama, would you please sing me my *bubby*'s lullaby?"

As Mama sang, the young man's eyes filled with tears.

"Thank you, Mama. Thank you for my *bubby*'s lullaby. I needed to hear that."

There, on an island so far away, a young soul was joined once again with the soul of his *bubby*. He had never forgotten her voice, never lost her words. They remained embedded in his heart, tiny embers waiting to be stoked anew. This is the *pintele Yid* that lies within each and every one of us.

To all the mommies and *bubbies* in the world, may your voices always sing. May your children and your children's children carry your words in their heart. May you ignite the fire in their souls with your love. And know that even if you do not see it now, the bond that you have with them is forever.

A Letter to My Father

Holding on to a parent's love

Dear Abba,

They say that time heals all wounds. I don't know. It's been more than twenty years, yet, somehow, there is still this crack in my heart that never seems to have healed. I miss you so. I close my eyes and see your beautiful face before me. I hear your voice as you say to me "Sheifele, don't worry. Everything will be all right."

I'll never forget the day we slowly walked the halls of Sloan Kettering Hospital together. I slipped my hand into yours, but I honestly don't know who was leaning on whom. You were undergoing the most difficult treatments and yet you never complained. "Rabbi, on a scale of one to ten, what's your pain level?" the nurses would ask. "Thank God, it's a zero," you'd reply, with that perpetual smile of yours.

You never wanted to burden us with your fears or pain. Visitors came and thought they'd bring good cheer, but instead you gave comfort and strength to us all. You lived with faith, genuine faith, until your very last day on earth.

Your enthusiasm for life and the souls that you were granted never waned. You would take the children outside to smell the spring flowers and feed challah to the ducks in the lake. You would sit on the floor and build blocks with the toddlers as the babies would happily crawl over your six-foot-two frame.

When my toddler was crying as his siblings played outside in the snow, you bundled yourself up and went out with my largest kitchen pot and spoon. I could not understand what you were doing, until you returned inside, carrying a pot full of snow with eyes shining. You set my son down on a towel, sat beside him and had a snow party together. His tears stopped in an instant. "You just need to get into your child's head sometimes, sheifele," you said with your loving laugh.

When we would come home for Shabbos and I'd be woken at 3 a.m. by a crying infant, I would wander into the kitchen to find you with your holy sefarim, humming the words as you learned.

"Give me the baby, Slovale. I'll hold him as I learn," you'd say.

"Are you sure?" I would ask. "It's three in the morning. Don't you need to sleep?"

Your face would light up and you'd laugh. "Do you know why babies wake up in middle of the night, sheifele? They're up to keep us learning Torah!" You would sing until your newest grandchild would slumber contently in your arms. I have no doubt that your words and prayers remain hovering above each child as they grow.

Abba, I remember sitting shivah for you, shocked that you were gone. We had only nine weeks to say goodbye. The shivah house was constantly packed. As "the rabbi" for more than thirty years, you touched so many lives aside from ours.

When you and Ema moved to North Woodmere, Long Island, you made it your mission to establish strong Jewish roots and reconnect people with their Jewish heritage. I understand that it was because you had both endured the flames of the Holocaust and lost your entire family that you were pained as you now watched a spiritual conflagration take place before your eyes. Through great dedication and sacrifice you opened up our home to the entire community, never judging, only reaching out to others with love. You taught me how to open my heart, and what it means to carry the burden of another. I watched as you and Ema shared in the joys and cried for the pain of our people.

That week of shivah, there were countless individuals wanting to tell us their stories about you. I looked around the room and wondered how one man could touch the lives of so many. From the corner of my eye, I noticed a little girl, sobbing. She must have been eight or nine. I didn't know who she was. I remember thinking: Why is this child crying for my father?

Her mother began to speak. "Your father was not only our rabbi; he taught us to love Judaism. When we decided to send our daughter to a Jewish day school, we had one difficulty. We couldn't help her with her homework. We had no background, no knowledge. At first, we would call your father with questions. And then one night, the Rabbi knocked at our door. 'I'm here to help you,' he said. Each night he would come to explain the work and teach us, too. How did he have the time and patience? I'll never know. My daughter and I are crying for our rabbi. We will miss him."

And I still miss you, even now. Sometimes I imagine how you would have danced at our children's bar mitzvahs and weddings and given our children your special blessing. But then I realize that you are surely watching and sending us your blessings from Above.

I remember, too, the time that you and I had a few precious moments in the hospital, alone. You had surrounded yourself with all your holy sefarim from home. You lined them up on the windowsill, transforming that gray dreary room into a place of sanctity. You motioned for me to bring a Chumash to you.

You opened to the portion of Vayechi when Yaakov Avinu became ill. You asked me to read. I tried but my voice broke. "Read for me, sheifele," you gently encouraged me.

My eyes blurred with hot tears as I read how Yaakov Avinu called his son Yosef and his grandchildren to his deathbed. He then bestowed his final blessing—the blessing of the angels...Hamalach Ha'goel.

You looked at me for a moment and then you spoke. "Slovale, I came to this country all alone. I walked through gei tzalmaves, the valley of death. I never thought that I'd see life again. And then Hashem blessed me with new life, with Mama and Zaydah, with your Ema, and our beautiful children. So, I understood that I, too, was given the berachos of the malachim. I know that I am leaving you soon. I am not sure when...Maybe it is a few weeks—maybe it is a few days that I have left here with you. I was thinking, sheifele. What can I possibly give you? What has meaning and value forever?" I began to sob and buried my face in my father's neck. I could not bear the pain. My father's tears mingled with mine.

"I leave you with my berachah, my child, the berachah of the malachim. May they accompany you and your children and children's children wherever you may go."

I will never forget that day. I hold onto your blessing and feel your love. With gratitude to my precious father,

Slovie

Love Them

Remembering our mission as parents

Here I am, basking in Jerusalem's golden light. A magnificent orange sun is rising. I catch its glow as my airport cab enters the holy city. My heart is pounding. In just a few moments, I will be holding my newest baby granddaughter, just four days old.

After what seems like eternity, I finally reach my destination. Though it is early morning, and the building is eerily quiet, I race up the stairs, luggage in hand. I knock, barely able to contain my excitement.

My daughter opens the door, and we happily embrace. Gingerly, she places little Elisheva Shimah in my arms. I kiss her soft silken head and gently put my pinkie into her hand. I smile as her fingers instinctively curl round mine. She breathes deeply, and I take in this miracle called life. I try to absorb the newborn scent, the eyes that suddenly flutter open, the delicate toes, and the curl of her mouth that becomes a smile. It is overwhelming. I am cradling a precious life—a gift from the Almighty.

As our children grow, sometimes it becomes easy to forget how privileged we are to be called "Mommy" and "Daddy." Carpools need to be driven, baths wait to be drawn, and hungry children clamor for supper. Our bills pile up as we try to deal with tantrums, mountains of laundry, homework sheets, and fighting siblings in the backseat of the minivan.

We wonder, "Am I really accomplishing greatness here? Do I genuinely make a difference in this world?" Each day seems to blend into the next.

You may never find yourself in Google Search for "Greatest Parents of the Universe," but you must not doubt the impact that your presence has on your family. Each soul is touched by your light.

The tears you lovingly wipe away, the bedtime story that you make time to read, the patience you surprisingly find when you feel weary and stressed, all teach your child a supreme life lesson. "I am loved." "I am cherished." "I have wings." "I have a soul." It is a lesson that resonates deep within your child's marrow no matter where life's journey may lead.

A woman approached me after a parenting lecture. "I look around this room," she began, "and I feel so inadequate. This mother is a lawyer, this one constantly invites guests, and this one is involved with charity work while she raises five children. What about me? What do I do that's so great?"

"Are you there for your children?" I asked. "Do you listen to them? Do you make time for them, guide them, and infuse them with your love?"

She looked at me for a moment. "Well, yes," she said, hesitantly. "But that's all I do. All I do is love them."

"All you do is love them? Are you kidding? That's *huge*!" I replied. "Do you know how many parents I meet who tell me that they cannot function? They are unable to love; they cannot control their tempers; they cannot get off their cells and just find the time to talk to their children. I hear about the dysfunctional homes in which they grew up and the poor role models who impeded their ability to be good parents. And you ask me if it is enough to just love your children? If you can give this gift of love to your child so that he knows that he is secure within his heart, along with transmitting a legacy of faith, then you have accomplished greatness here."

It is not easy for today's families to prevail. One out of every two marriages end in divorce and those that remain are often steeped in misery. Financial pressures eat away at the serenity and peace that was once found within the walls of our homes. Many parents return from work exhausted, their nerves frazzled. Children go through emotional and physical trials that test our spirits as parents.

At the same time, our children are engrossed in their gadgets and cell phones. They text their friends at the dinner table, and we find it impossible to communicate with them. Parent's devices keep buzzing. Instead of growing closer, we grow further apart and hardly speak to each other anymore. The fabric of our home is crumbling.

As parents, we have an incredible opportunity to fill our homes with blessing. We can teach our children how to handle life's challenges with faith. We can transmit to them the ability to stand up for truth and kindness. We can show them that one can go through adversity, yet remain strong, and that success does not have to breed arrogance. We can take the time to stop whatever we are doing, look at our children, and hear them. We can turn off our cell phones and talk to our kids again. And then, we can proudly raise spiritual children who are morally anchored.

My stay here in Israel has come to an end, and I must return to the States. It is extremely difficult to say goodbye. Images of those first few moments when I arrived play in my mind. My heart is heavy. Israel is a world like no other. Jerusalem's stones speak volumes. The pull of our land and the pull of my children tug deep inside me. What can I say? What am I thinking?

I am holding onto this thought, my friends. Long past the time that you've sang your last lullaby, your melody accompanies your child each night as he goes to sleep. Your image and all that you stand for accompanies your child throughout his life. As I look at my children and hold my granddaughter close as we say our goodbyes, I know that they will carry my voice with them.

Sunrise, Sunset: Marrying Off Our Daughter

Sharing wedding words and wonders

As a little girl, I loved the wedding scene in *Fiddler on the Roof*. My favorite scene was watching the flickering candles light up the night as the white chuppah fluttered over the young bride who circled her groom.

And then Tevye, the bride's father sings: "Is this the little girl I carried? Is this the little boy at play? I don't remember growing older, when did they?"

Sunrise. Sunset. Swiftly fly the years.

As my husband and I walked our youngest daughter to the chuppah, I lived the words of this song. With God's magnificent sunset as the backdrop, I held my daughter's hand, and a stream of emotion enveloped my heart.

All my life, I had prayed for this very moment. And now that the moment has come, I am filled with wonder. Where did all the years go? Wasn't it just yesterday that I held this little girl in my arms, cuddled with her, stroked her cheeks, and wiped away her tears? When the others grew too old for bedtime stories and giggles with mommy, this was the child whose little hand fit perfectly into mine. I held onto childhood laughter, bike riding with the wind, and hot chocolate with marshmallows floating on snowy winter nights. Who else would sing with me at the top of our lungs and dance around the house till we would fall down breathlessly together?

How I would smile when she would totter in my shoes, put on my "mommy things," and make believe that she was me. Each Purim, we would dig out the little bride costume, the veil, and the crown, and look in the mirror together with dreamy eyes.

When she was a little girl, we would read a story called *Love You Forever*. At the end of the book, my daughter would lean in and listen as I'd sing the last words on the page.

"Love you forever. Like you for always. As long as you're living. My baby you'll be."

I would kiss her silken curls, we would sing the *Shema*, and say a prayer for all our loved ones. I'd watch her eyelids slowly close, listen as her breaths deepened, and think that these days would last forever.

The other night I took out a folder I've kept, tucked in the bottom of my closet. Stacked inside are all the cards my little girl ever gave me. Colorful pictures before she was able to really write. Big red hearts, a smiling sun and rainbows with the word MOMMY spread across the page. Happy feelings somehow fly out of the papers spread across my floor.

Then the letters begin. Each carefully written as my baby starts to string her words together and embrace life. "Dear Mommy," they each open. "I love you so much."

My heart melts as I see her childish scrawl. First grade. Second grade. Where did the time go?

Homemade Mother's Day cards, birthday wishes, and some, just because.

I read and re-read. A little tear trickles down my cheek.

> *Dear Mommy,*
>
> *I love you so much and when I get married, I will miss you soooooooooo much, but now is not then and now I wish you 2 words—Happy Birthday. I love you mommy.*

Well, then is now.

It is time to thank God for the gift of life that I have been given to watch over. For the joy of bringing children into this world. For the hugs, the kisses, the triumphs, and yes, even the tears. For the privilege of carrying this soul inside of me and then trying oh so hard to create a path, despite it all, so that I know that my parents, *zeidies*, and *bubbies* live on.

When I was a little girl, one of my favorite places in the world to be was in my grandparents' home. Despite the darkness of their lives, they gave me only love. When my Zaydah would bless me, his soft white beard would flow over my face. I felt safe, even strong somehow. He would place his hands on my head, whisper the holy words and cry. I was named for my Zaydah's mother who was killed in Auschwitz. Perhaps, the grief of the past and the hope of the future collided. *Sunrise. Sunset.*

I see my little girl now grown, beginning life anew.

I have hopes and dreams. I have prayers that soar.

It is hard as well to know that those days of my little girl are memories now to be carefully taken out and gingerly revisited.

Sometimes, we wish we could go back in life, but no. The caterpillar becomes a butterfly, and it is time to spread your magnificent wings and fly.

I love you my little girl.

I pray that you build a home, together with your wonderful *chassan*, filled with Torah, blessings, and joy. May the footsteps of your *bubbies* and *zeidies* create a path for you so that you always find your way. May their tears, their sacrifice for our people, their legacy, and their wisdom shine as a beacon of light for you always.

xo

Mommy

Bas Mitzvah Reflections

A letter to my daughter upon her bas mitzvah, April 19, 2010

Dear Aliza,

Twelve years ago, there was still much sadness in my heart… I missed my Abba, your Zaydie, on whose shoulders you had never been carried. And then, the night that Pesach was over, great joy returned. Your sweet soul brought life again into this world.

I remember singing the Shema to you that very first moment that I held you. Your tiny little hand curled round my one finger. Holding you brought me peace. I was comforted.

We asked your Bubba for a name. Bubba, your beloved grandmother, is the "keeper of the names." After surviving Bergen-Belsen as a little girl and losing her zeidy and bubby along with so many cousins, aunts, uncles, and life as she knew it, Bubba refused to relinquish their names. Until today, your Bubba holds onto their sacred memory and tenaciously remembers each and every name.

Bubba likes to tell the story of how, when I was first born, the nurse entered the room and asked for my name to record on hospital records.

"Slova Channah," Bubba said.

"I'll come back when you're feeling better, dear," was the nurse's immediate reply.

I have always carried the name of my great-grandmother, Rebbetzin Slova Channah, proudly. Knowing that my name is unusual and certainly not typical American never daunted me. As a little girl, my name seemed to whisper to me and remind me of whom I am.

So, when you were born, of course, we came to Bubba and asked for your name.

"Your Abba Zaydah had a most beautiful sister," Bubba told us. "She was known to be kind and wise, always with a bright smile and great love for life. She was taken away by the Nazi Gestapo…never married, never seen or heard from again. Abba Zaydah missed his sister so. Her name was Fraidel, which means joyful. It is a perfect name for our sweet baby. Let's add the name Aliza," Bubba advised. "Aliza is the Hebrew version of the Yiddish Fraidel. With Hashem's help, this baby will always bring us joy."

The name Aliza Fraidel became your noble legacy.

I tell you all this, my precious Aliza, because now it is your turn to bear the torch. Turning twelve is the age of understanding, for you, my sweet child. As you come to embrace the mitzvos with new understanding, it is important that you know from whence you've come.

We live in such difficult times. I know how hard it is to grow up in today's world. So many challenges, so many fears. I know that, at times, your world will seem overwhelming. Even frightening. My precious Aliza Fraidel, never forget from whence you've come. Never forget your name.

Take this legacy with you, wherever you may go. Remember, too, that the root of the word neshamah, soul, is shem, name. If you would like a window onto your soul, grasp onto your name and never allow its presence to leave you. You have been called after a most righteous woman who died al Kiddush Hashem, sanctifying the name of God. Her holiness will accompany you throughout your life. You will always be reminded of your noble mission, just as I have been, as your name gently whispers to you and reminds you of your roots.

At your bas mitzvah, we asked Bubba to say a few words so that she would give you her blessing. The girls in your class were sitting in front and Bubba took a moment to look at them before she began to speak.

"I know that it seems strange to you that I am crying, but you see when I look at all these beautiful girls sitting together as one, I am overwhelmed. When I was a little girl, there were no bas mitzvahs. There were no girls laughing, singing, and dancing together. We did not even know if there would ever be more Jewish little girls. We could not imagine that we would survive. And here you are! A new generation ready to stand up and live a life of Torah and mitzvos. Girls, who, with Hashem's help, will one day build their own Jewish homes and bring new light into our world. Who would have believed this?

"And so, I want to thank Hashem for allowing me the privilege to rebuild. We came from the ashes and now look! Hashem has, in His great kindness, blessed me with children, and grandchildren and great-grandchildren! All loyal to His Torah, all walking in the path of our people."

Bubba asked you to come up so that she could bless you. As you stood before her, Bubba placed her hands on your head and, through her tears, gave you her berachah.

As your mother, it seems daunting for me to put my blessings for you into words. Words are limiting and my hopes and prayers are boundless. I have so much to say, so many supplications rest within my heart.

You know, Aliza, that since you were a baby, we had a tradition together. I would sing you the Shema, and you would fall asleep contentedly in my arms. As you have grown, you still fall asleep with a prayer on your lips, but you have added your own traditions. Each night you conclude your bedtime prayers with a private plea to God. You ask Hashem to bring refuah sheleimah, a full recovery and healing to those who are ill. And then I hear you say the names of so many—mothers, fathers, children, babies, all in need of God's healing balm. You do not even know many of these people, but you have heard their names being given for Tehillim.

I pray that you forever feel compassion for others. I pray that you walk in the ways of our mothers, Sarah, Rivkah, Rachel, and Leah. I pray that you forever remember your name, your legacy for life, and your holy roots. And as you grow into a bas Yisrael, a daughter of Israel, may Hashem bless you with all His blessings, watch over you, and guide you so that you may be a source of true nachas to our family, our people, and our God.

I love you forever.

xo

Mommy

Letter to My Son on His Wedding Day

This is the message I want you to always remember

My Dear Son,

Was it not just yesterday that I cradled you in my arms, your little fingers curled around mine?

I can still see your newborn body rising with each breath, feel your silken little head, and hear your innocent wail. How have the moments passed by in a flash?

You were born on the holy day of Shabbos.

After Havdalah, your grandparents, Bubba and Abba Zaydah, came to meet you. They brought your little siblings along. Laughter and shouts of "mazel tov" filled the room. We walked together to the nursery to find our baby. Amidst the bundles of blue and pink we finally found you, eyes wide open.

My father motioned to me to come close.

"Slova Channalah," he said, "yesterday this little neshamale was studying Torah with the malachim in the heavens above. Now he is here with you. Teach him. Guide him well. He is a priceless gift, a pure soul. Watch over him, my sheifele."

I've tried my best to follow your Abba Zaydah's words. I never imagined he would not be at my side as you grew.

You had just a year together, but oh, how you loved one another! Your favorite place in the world would be nestled contentedly on your Zaydie's shoulders. You had a language of your own. When it was time for us to say goodbye and leave, you would hold on tight, protesting with tears. Then came that awful time. Abba Zaydah was taken to Sloan Kettering. I asked permission for you to visit. A joyful toddler radiating energy through the halls of Sloan! Your sunshine illuminated the hospital walls and pushed a bit of the heavy darkness away.

You've always had such spirit and life.

I remember one cold morning, when we were on a family ski trip. The air was frigid. It was early and eerily quiet. Around us, people were moving slowly, holding their cups of coffee close and trying to wake themselves up. You were a child of three, running and singing at the top of your lungs.

A man stopped us. "Hey kid!" he called out. We both froze for a moment. "Never lose that! You hear? Never lose that! It's awesome."

You taught me how to play hockey, baseball, and football. Nights you'd drag out your hockey net and we'd take turns being goalie (and I'm no goalie). Abba and I would love to watch you play. We'd cheer you on wildly as you'd slide in the grass and yell "safe!" But greater than any sport, you taught me how to cheer for life, to be in the moment, and relish each experience absolutely, just as you did. You've opened my eyes to the wonder and magic of this world.

I wish your Bubba could be here with you today.

Each Friday night, when you would share your words of Torah at the table, Bubba's eyes lit up. If others may have gotten a little distracted, Bubba would say "Don't worry, sheifele. I am listening." You'd smile at each other and keep going.

You've been blessed with the gift of grandparents who have loved you, who made a path for you. Despite the fire of the Holocaust through which they lived, they ignited the fire of faith within your soul. Your Bubba whispers to you from above: "Don't worry. I am listening."

When Shabbos would come to an end, you would walk over to Bubba's house and sing Havdalah for her. After extinguishing the flame of the candle, you'd laugh out loud together so that your week would be one of joy. Then Bubba would place her hands on your head and bless you. That last year of her life, you would return home with glistening eyes. I know that Bubba wanted so much to have more time with you, and you with her. As you walk to your chuppah, I know that you will be looking for your Bubba. Me too.

Here's what I can tell you. The same message my father told me as I was about to begin this new season of my life.

"Before we go, I want to tell you this. My Slovelah, all the zaydahs and bubbas in the heavens above are here with you tonight. All the holy neshamos come down to walk with you. Never be afraid in life. No matter what happens, you are never alone. Your zaydahs and bubbas are with you."

I have carried those words in my heart all these years and now, it is my turn to pass the message on to you. There are those whom we loved mightily, and it hurts when their days with us come to an end. But know that they have made a path for us, prayed for us, and created merit and blessings that remain forever. We have memories and moments to hold onto. Time can never take that away.

As you and your bride build your own home, with God's help, I pray that you take the legacy of your past and bring blessing into this world. I thank God for giving me the privilege of carrying your soul and raising you together with Abba. I have watched you grow from a little boy into the young man that you are today. Along the way, you have inspired me to swim upstream, as you like to say. To try harder, be more, and discover the strength that lies within.

Mazel tov, my dear son.

May Hashem bless you, watch over you, carry you, and grant you peace.

I give you my prayer: together may you establish a true mikdash me'at, a sanctuary filled with holiness, and generations who bring nachas to our people and our God.

I love you with all my heart and soul.

Mommy

My Father's Gift of Silence

Sometimes, it's what we don't say that becomes our greatest gift

When I was a little girl, a couple in our community went through a terrible tragedy. They lost a young child and were in deep despair. Shortly afterward, my mother ran into the father at the local supermarket. He turned to my mother and said, "Your husband saved our life. He was the one, more than anyone else, who helped us get through this incredible loss."

When my mother returned home, she wanted to know what my father could have possibly said that made such an impact on this couple. What message of solace and comfort was given to lift them from the dark abyss of despair?

"What did you say?" she asked him. "I know that you went over to their home and spent time with them. What did you tell them?"

My father's reply baffled my mother.

"I said nothing. What could I possibly tell a couple who just lost their child?"

My mother asked my father about his conversation numerous times. She wanted the secret to his lightening of their heavy load, but my father insisted that he had said nothing.

A few weeks later, the couple came over to our home. Now was my mother's chance. After sitting down for a few minutes and giving the couple refreshments, my mother gently said, "You told me that my husband saved your life. He helped you the most when you went through your awful grief. What did my husband say?"

The man paused. He then gave the secret of my father's consolation.

"Rebbetzin, your husband did not say one word."

My mother could not comprehend the response.

"The rabbi came over to our home. He walked over to me without saying anything. And then he reached over to me, took my hands into his, and hugged me with all his heart. I looked up and saw the rabbi's face. There were tears falling from his eyes. You cannot imagine what that felt like for me. The rabbi felt my pain. I was not sitting alone in my suffering."

My mother was quiet, absorbing the message this man, whose life had been turned upside down, was giving.

"Your husband did not speak. I didn't need him to give me words. I needed his heart and soul."

When I recall this story about my father, I realize an awesome truth.

We sometimes think that we must fill space with words. We have someone in our lives who is going through difficulty, we know someone who is facing sorrow and sadness. We are at a loss. What do we say? What do we do? How do we make this all better?

Even in our pre-pandemic world, there were many who were walking around as if they had been given a punch in the gut. There was too much suffering. And now, having been forced to deal with a lockdown has strained relationships. Teens have expressed anxiety, loneliness, and feelings of despair. Children have experienced erratic school schedules;

they've missed their friends. Parents have found themselves frustrated and frightened. We have gone through a chaos like we have never experienced before.

What is the greatest gift that we can give our loved ones?

I turn to the wisdom of our sages that has anchored us for thousands of years. "I have been raised amongst the wise and I have found nothing better for the body than silence."[2]

When you want to give of yourself, give a *lev shome'a*, a listening heart. Sometimes a person in pain needs you to stay silent. Feel their pain. See their suffering. And say not a word. Just show that you are here for them, that you won't turn your back on them. You are not too busy or tired, too absorbed with your own problems and life, to put aside your troubles for theirs.

A listening heart means that we do not simply hear with our ears. We don't keep talking, giving ideas or solutions or judgment calls. We are silent and open our most inner self to the anguish of another. That's it. And with this gift of silence comes an understanding that we are fully present. Perhaps, we can't fix anything or take away the pain, but we can feel. In our silence comes compassion, understanding, and empathy. And we can share the load.

This was my father's message to me during his life. There were times when I faced disappointments and fears as we all do. My father never filled the space with empty words. All I had to do was look at my father's face, see his shining eyes, feel his strong hand hold mine, and I knew that I was not alone. His presence spoke louder than any word.

In the final days of my dear father's life, it was now my father who was facing the challenge of his life. It was my turn to show that I had absorbed his deep wisdom.

I recall sitting at my father's bedside, just the two of us. I struggled to find the words. My father took my hand in his. There were moments where we said nothing. What is there to say?

---

2 *Pirkei Avos*-Ethics of the Fathers, 1:17.

I looked at my father's face; I saw his pain as he saw mine. We both shed our tears. Our hearts ached. Silence filled the room. I knew that more than any words I could say, I would give the gift of a listening heart. I would be there for my father, and he would know that he would be loved and remembered. Forever.

My Moment of Truth

One cold day in January, I experienced my own personal wake-up call. My beloved father was a patient in Memorial Sloan-Kettering. In just nine weeks we watched my father's broad frame wane. Though he never lost his dazzling smile and warm love, my father's energy slipped away a bit more each day. The doctors mapped out a treatment plan. My mother and my siblings spent our days and nights by his side. We plastered the room with happy photos of grandchildren. My father asked that we bring his holy *sefarim* from home. He also requested a huge blowup picture of our Zaydah—known in Hungary to this day as "The Miracle Rabbi," Rabbi Asher Anschil HaLevi Jungreis—to be hung facing him on the wall in his room. The room was transformed. Then a procedure went terribly wrong. I recall the sickening feeling of overwhelming fear in the pit of my stomach. My father courageously reassured us that everything would be OK. We were supposed to be the ones giving my father strength. Instead, he was the one who soothed our souls. "*Sheifele*, it will be good. Don't worry." His smile and sense of calm filled the dread in my heart.

One day I arrived at the hospital and the door to my father's room was ajar. I approached his bedside, kissed his cheek, and held his hand. My father's eyes slowly closed. A nurse walked in and asked me to give my father a few moments. She set up a screen and told me that I could step behind it. I sat down on a chair and took out my book of *Tehillim*. The room was silent. I heard the nurse speak softly to my father as I continued praying. Suddenly I heard a most awful sound. I couldn't place it. I had never heard this sound before. And then it hit me. My father was crying. My beautiful Abba was sobbing out loud. I froze. I didn't know what to do. The sound I heard emanated from the depths of the soul.

"Rabbi?" I heard the nurse say. There was no response. The haunting sobs continued. "Rabbi, are you in pain?" she asked. "Because this should not be hurting you. I am almost done, Rabbi."

My father finally spoke. "No," he replied, as he wept. "Don't worry. I am not crying now because you are causing me pain. My heart is heavy."

"What is it?" she asked. "Oh," my father cried out. "I know that my days here are coming to an end. I don't know when, but I do know that it will be soon. Only God knows, and I will be facing my Creator. I am scared. I am so scared. I will have to answer for my life."

My father's anguished wails shattered my heart.

"But, Rabbi," I heard the nurse say, "you are the kindest, gentlest, and most humble human being I have ever met. You have done so much good in your life. You are a rabbi. You don't have to be afraid."

I slowly made my way back to my father's bedside. I looked at this giant of a man and was awed with the transparency of his soul. He was all truth. How blessed was I to have been given my time with him. What a void I would be left with. My father's whole life was living Torah. He did not just study, he breathed Torah's wisdom day and night. He took the mundane and made it holy. He cared for us with all his heart and transmitted his legacy of life and love.

That day, I entered the realm of Yom Kippur in January. I received a wake-up call and understood what it means to make a *cheshbon ha'nefesh*, a true accounting of our soul.

I have tried hard to carry my father's soul-wrenching message with me. Life is fleeting. Love is fragile. Make the most of every moment. Treat the people in your life with care. No one is here forever.

And ask: How will I answer for my days, my words, and my deeds?

Missing My Mother, Rebbetzin Esther Jungreis

To the world, she was a survivor and trailblazing visionary. To me and my siblings, she was our mother who was always there for us.

GETTING UP FROM SHIVAH

These are most difficult words for me to write. Today, I got up from sitting *shivah* for my beloved mother, Rebbetzin Esther Jungreis. For seven days, I opened my mother's front door, waiting for her beautiful smile to greet me. I walked into my mother's kitchen where photos of all her children, grandchildren, and great grandchildren plastered the walls. I looked for her, but her chair was empty. The pain is raw. Where is my beautiful Ema?

To the world she was "the Rebbetzin"—the Jewish soul on fire—powerhouse, visionary, survivor of Bergen-Belsen, founder of Hineni, charismatic speaker who packed Madison Square Garden, trailblazer in the world of outreach, and a woman who fearlessly traveled across the globe igniting the spark that she believed lay dormant within every Jew.

While sitting *shivah*, we met people who came from far to share their stories of connection. Some spoke of her blessings that brought children and healing, others of her Torah teachings that helped bring peace to their divided families. Couples who met through her matchmaking shared pictures of sons and daughters who bring joy to our people. Men and women recounted incredible tales of being inspired to discover Judaism and leave assimilation behind.

My tears joined with those who came to offer consolation. They tried hard to express their words, but many simply could not speak. The grief was overwhelming. Over and over, I heard, "We lost our *bubby*." "We lost our Torah *ema*."

A great light has been extinguished. Our world has dimmed.

To me and my siblings, "the Rebbetzin" was our *ema*. She was my mother who was always there for me, loved me, guided me, and gave me life. After each baby, I would return home where my mother rocked my newborns, bathed them, and sang our Mama's Yiddish lullabies softly in their ears.

To our children and grandchildren, she was "Bubba." How she adored us and made each child feel as if he were "the favorite one."

Whenever we would visit, Bubba would insist on walking us to the door. We kissed Bubba and said goodbye. My mother placed her hands on our heads and gave us her blessing. She would always shed tears. Once outside, she would call us back. "One more blessing," she would say.

I recall once saying, "But Ema, you *bentched* me already." I felt badly seeing my mother, toward the end of her life, stand by the door, carefully holding onto her walker.

"As long as I am alive, never say no to a berachah. Always come back...and I will give you one more berachah."

As I reached the bottom of the driveway, I would turn. Bubba was still standing there. Her lips were moving. She was whispering her blessings. She'd wave, and I would wave back. A few more steps before her figure was just a dot. But I knew that she had not budged. She was still watching, not letting me out of her sight. Constant prayer on her lips.

When my mother was a small child, before deportations to the concentration camps had begun, young Hungarian Jewish men were drafted for slave labor.

Szeged, my mother's hometown, was their stopover. Zaydah, my grandfather, was the rabbi of the city, so my grandparents' home became their refuge. Soon after, they were shipped away. These young men were forced to wear yellow armbands identifying them as vile Jews. But at my grandparents' table they were transformed. They studied the holy books and were enveloped with love. Yellow badges of shame became badges of honor. When the hour would come for them to take leave, Zaydah would place his hands on each young man's head. He would cry as if they were each his very own child and give his blessing. Then he would accompany them to the door and whisper blessings until they were out of sight.

Out of the ashes, my mother brought Zaydah's blessings home to us, the next generation. She, too, would whisper her blessings till we were out of sight. Though I grew up in the United States of America, my mother transported me to another place, and another time. Holy souls of my *bubbies* and *zeidies* have always been hovering.

As long as my mother remained alive, I felt secure in the spiritual womb of her prayers and blessings. Who will pray for us now? Who will bless us? Who will see the hidden miracle that lies within each of us?

My mother brought the Jewish nation home with her love and unwavering belief in God. The flames of the Holocaust that consumed our great-grandparents, grandparents, aunts, uncles, and infant cousins only strengthened her conviction.

As our children grew, all the cousins would sleep over my parents' home for Shabbos. Friday night, after the meal, they would run down the stairs and quickly get into their pajamas. "Bubba, tell us a story from when you were a little girl." These were always stories of triumph of the spirit.

My mother would share how, when she arrived at Bergen-Belsen, terrified, she stood in the freezing cold, eyes glued to the ground. She then put her hand in her pocket and felt a crumpled piece of paper. Somehow her father had placed the words of the *Shema* in her pocket. "It was only a piece of paper, but it told me that I was not alone, that my God lived. Slowly, I lifted my eyes."

My mother connected us to those holy souls who came before us. She made us understand that our past is embedded into our future. We cannot possibly stand if our tree is rootless. The slightest wind will blow us away.

She taught us how to live with hope. "Never give up!" she would say. "Pray! Jewish people pray!" she implored. I can hear my mother's voice now as I write these words. Until her last day here on earth, my mother never stopped davening. Oh, how I miss my mother's powerful prayers.

She created a legacy of *emunah*, pure faith. She entrenched within me the understanding that no matter the darkness, we are a nation of miracles. "Look at me!" my mother would say. "I should not be here. But here I am. And Hitler, *yimach shemo*, is gone!!"

Hashem is watching over us. Never stop believing. Never be afraid.

"Seven times a *tzaddik* falls! But he gets up. And then he falls and gets up again," she would declare with strength and passion. No matter how many times you have fallen, and no matter how hard your fall was, there is no barrier between us and God. Hashem is our Father, waiting to hear from us, waiting for each of us to come home.

Ema, my heart is full. I miss hearing your words. Your seat at my Shabbos table is waiting for you. That final Shabbos that you were home, we were waiting and waiting to see your shining face at our door. Dov, our two-year-old grandson at the time, kept peeking behind the curtains. "Maybe? Maybe Bubba is coming?" he kept insisting. But, no. It was not to be. Your strength was waning.

We ache for your blessings. I grasp onto snippets of memories, trying to remember all your brilliant wisdoms.

Thank you, Ema, for your footsteps. We will try to kindle your light and continue your mission.

And please, Ema, pray for us in the heavens above. Because we are all your children.

Epilogue

I have tried to relay to you the love and legacy that I have been given. Each day I thank Hashem for the wisdom and teachings of my parents, my grandparents, and all my holy ancestors who walked before me. Growing up in my parents' home was a lifetime lesson in *mesirus nefesh*, faith under fire, and the power of the human spirit. I have witnessed the meaning of resilience, love, commitment, courage, and strength. I have watched my parents and grandparents miraculously rebuild after suffering inhumane devastation and loss.

We each have the ability, even more so, the responsibility, to bequeath our own personal legacy to our children. *Chinuch*, true Torah based parenting, is the nurturing of our children not only physically, but morally as well. This is the definition of "*peru u'revu*"—to reproduce the best of our spiritual energies until we see in our children a reflection of the light that shines within each of us.

In one of the final moments I had with my mother, we were alone in her hospital room. My mother's eyes were closed shut. The sound of beeping machines filled the room. I was not sure that my mother could hear me, but I knew that I must speak these words.

I took my mother's hands in mine and whispered gently.

"Ema...I want to say thank you. I wish I would've said this to you before, and I am so sorry that I never did. I want to give you my *hakaras hatov*, Ema. You gave me life. You gave me everything I know, everything I am. You gave me a *derech*, a path forever, to reach out, to teach, to love, to have *emunah sheleimah*. You created Hineni and gave us our Hineni family. You loved Am Yisrael. And, Ema, you always made us feel loved. We constantly knew how much you cared about us, worried, and davened for us. How can I ever say thank you enough, Ema? You suffered, you triumphed, you lived with passion in your soul, and you never stopped doing and believing. Please be *moichel* me for any hurt I may have caused you. Oh, Ema, I will miss you so!"

I kissed my mother's hands as my tears fell freely.

And then I saw the silent tears that begin to trickle from my mother's closed eyes. My words had been heard.

I took a tissue, wiped away each hot precious tear and felt as if I was touching fiery holiness at that moment.

How painful it was to say goodbye.

THE WEEK OF SHIVAH countless people came through our door. Many were strangers to us. My mother's worldwide reach had been endless. Friday morning, as we approached Shabbos, an elderly woman sat in the chair in front of me.

"So let me ask you this," she began. "Your mother would tell the story of the shofar of Bergen-Belsen. She described how your grandfather and the rabbis in the camp secured a shofar to blow for Rosh Hashanah. How the Nazis beat the Jews as they stopped to listen to the piercing sounds that filled the air. Well, I don't know. I was also in Bergen-Belsen, and I never heard a shofar there. How do you know it's true? When did it happen? What year?"

My sister and I were sitting beside each other. I could not look up. My energy had been completely sapped. I put my face into my hands and started to silently weep. "Ema! Where are you? Why didn't I ask you more questions? What do I do now? How can I know the answers? Ema, why did you leave us?"

The woman got up and left.

I was depleted.

The moment her seat became empty, another woman came to take her place. She sat in that exact seat. I did not have the strength to continue and kept my eyes closed.

"You do not know who I am," she began. "I live in Israel and just happened to be down the block being *menachem avel* a close family member. I heard about the loss of the great *rebbetzin*."

I remained quiet.

"I came to share a story with you. The story of the shofar of Bergen-Belsen."

My heart began to pound. I looked up. "Say that again?"

"I am here to share the story about the shofar of Bergen-Belsen."

"What? Why do you want to speak about the shofar?"

"Because I have it."

"You have the shofar?" I asked in disbelief.

"Yes. I live in Neve Alizah. After the Hungarian Jews managed to get their hands on the shofar, it was smuggled in a pot filled with liquid to the Polish camp. The two camps were separated by barbed wire. My mother-in-law's father was the rabbi who blew the shofar in the Polish camp. Years ago, your mother spoke in Neve Alizah before Elul. She told the story of the shofar of Bergen-Belsen. My mother-in-law was there. She ran home to get the shofar and show it to your mother. Who could believe that the shofar had made it to Eretz Yisrael? The Nazis, *yemach shemam*, were gone, but the shofar had survived! How your mother and my mother-in-law hugged and cried that night! Each year we blow the shofar as testimony to the *emunah* of Am Yisrael and to the *nes* of our nation."

At that moment I felt a surge, a life force, restored within me.

And the thought that went through my mind was "*Al titosh Toras imecha*—Do not forsake the teachings of your mother."[1] My mother was speaking to me. She was still guiding me, teaching me, and empowering me.

She may not be with me physically, but her *neshamah* is watching over me. I am not alone.

As the sun began to set, and I kindled my *Shabbos licht*, I was filled with emotion. Though the loss was searing, I had been given the ultimate solace. I gathered my children round and told them the story of the shofar of Bergen-Belsen. I relayed the hurt in my heart as I had sat *shivah* that day and the gift of strength that had been orchestrated from

1 *Mishlei*-Proverbs 1:8.

Above. Once again, I saw how the past and present collide, creating an explosion of living faith.

As I close the pages of this book, I ask that you, dear reader, take my stories, life lessons, and teachings to heart. Create homes filled with compassion. Inspire your children to live with purpose and mission. Discover the power of strong roots. Infuse your children with faith. Ignite their *pintele Yid*. Nurture their souls with love and patience. Believe in each child's inner greatness. Never give up on a *neshamah* and never give up on yourself. You are raising the future of our people. What a sacred mission!

Dear reader, may your homes be filled with blessing and light.

About the Author

Slovie Jungreis-Wolff is an acclaimed author, renowned lecturer, and parenting instructor. She is one of the most sought after and passionate speakers in the Jewish world today. Slovie is the leader of Hineni Couples and has taught about life, relationships, and marriage for more than thirty years. Slovie's groundbreaking parenting handbook *Raising a Child with Soul*, published by St. Martin's Press, has been a source of guidance to parents and families all over the world. She has given workshops and lectured extensively throughout the U.S., Canada, Mexico, Panama, Europe, and Israel and has addressed thousands at South Africa's Sinai Indaba by the invitation of Chief Rabbi Warren Goldstein. Slovie is a popular columnist for the renowned site Aish.com, where her articles about life and Judaism have inspired people worldwide. Her parenting workshops on JewishEbooks.com have reached audiences around the globe. She is currently a teacher at Manhattan High School for Girls and a columnist for *Ami Magazine* and *The Jewish Press*. Slovie is the daughter of Rebbetzin Esther Jungreis and continues her mother's legacy of rekindling the spark within every soul.